Life in Her Hands

Life in Her Hands

The Inspiring Story of a Pioneering Female Surgeon

AVERIL MANSFIELD

EBURY SPOTLIGHT

Ebury Spotlight, an imprint of Ebury Publishing
20 Vauxhall Bridge Road
London SW1V 2SA

Ebury Spotlight is part of the Penguin Random House group of companies
whose addresses can be found at global.penguinrandomhouse.com

Penguin Random House UK

Copyright © Averil Mansfield 2023

Averil Mansfield has asserted her right to be identified as the author of this
Work in accordance with the Copyright, Designs and Patents Act 1988

First published by Ebury Spotlight in 2023

www.penguin.co.uk

A CIP catalogue record for this book is available from the British Library

Citation acknowledgements

'Just an Old Fashioned Girl', written by Marve A. Fisher
'If You Were the Only Girl (In the World)', written by Nat D. Ayer and Clifford Grey
'The Lion and Albert', written by Marriott Edgar
'In My Liverpool Home', written by Peter McGovern

All images from the author's private collection, or copyright of the following rights holders:

The Times / News Licensing
Kathryn Cusimano / Imperial College Healthcare NHS Trust
Arthur Dickson Wright
Cartoon by Mel Calman. © S. & C. Calman
Paul Cox
Blackpool Gazette & Herald Ltd
Ernest H. Cooper
British Red Cross
Blackpool Collegiate School for Girls
Gaunt, Bond Street
Simpsons Photographic Service Liverpool
Kaye Photography Liverpool
Imperial College Healthcare NHS Trust Archives
PLC Photos
B. C. A. and Buckingham Palace
British Medical Association

The publisher has made serious efforts to trace various copyright owners and has been unable to do so. The publisher is willing to acknowledge any rightful copyright owner on substantive proof of ownership and would be grateful for any information as to their identity.

ISBN 9781529149968

Set in 13.5/16pt Garamond MT Std
Typeset by Jouve (UK), Milton Keynes
Printed and bound in Great Britain by Clays Ltd, Elcograf S.p.A.

The authorised representative in the EEA is Penguin Random House Ireland,
Morrison Chambers, 32 Nassau Street, Dublin D02 YH68

MIX
Paper from responsible sources
FSC® C018179

Penguin Random House is committed to a sustainable future for our business, our readers and our planet. This book is made from Forest Stewardship Council® certified paper.

For Jack and my family

Contents

1. In the Beginning	1
2. Secondary School	22
3. Off to Liverpool	36
4. Life as a Doctor	66
5. Becoming a Woman in Surgery	79
6. End of Training	106
7. Early Years of Consultant Practice	124
8. Jack Appears in My Life	139
9. And Now for St Mary's	163
10. What Is a Professor?	193
11. Winding Down	214
12. Retirement	228
Acknowledgements	263

1
In the Beginning

My parents met in Blackpool in 1928. My mother, Olive Atkinson, one of four children and the daughter of a fireman, was from Accrington. My father, Ralph Dring, one of six children, was born in Hull but moved to Wales as a child, where he and his father built a house for the family in Gower. The Drings seem to have lived a fairly hand-to-mouth existence. My father sold fish from a horse-drawn cart in the Mumbles area for a while, before he travelled to Blackpool from Swansea seeking work in the 1920s, when employment was hard to find.

Olive and Ralph met on the Pleasure Beach, where they had both successfully found employment. He was doing maintenance work and she was a cashier, and their love developed over a series of strolls along the promenade and occasional visits to the cinema. They enjoyed very little privacy, but in spite of that, they soon realised that they wanted to be together for life. They were denied permission to marry by my grandfather Atkinson, because the prospective groom was only earning £2.10 shillings per week. Rather daringly, they married on my mother's twenty-first birthday, when permission was no longer required. As Dad's wages had in fact by then been reduced by 5 shillings a week, there would have been even less chance of permission, so it was really their only option. Luckily the rift soon healed, and although life must have been quite tough at times, they were a happy couple and were to remain so until my father died aged 72, close to 50 years later.

My mother hoped to fall pregnant as soon as she and my

father were married, as did one of her close friends and also her sister-in-law, who had both married around the same time, but none had any luck. Then, after five years, by a happy coincidence all three women became pregnant at the same time, so there was joy all around.

Of course, there was no NHS in the 1930s. A few weeks after my mother discovered she was expecting, she approached a doctor, choosing her entirely on the grounds that she was female. Dr Coope, a GP, was responsible for arranging a place for the birth and for checking the pregnancy's progress. This largely consisted of blood pressure checks and physical examinations. In the later stages of the pregnancy, my heart could be heard through a foetal stethoscope, but this was many years before ultrasound was invented, so there was no imaging of any kind.

Dr Coope was a tiny but tough lady, and so she needed to be, as my mother was in labour for about 48 hours and eventually required forceps to deliver me in a nursing home at the substantial weight of 10 lbs 7 oz. As a result of this difficult birth, my mother required surgery and was told that she shouldn't have any more children. Her operation was then quite dramatically followed by a life-threatening pulmonary embolus (a blood clot in the veins that moves through the heart into the lungs). The story of this embolus was to become part of our family folklore. My father was summoned to the hospital and told that his wife was at death's door. She was instructed not to move a muscle for fear of further embolism, which would have been fatal. It was a tale of great drama and it fascinated me as a child. It perhaps explains why my first foray into research as a doctor was on the subject of deep-vein thrombosis and pulmonary embolism.

In 1937, the year of my birth, there was little or no real

understanding of the causes, prevention or treatment of such thromboses. The circulation of the blood, on the other hand, was well understood: the heart pumps blood into the arteries, and blood returns to the heart through the veins, aided by the contraction of the calf muscles. It was also understood that if a clot formed in the leg veins, it could move from there to the heart as a pulmonary embolus, hence the advice to remain immobile. The majority of such clots remain in the leg veins and undergo 'reorganisation', which is a technical term for the process by which the body attempts to reopen the blocked vein. This in itself can result in long term problems in the body's deep veins, leading to the less efficient return of blood to the heart. It is, however, not fatal, which is why complete bed rest was the preferred, and in fact only, treatment of embolisms available at that time.

Happily, my mother survived and the postpartum surgery was a success, though there were to be no more children. But despite being an only child, I was never lonely; my parents were from large families and we lived in close proximity to my uncles and aunts, and therefore to my cousins.

At that time there was little fear of the big outside world, so playing in the street was a very normal part of life – there were scarcely any vehicles – and I mingled with other children, including my cousins, every day. We were much more afraid of treading on a crack between paving stones than of any stranger. Balls were the main staple of our games, but there were also several that involved chalk marks on the paving stones and a complex series of movements, sometimes accompanied by singing. I suppose they were variations on the game Hopscotch. Everyone owned a skipping rope and we were constantly on the move with one activity or another. There was very little danger of obesity back then!

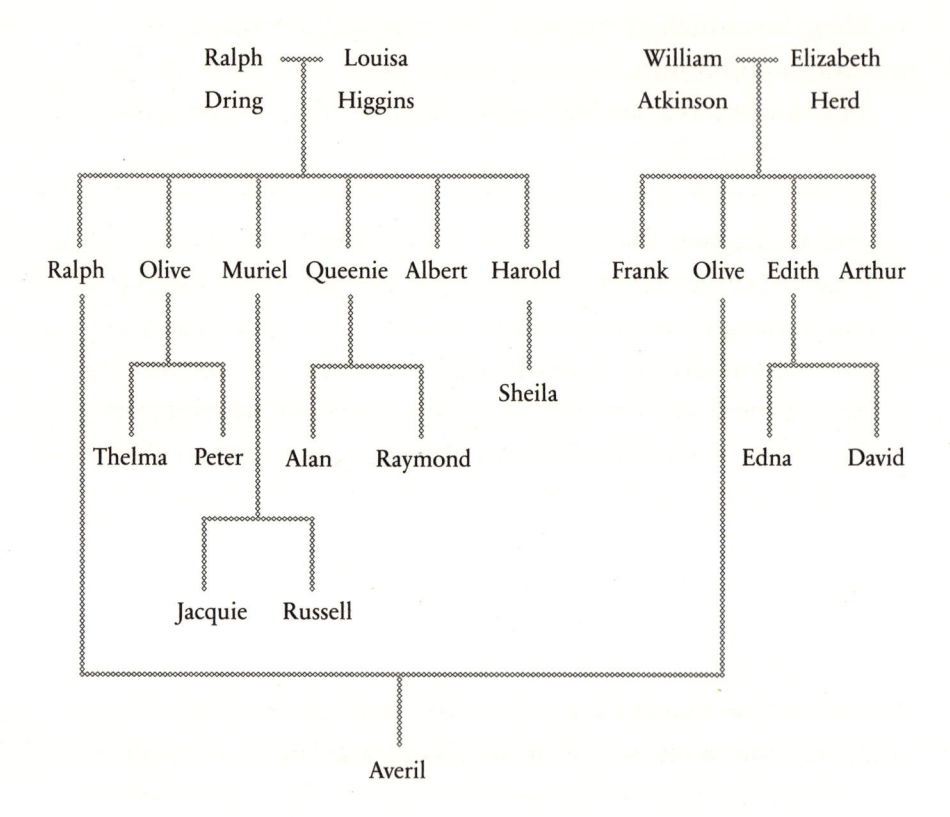

```
      Ralph ∞∞ Louisa                William ∞∞ Elizabeth
      Dring      Higgins              Atkinson    Herd
        |                                  |
  ┌──┬──┼──┬──┬──┐              ┌────┬────┼────┐
Ralph Olive Muriel Queenie Albert Harold  Frank Olive Edith Arthur
        |     |      |              |              |
      ┌─┴─┐ ┌─┴─┐  ┌─┴─┐          Sheila         ┌─┴─┐
   Thelma Peter Alan Raymond                    Edna David
            |
          ┌─┴─┐
       Jacquie Russell

                    Averil
```

My parents moved into a council house in Layton, Blackpool, when I was two years old. The day of the move is still vivid in my memory. However, no matter how hard I try, there is not a glimmer of any memory prior to that. I presume that the shock of the new imprinted the day on my mind. I can see the main room and the family members who were helping with the move, including my aunt Elsie and her husband, my father's brother Harold, in great detail. I particularly remember the extreme difficulty of the back doorstep. It was the exit from the kitchen into the back yard and therefore, to me, a highly desirable route to freedom. It was steep and I can clearly remember trying to work out how I was going to tackle it. Eventually I turned round and slithered down it on my knees. Job done!

The house was a semi-detached bungalow on a corner plot at No. 11 Wembley Avenue. There were two bedrooms and a large attic, which was eventually to become my bedroom. We moved in the year that the Second World War began.

One important change resulting from the move was that I began to sleep through the night, having been a difficult, restless sleeper previously. Apparently, not long after the move, my father sat me down on some carefully spread-out newspaper and gave me a brush and some paint so I could decorate my own bedroom. He was certainly of the opinion that a feeling of ownership of my room was the turning point in my sleeping habits.

My father was a smoker. It was his only luxury and it is impossible for me to imagine him without his inevitable Woodbine or Player's cigarette. My mother never smoked, and such tolerance is hard to imagine today, but it was fairly common then. I had a chronic cough as a child and was taken to see a number of experts, but not one of them attributed it to the smoke that surrounded me as I grew up – at home, in the car, simply everywhere.

We also had a coal fire in the living room, with an oven alongside it in which any baking was done with heat from the fire. It was the only source of heat for the whole house and as such it was the focal point for the family. My bedclothes would be draped around it prior to bedtime in order to warm them, before a rapid transfer to the bed, possibly with a hot water bottle too. The coal smoke did nothing to help my childhood coughs.

My mother did a daily shop because there was no refrigeration and the grocer's store was close by; it was visible from our house. She cooked and did our washing without any mechanical aids, and she always kept the house clean. We had an allotment, which meant we usually had vegetables, and because my father was vegetarian, my mother and I had a tad more protein to share between us. Dad stopped eating meat while quite young, as the result of a visit to an abattoir; it was very unusual to be vegetarian then. He did, however, continue to eat fish and was quite the amateur fisherman when the opportunity arose.

By the time he had moved to Blackpool, my father was an oxyacetylene welder and cutter. Although his work was extremely hard, it did save him from being called up into the armed forces, as it was a reserved occupation. As children, my friends and I were shocked by the steady departure of the men in our lives. I was the lucky one. Dad felt guilty that his job meant he did not go to war when so many were being sent to perilous situations, but it was wonderful for me to have him at home. Every day except Sunday, he worked from 8am until 6pm, and he would be outdoors in any weather for most of that time. The conditions in which he worked were appalling, though never as bad as might have been the case if he had been called up into the military.

His first experience of his new skill was taking down the Big Wheel in Blackpool, during which the workers were exposed to the heights and the elements with no safety harnesses. But it was a job, and they were scarce. Once that was completed, he found work near our home, on Talbot Road, in a scrap metal yard. I can only imagine that in the yard there might have been some swearing, but if there was, it was never brought home. In fact, I never heard anyone swear when I was a child. My father was always my most important role model, which is possibly why I was never known to swear in the stress of a difficult operation. There was also a very limited vocabulary around the home when it came to personal matters and, in addition to expletives, there were many words that I simply never heard spoken. As such, when the 'facts of life' were later taught to me, it was in rather vague language that left many more questions than answers. Procreation generally did not seem to be desirable. I think it was a deliberate ploy to make sure there were no unplanned pregnancies!

Dad was paid in cash at the end of the week, always in a brown envelope. He would bring it home intact and then my mother would determine its distribution. He was given his 'pocket money' and the rest was shared out into the pots on the mantlepiece for our various expenses: the doctor, coal, electricity, rent, and so on. Most working-class families at the time had a similar system to ensure they lived within their means and didn't go into debt, which was a great fear, and the word 'workhouse' a dreaded threat. Unexpected expenditures – such as my mother's operation – always added considerable anxiety.

There was no phone in the house, so we made all our calls from a black phone inside an iconic red Post Office telephone box on an island in our road. It was visible from home, so on the rare occasions when a call was required, we could check that it was unoccupied in advance and time the visit perfectly. You needed pennies to make the call, and if it failed to connect, you got your money back by pressing button B. As children, my friends and I could never pass such a box without trying button B, and just occasionally we became rich instantly.

In addition to his day job, my father became the local fire warden during the war. Using his skills with metal, he created a wonderful fire-fighting machine and left it outside our front door for the neighbourhood to use in case of emergency. Strangely, it survived the war but was stolen as soon as it ended and we never saw it again. The other notable item that Dad made using his welding skills was a wonderful scooter for me. Streamlined and painted red and gold, it was my absolute pride and joy. I went everywhere except to school on my beautiful scooter.

Initially, when the air-raid sirens sounded, we sheltered under the stairs that led to our attic, as so many families did. It soon became evident that this was not safe, so Dad set about digging a shelter in the back yard and lining it with metal. It might have been one of the famous Anderson shelters, no doubt with some original features of Dad's own too. I remember that there were steps down into it and seating inside, where there was a pervasive smell of damp earth.

There were many aspects of the war that, to me as a small child, seemed fun. Even the air raids were exciting and I did not perceive any real danger. Indeed, there was not much danger in Blackpool; the Tower provided a useful landmark for navigation, so while we often saw enemy air traffic and heard the accompanying sirens, there weren't many actual air raids or bombs.

Our house had to be completely blacked out so that no glimmer of light could be visible from the outside. Of course, there were no street lights then, so nocturnal excursions were always in total darkness, unless there was a moon.

We took the privations in our stride and were proud to carry our gas masks. Evacuees arriving from distant parts, labelled and clutching gas masks and not much else, also added to our excitement. I did not find living on rations to be a hardship. I knew no better and we were not seriously hungry, but it must have made life difficult for my mother. Purchases were entirely governed by the limitations imposed by our ration cards. A limited range of vegetables was usually available but staples like butter, eggs and meat were more of a luxury, as was fruit. Rice was only available for puddings, and pasta was simply unheard of. Eggs were preserved in a gelatine-like substance called isinglass; my mother used a large crock pot for hers. At school we got our daily third of a pint of milk and our orange concentrate, and about once a term we were invited to take a jam jar in to collect our chocolate powder 'from the Americans'. I often succumbed to the temptation to dip my finger in the jar on my way home.

When the war ended, there was a huge street party. Somehow, as if by magic, the necessary ingredients appeared and a great range of delicious food was prepared in quantity. My mother made brandy snaps, and to this day, they remind me of that special event. There were, however, several foods that I never tried in my childhood – I was in my teens before I even saw a banana or a pineapple, for example. I purchased my first sweets, some pear drops, in the tuck shop adjacent to my secondary school when I was in my early teens. I remember feeling seriously wicked in doing so.

My mother was not employed, so she was always at home throughout my early years. I was keen to learn from her and she was happy to teach. She had in fact wanted to become a teacher but was told she had to leave school at 14, and also that she was too frail – although she went on to live to the age of 84! I vividly recall learning to read with Mum while I sat on a swing that Dad had made in the yard.

I looked forward to starting at Layton Primary School, which was a short walk away from home. On my first day, my mother took me there. When we arrived, she said, 'You will be able to find your own way home.' At the end of the day, I simply walked back by myself. From then on I walked to and fro without an adult every day, and my mother would always be at home when I returned. It seems strange now to imagine such freedom, but it was very normal then, and apart from some anxiety at the end of the first day, I was not concerned by it.

Education was provided for all children at no cost, but health care was a cause for worry, as it had to be paid for. There was a pot on our mantlepiece labelled 'Doctor' and, of course, a portion of the contents of Dad's brown envelope went into the pot regularly. Visits to the GP only occurred when there was some kind of serious concern. I well remember the arrival of the National Health Service in 1948 and particularly the enormous relief felt by working-class people when that particular pot on the mantlepiece was no longer required.

Dr Philip was our GP and his house was visible from our home. We always would wait until the queue at his door had disappeared before venturing out to see him. There were no appointments back then; we would simply turn up at the surgery and we were always seen that same day.

Dr Philip was a kindly man, and his son initially went to the same primary school as I did. We were great friends and, indeed, competitors. Although Dr Philip was a man, the other doctors I came into contact with were mostly women. I had a special affection for our school doctor, a lovely, gentle woman who I felt really cared about us. In many ways, she was an early role model for me. In hindsight, I think it was important that I saw women doctors as quite normal from a young age. It meant that being a doctor myself was something to which I could readily aspire.

Like many children at primary school, I developed a verruca

on my foot at one point and I remember waiting in a queue at the school clinic to have it treated. A boy in front of me graphically explained what would happen. 'The nurse has a pair of sharp pointed scissors and she sticks one point on either side of the verruca and then digs in and twists and pulls it out.' I am amazed that I stayed in the queue.

Scarlet fever and diphtheria were also rife at the time, and as children we were acutely aware of the risk of potentially having to suddenly leave school for treatment at a sanatorium. During one outbreak, my mother sat me down to explain what was going on and reassure me that if it happened to us, I would still be well cared for, just not by her. I concluded that it sounded like an experience I might enjoy, but it never came to pass.

I did once have to go into hospital, when I was aged seven or eight, to have my tonsils removed. I felt no fear. I walked to the operating theatre myself and the only time I became worried was when I thought they might start to operate before I was asleep. The anaesthetist said I was to keep answering his questions as he put me under, but when I could not understand one of his questions and so fell silent, I momentarily feared the worst. Apart from having to eat porridge, which I disliked, there were no problems after the operation.

The only other major medical problem I developed as a child was a large abscess in my neck, when I was six years old. This was a not uncommon problem and the solution was quite a simple incision. Mine took place in the GP surgery under a so-called local anaesthetic while I sat on my mother's lap. In fact, the skin was simply frozen with ethyl chloride spray. I am not sure whether the icy spray or the knife was the worst aspect, but either way, my scream must have penetrated the air for miles around.

The abscess was dealt with immediately and expeditiously, but it was unfortunately followed by torticollis. This means that my head was fixed in position on one side, and it took weeks of treatment and exercises to correct. I remember feeling guilty, as I was certain it was my fault that it had happened.

While I was at school, all the children of my age group were sent regularly to get ultraviolet rays, which were meant to improve our health. We stripped to the waist, wore dark goggles and paraded around the ultraviolet lamps. There were clearly no concerns then about melanomas!

I loved going to primary school. The teachers wanted us to learn and we wanted to fulfil their ambitions for us. The headmaster, Mr Singleton, was superb and personified the highest ideals of education, drawing out the best that his flock could achieve, giving us every encouragement and getting to know us all as individuals. It was a wonderful foundation for me, for which I have always been grateful.

The school classrooms were arranged around two quadrangles, with the assembly hall in the middle. My desk partner and fierce competitor was Alastair Philips, the son of Dr Philips. We both always wanted dearly to be top of the class, but despite this, we remained good friends. At one point I even planned to call my first child Alastair! My little world was shattered when his parents sent him off to Gordonstoun School; we did meet again many years later, when we were each working as quite senior consultants.

Before starting school I had been a shy child, sometimes painfully so. I often hid under my mother's coat when we met her friends. She decided to combat this with ballet lessons, which were to be the first of many extracurricular interests that I followed in my early years. I happily managed to get over my shyness eventually. I recall getting up to sing 'Hey Little Hen' at a church fête once, much to my mother's astonishment.

St Mark's Church was the centre of the local social – as well as religious – life and I participated in many different activities there, ranging through music, drama and dancing. I became a proficient performer of monologues and knew quite a few by heart, including 'Albert and the Lion' and 'Sam, Sam, Pick Oop Tha' Musket', both of which were popularised by Stanley Holloway of *My Fair Lady* fame. We performed a lot locally and there was once even a poster describing me as 'Layton's Little Wonder Child'. My parents saw that I could quickly and easily learn things by heart and I think they quite enjoyed my local childhood stardom. I never questioned it and simply saw it as part of growing up. In later life, I appreciated that it was helpful to have learned how to speak in public and project my voice. Much later, as a consultant, I frequently advised young trainees who were giving their first presentations to think of themselves as actors on a stage who had to engage their audience.

My father played a key role in the stage productions at the church hall, as he was skilled and able to make scenery out of nothing, or at least nothing very much. He was both practical and artistic and he could see the potential in any old scrap of discarded material. This ability really came into its own after the war, when the war surplus meant there was a wealth of no-longer-needed materials to work with. I vividly recall that when we sang at the Festival of Britain, the Blackpool Girls' Choir was dressed in outfits made from cream parachute silk.

Because my mother had taught me how to read before I started school, I often found myself marking time in the classroom in the early days. There was talk of putting me up a year, which my mother sensibly declined, and it all worked out in the end, as the abscess in my neck meant that I was off school for a few months. When I returned, the wonderful Miss Mills came into my life and she gave me a copy of *The Wind in the Willows*, my first real book, which I treasured.

There were few books in my home or in the homes of my friends, so the local library was the place to go to for reading materials. It was quite a small single-storey building centrally placed by the roundabout in Layton, but its contents were invaluable. I believe strongly that it enabled me to see beyond the horizon of Blackpool and imagine the possibilities that existed in the wider world. Prominent among the discoveries I made there was the world of science and medicine. There was also a bigger 'reference' library in Blackpool where more difficult topics could be pursued. I read about medicine in fiction initially and, because I was fascinated by it, I started to look at its history. In particular, the field of surgery had me gripped and wanting more. The idea that someone would, for the first time ever, open the chest of a patient, not knowing whether they could survive such a major intervention, was captivating stuff for me as a small child. I simply wanted to learn more about this fascinating world, and if possible, to become a part of it. At about eight, I decided that I wanted to be not only a doctor but a surgeon. My perspective back then was, and still is, why not? It was something that held my interest and I had no reason to suppose it would be unusual. I had always felt a desire to fix and mend things, and even at that young age, I saw the attraction of working within a developing area of science. I think some of these ideas came from Arthur Mee's *The Children's Encyclopaedia*. The library had an old copy and I longed to follow the instructions to make, for example, a go-kart. But best of all would be to fix the human body in the ways that I had seen in other library books.

So, I was a budding scientist and quickly developed the habit of carrying out chemistry experiments in our kitchen at home, where I had a Bunsen burner and chemicals that could be bought seemingly without restriction from Mr Iddon in the local chemist's shop. I made my own Petri dishes in the pottery class at school; they were crude but functional. There were sometimes some pretty pungent results and my mother wisely insisted that I should always have the back door open. Fortunately, nothing more serious than an occasional bad smell resulted from my experiments.

By this time, my bedroom was the attic space of our small semi-detached bungalow. I fitted it out with all the gadgets I could create using anything that was surplus to requirements. Doors, windows and light switches could all be controlled from my bedside via discarded parachute cords or hooks and pulleys that I manipulated along the curtain rail.

I liked to use my hands and performed many surgical procedures on my toy panda. It was repeatedly subjected to appendicectomy. I would insert an eraser into the abdomen, remove it via an incision and then sew the panda up again. One of my other early patients was an injured cat that I found abandoned in the road. He had been run over by a bus and his leg was broken. Initially, he seemed destined to be put down, but I persuaded my reluctant parents to allow me to keep him. I splinted and bandaged his leg and cared for him. In time, Snoeky was restored to health and became my great friend.

My biggest worry as a child was always money, as the family finances were obviously limited. The contents of the brown envelopes just about covered our weekly requirements, with little to spare and very few luxuries. Despite that, my family enjoyed playing cards for small amounts of money. This was a source of considerable concern to me; it seemed totally out of character with my parents' otherwise careful existence. I would go to bed, leaving my mum and dad and aunts and uncles playing a game called Halfpenny Nap. Sometimes, I used to creep down the stairs and sit out of sight on the bottom step, making sure that we had not lost all our money in halfpennies.

Most of my clothes were secondhand and I can remember the reluctance, indeed the dread, I felt when being taken to the home of older children to try on their cast-offs. Nothing was wasted and repairs and darns were the norm. I did have one new dress because when my father saw it, with its beautiful red, white and blue pleats, he decided he simply had to find the money for it somehow. He had pocket money for his cigarettes and an occasional beer, and I expect that was the source. I remember that he would sometimes take me 'Christmas shopping' after the shops had closed. I thought everyone did the same, and for me, window shopping was the best kind of shopping anyway.

The wireless provided entertainment, and there were board games and card games for the adults. I very much enjoyed the comics *The Dandy* and *The Beano*, and one of my nicknames was Pansy Potter – the strongman's daughter from *The Beano*. Only last Christmas, my stepdaughter Lesley sourced and purchased a plate with Pansy Potter on it for me.

Music has always been a big part of my life, and an important early influence was a radio programme called *Music While You Work*. Just writing those words brings its theme tune into my head. Every morning before I started attending school, my mother and I would have it on as the background to our activities. There was also a programme called *Friday Night is Music Night* that I listened to often, though I had never seen an orchestra or indeed any musical instruments other than a piano at that time.

I wanted to be able to play music for myself and I decided

early on that it had to be the piano. Dad purchased an old piano and had to cut off its legs to get it into the house. He then restored it once it was inside. My first lessons were when I was around eight or nine, with a Miss Spafford. She was enthusiastic but unskilled, and I soon lost motivation. I was not given to doing much practice, so my mother stopped the lessons, which my parents could ill afford, and it was not until I pleaded to be allowed to return that I began to take it seriously under the tutelage of a new teacher, Mrs Perry. She was a well-respected instructor and made learning a great pleasure.

I have no recollection of taking examinations nor of any associated anxieties, but I did achieve Grade 8. Like many young musicians, I entered competitions and won prizes, but music was never a serious contender for my ideas of a future career. When I was about to leave home for the first time to go to university, Mrs Perry wisely said to me that if I ever became lonely I should simply find a piano. 'Sit down and play and you will find friends.' I was to make use of that suggestion on my very first weekend in University Hall in 1955.

Some members of my father's family had remained in the Swansea area through the war and we would often visit them for the summer holidays. Dad's sister Queenie was married to Reg, who was a train driver and my dad's best friend. My absolute favourite cousin was their son Alan. He was older and always looked after me. He would carry me through the nettles and pick a rose for my bedroom. He had thick, gently curly black hair, a joyous smile and, of course, a lovely lilting Welsh accent. We were such good pals.

The nearby beach was our playground, except along the Swansea Bay, where land mines had been placed during the war. From the cottage at Clyne where we stayed, we could watch the Blitz on Swansea without, as children, any realisation of the enormity of the damage we were witnessing. But elsewhere on the Gower Peninsula, there were great places to play – sea and sand and rock pools. Dad and I would go crabbing in the rock pools with a crab hook that he had made using his welding techniques. Picnics on the beach consisted of paste sandwiches or sometimes sandwich spread, all with a dusting of sand! We often bought trays of tea from the local kiosk and took them to the beach.

Incredibly, even during the war it was sometimes possible to buy an ice cream. The greatest treat of all was to go to Pablo's in Swansea and join a long queue in the hope of successfully buying one. Our ambition as children was that one day we would try the knickerbocker glory, which was the absolute best that Pablo had to offer.

I remember the bus trundling along small lanes to the remote beaches around the Gower, and how the tree branches would brush the sides as we passed. There was an endless choice of beaches; our favourites were Rhossili and the well-named Worm's Head. Uncle Reg and my dad would retire at the end of the day to the Woodman pub in Blackpill, whiling away an hour or two stretching out a small beer each, which was all they could afford. I slept on an inflatable mattress in the lounge, which would be unceremoniously deflated by my cousins whenever they felt it was time to get up.

My other relatives remaining in South Wales were my dad's sister Muriel and her husband Frank. They had two children, Ian and Jacquie. Muriel was an exciting and vivacious woman with a great sense of humour with a touch of naughtiness. It was to her house that, rather surprisingly, considering her naughtiness, my parents allowed my first night away from home without them when I was in my early teens.

Dad's third sister was Olive and she was married to Tony,

who was her second husband. They lived in the next street to us in Layton and had two children: Thelma, by Olive's first husband, and Peter. Auntie Olive was the smart lady of the family. She always wore good clothes and had well-dressed hair. Apparently, she had initially wanted to become a nurse, but had left the training after fainting at the sight of blood. That might go some way to explaining my family's lack of confidence when I later declared my intention to become a surgeon! After all, Aunt Olive's brush with becoming a nurse was the nearest any member of the family had come to having a formal profession, and no one had ever been in higher education, let alone university.

Olive went on to become the manager of a very posh dress shop called Diana Warren's, on Blackpool Promenade. Later in life she was to take on the same job in New Bond Street in London. When I qualified as a doctor, she invited me to the shop, where Diana Warren herself gave me the smartest suit I have ever owned. It was really too small for me, but I was instructed by my aunt to breathe in deeply and to wear it with my (non-existent) corset when I got it home. In other words, do not look a gift horse in the mouth!

Aunt Olive must have forgiven me for once wandering into her shop in Blackpool, hand in hand with Alastair Philips, when we were around six. We had strayed from our class after a school trip to the Blackpool Circus. She put us two waifs and strays into a taxi at once and sent us packing!

I always admired Aunt Olive's well-cared-for hair. As children we had our hair looked after by our parents. I didn't visit a hairdresser until my late teens. Indeed, I was even quite scared of the idea of the hairdresser, for two reasons. The first was that I had seen flames being used on men's necklines in the local barber's shop and I did not fancy that experience. The second was that there were some very strange contraptions hanging from the ceilings of hairdressers at that time, with wires and electricity. They were for giving hair a permanent wave, or a perm. All best avoided, in my opinion back then. Mostly, my hair was in plaits or bunches; I would very occasionally curl it. The process for curling hair was as follows: strips of cloth were tied to the ends of a bunch of wet hair, then twisted and tied up so that when dry and released the next day, the hair was curled. Sooner or later everyone wanted curls, and 'home perms' could be purchased in the chemist's shop. DIY hairdressing occupied many of my friends and family for hours.

Dad's brothers were Harold and Albert. Harold was called up for the war and ended up in Ceylon, as Sri Lanka was then known. He and his wife Elsie had one child, Sheila, who was also born in 1937, just a few weeks after me. We spent a lot of our youth together, especially at dance class, and dancing was eventually to become her career. She easily passed the Eleven-plus and decided to go to Elmslie School for Girls. It was not a particularly academic school, although it did have a most attractive purple and yellow uniform! Gradually, we went our separate ways, though we never lost touch. Our worlds were miles apart but she had no close family. I wanted to be supportive and, indeed, I loved her. I was at her side when she died of a stroke after receiving thrombolytic treatment for a heart attack in University College Hospital in London.

In the time leading up to her death, Sheila had asked me to look after her cat when she died. I agreed, though I knew that it would be difficult to do so. But a promise is a promise, so I said to my husband Jack that we would have to take care of this cat. I discovered at the funeral that no fewer than six of her friends had been persuaded to agree to take it in, and one of them was very keen to do so. Thank goodness!

Albert was the most financially successful of the six Dring children. He joined Woolworths on the shop floor in Blackpool and worked his way up to become a board member, buying shoes for the chain around the world. With his wife Phyllis, he eventually settled in Chorleywood, near London. They had no children. It was Albert and Phyllis who generously gifted me my much-treasured record player, which became my first means of listening to recorded music. My first purchase was a recording of the 'Karelia Suite' by Sibelius, which I played to its destruction. Mostly, I enjoyed recordings of classical music, largely symphonic, and almost always borrowed from the library.

Another important person in my childhood was my friend Jean. She and her parents lived two streets away and we went to the same school, though she was one year ahead of me. She had the huge misfortune to lose both her parents to cancer in the early days of our secondary education. I visited one of them in the Christie Hospital in Manchester, and the ward filled with people in the end stages of cancer was overwhelming for me as a child. I thought I was going to faint and feared that if I did, it would be the end of my hopes for a medical career. Thankfully, I managed to stay upright.

My parents were a great help to Jean and continued to be supportive of her throughout their lives. She married and now lives in Holland, and I think of her as a sort of sister even today.

After we passed the Eleven-plus, Jean and I both had our secondary education at the Blackpool Collegiate School for Girls, the best local school for girls. It was there that, for the next seven years, I progressed towards my dream of attending medical school.

2
Secondary School

When I began my new life at the Blackpool Collegiate School for Girls in 1948, there was an immediate and evident difference from primary school. There had been no uniforms there, but here we wore navy blue gym slips with white shirts and a tie, which I had to learn to put on. There was also a porkpie hat, and heaven preserve you if you were seen outside without it! One day, I clearly recall setting off to school in my pixie hood, which my mother had made me. It was warm and cosy and covered my ears; it was also very much not within the school rules. I had simply forgotten. Miraculously, I got away with it but I was never to make the same mistake again. I had a miserable day of prolonged anxiety.

My primary school had been a warm and nurturing place, where few restrictions were imposed on us. Here, however, we were subjected to strict rules, such as not talking in the corridors and always wearing our uniforms correctly. I was a girl who tended to obey the rules, as were most of my classmates. We simply did as we were told. Secondary school would prove to be quite a disappointing experience for me, with little of the encouragement that was so freely provided at my primary school.

The school was on a large site with adequate playing fields for hockey, netball and tennis. I was not an enthusiast for sport but did what was required and developed into a reasonable netball and tennis player. The school houses, named after local landmarks, were Pendle, Parlick, Longridge and Bowland, the latter being my house.

Generally, I walked to school, which was just over a mile away, but there were occasions when my father would miraculously appear in his van beside me and my friends as we were walking to school in the rain. This was typical of my father. I still can imagine him now, standing in a downpour in the yard where he worked and thinking about how we would be getting wet on our way to school. So, if he could, he would come along in his work van and hope to find us en route. My cousin Peter would sometimes get off his bike and walk with me when he was on his way to St Joseph's College, known to all as Holy Joe's, which was next door to my school. Very occasionally, we took the bus for about half the journey, at all times wearing our hats, of course.

The school day always began with assembly, at which the whole school would sing a hymn and listen to announcements about activities and events. The head was called Mrs

Robinson and she had a strong Scottish accent. Sometimes her announcements caught our interest, and never more so than when a summer job was announced to go 'rice picking in Persia'. There was a rush of interested applicants until we discovered that what Mrs Robinson had actually said was 'rasp' picking in Perthshire'. Which wasn't quite so exciting.

After assembly we would march out and return to our allocated classrooms, where we'd stay for all of the lessons that did not require specialist equipment. We were streamed according to overall ability and I was always in the top stream, though not at the top of the class. Some subjects, such as mathematics, came very easily to me and I did well. This may in part have been the result of our maths teacher's abilities. Miss Mason was a superb teacher.

We all loved Miss Astle, who taught geography and had the ability to bring the whole world to light. She was a model for us in every sense, including the physical, as she was a happy, vivacious blonde beauty. Sadly, I struggled with history, which seemed to me dull and irrelevant. In later life, I came to wish I had taken a greater interest.

I enjoyed Shakespeare as it allowed me to use some of my acting skills and I even won some prizes, but our book choices were generally not at all inspirational until the sixth form. Someone decided that at that stage the scientists should have a weekly class in the humanities, and I still have the brilliant reading list that our teacher gave us. At last, books to enjoy, books that restored my early love of the written word. One of the first that I read and adored was Dodie Smith's *I Capture the Castle*.

However, my greatest love was science, and in this area the teaching was undoubtedly disappointing. I think it would be fair to say that the school's strengths were not in the direction of the sciences, as a scientific education was then not really seen as appropriate for girls. The boys' grammar school, for example, had a notably better science department. Of course, as a prospective medical student, science was my greatest focus and need. My mother had received little formal education but was intelligent and aware of the school's deficiencies. By this time she had accepted the inevitability of my application to medical school and was determined to help me. She bought the A-Level syllabus in advance, in order to ensure that I had covered all the relevant subjects for the exams.

Our biology teacher, Miss Wright, was a jolly, rounded person who loved botany and, in particular, lichens. Her grasp of the syllabus was limited, but she did at least provide the basics. It was much more difficult to make up for the deficits in chemistry and physics teaching, as the practical aspects needed professional guidance. Sadly, the best chemistry teacher had to quit because of a family tragedy and following that, the whole class struggled. Nonetheless, I passed the exams with a sufficient grade to get me into medical school and I even managed a distinction in biology.

Right from the start, our friendship groups were largely associated with the subjects we enjoyed, so most of my friends were, like me, budding scientists and also decent musicians. At the end of the school day, we would all amble homewards in groups and linger on the street corners where our routes parted in order to have that extra five minutes of chat that seemed so vital at the time. We would be laden down by our satchels, which contained our vital possessions: books, pens and paper – there were no electronic devices then. Chatting was the equivalent of modern-day calls and texting, but of course it ended as soon as we parted company.

My best friend, however, lived a long way from school, so

was not part of the group meandering home together. Sheila was a farmer's daughter and both of us were set on becoming doctors. She was tall, utterly dependable and very honest. We both loved learning about animal life, but had no inclination to become vets. She once brought a mouse from her family's farm into school in a box. When she opened the box, she found that, much to her surprise, it had given birth to six little mice!

Anyone who misbehaved was punished by detention; the pupil in question had to stay behind at school for an extra hour and complete a task. Writing lines was a popular punishment, though to my mind, it was of no possible benefit to anyone. When I became a prefect and had to devise such punishments myself, I gave my hapless victims the civil service arithmetic tests to work through instead. I enjoyed doing them and they were beneficial, so I thought, *Why would not everyone find them useful?*

In my early teens I had the opportunity to do an exchange visit with a French girl, Catherine. I was in my fourth year at secondary school when decisions had to be taken about O Level subjects. I needed a language in order to go to university, and in my mock exams I had got 33 per cent for both Latin and French, so it was a good idea for me to strengthen a language.

My classmates and I travelled as a group with the French teacher, Miss Taylor, taking the train, the ferry and the train again into the Gare Saint-Lazare in Paris. The journey was a great adventure as I had not travelled abroad previously, though it was daunting to be in the company of a teacher all day long. Some girls became seasick on the ferry, but I was luckily not so afflicted and quite enjoyed my first trip to sea.

Our hosts were waiting for us at the train station and I recall standing there and hoping that someone nice would call my name. I was the guest of the Chollet family and was taken to their Paris apartment, a vast place on rue de Monceau, close to Parc Monceau and the Arc de Triomphe in the 8th arrondissement. I was driven from the station in a luxurious Citroen and I remember Monsieur Chollet (and just about every other driver we passed too) making liberal use of the car horn.

We took an ornate lift from the ground floor up to the family's apartment and to me it felt like something from a film. On emerging from the lift, we entered a huge area that was probably a complete floor of the apartment block. There were several bedrooms and bathrooms; it was clearly a world away from my home in Blackpool. I had one small suitcase with all my limited possessions in it and I remember feeling very small and lost on my first night away from my family.

It was difficult to communicate initially, and I remember hearing Monsieur Chollet ask his wife, 'Does she not speak *any* French?' By the time I had worked out a response, it was too late for me to say anything. However, they were a large family and, in addition to Catherine, there were some friendly younger siblings. Jacques was just five and making all the same mistakes with French as I was. *'Non, non, non,'* he would say, and then teach me as he was himself being taught.

In addition to their grand apartment in Paris, the family had two other homes, and I spent most of the trip at one of these, a cottage in Gif on the outskirts of Paris. We were plagued by mosquitos, but that was really the only problem and I had a very happy time there. It was an idyllic existence, cycling around the local area (which I was not allowed to do at home), picking soft fruits, eating lovely food and slowly becoming quite fluent in French. Cycling was, for me, a particular treat, though it also made me feel quite guilty. I had longed for a bicycle as a child, and when I was 12, one eventually materialised. I was thrilled.

However, my father restricted my cycling to our most local streets and I was absolutely not allowed to go on the main roads. Here in France, I was free, though I felt anxious that my father would not be pleased if he knew. There was some concern from the Chollets that I did not have appropriate footwear for cycling, so one day they took me to the market and bought me a brand-new pair of shoes. As someone very used to hand-me-downs, this struck me as an incredibly generous gesture.

Every Sunday, the grandmother of the Chollet family would make baba au rhum, which seemed to me a huge amount of effort for little reward. To everyone else, though, it was the pièce de résistance of the big family meal.

After three weeks in France, Catherine and I travelled to Blackpool and to my parents' tiny council house, which could not have been more different from the grand French abode. I was of course aware of the contrast between our respective homes, though it didn't trouble me. By this time we were used to chatting in French and indeed I was even thinking in French, so I benefitted hugely. Rather more than my opposite number, because even in England we continued to converse in French.

On my return to school, I nonetheless chose to take Latin over French at O Level, which perhaps seems quite perverse, but it was a good decision. Latin is very useful to a medical student. Moreover, the exam was almost two weeks after all of the others were finished, so I was able to settle down to work and was proud to earn a distinction.

My first musical experiences at secondary school were not so good; I was not up to the required standard. I was not much good at sight-reading and my hopes of becoming a school pianist had to wait until I made progress in that regard. Later, however, I was able to play at many school events and sing in the choir. I even went on to conduct the house choir and guided it through various interhouse competitions.

My best choir experience, however, was with the Blackpool Girls' Choir. We were conducted by a charismatic Mrs Dunkerly, who also gave me some singing lessons. The choir had a weekly evening meeting where we rehearsed a wide variety of part songs for girls. We entered competitions for choirs and did enjoy some success. We were young teenagers and of course the boys were denied this sort of experience because of their changing voices. Membership was by invitation and I am sure Mrs Dunkerly had talent scouts around all the local schools.

If my memory is correct, when we sang in a competition at the Festival of Britain – dressed in our parachute silk outfits, of course – we won a prize. My memory is not in doubt about the accommodation, however. I vividly recall sleeping on bunks in the underground tunnel at Clapham Junction, which had served as a shelter during the war. Trains ran in the tunnels above us through the night and provided an interesting nocturnal accompaniment.

Under the guidance of Mrs Perry, my piano playing progressed in leaps and bounds. I came up to the standard required of school pianists and was delighted to eventually become one. This meant playing for the daily assembly, which involved gentle music as the school gathered together, a hymn and finally a rousing march as students filed out. All very good preparation for becoming a 'useful' pianist at university, when I would find myself playing for choirs, chamber music, dances and other events.

I was involved with a wonderful amateur drama festival too,

for which one-act plays were performed at the Grand Theatre in the centre of Blackpool. I was used to performing as part of my many out-of-school activities and loved it. As usual, my father made the scenery both for these plays and for other events like local pantomimes. One opening scene was in a French kitchen, and Dad had a kettle on the stove and used dry ice to create the steam. Unfortunately, it drifted downwards rather than upwards as steam would usually, but it was as good as we could muster and was greatly appreciated by the audience, with prolonged applause when the curtain rose.

I had lots of hobbies and interests to keep me busy and, on one occasion, the head advised my mother to start a society for saying 'no' for me. Old habits die hard and I am still generally more inclined to agree to do something than to say no to it. I have sometimes been advised to be more assertive, and for me this translates into being more likely to decline rather than agree. But what a dull world it would be if everyone responded to requests for help or invitations to participate with the word 'no'.

When I was young we had a golden cocker spaniel at home called Rusty, and sadly I was to learn about the complexities of head injury through him. We once had to place Rusty in kennels while we went on holiday. On our return, the kennel said we could not collect him immediately. We later learned that while the dogs were out exercising together, a fight had broken out, which had been resolved by a stranger throwing a brick that had hit Rusty on the head. In the following weeks he developed a new and aggressive personality. He had until then been a gentle and loving friend, but the injury had turned him into a growling and rather vicious, even frightening, animal. One day I was walking home from school and happened to notice that the vet's car was parked nearby. It was a very distinctive and desirable maroon VW Karmann Ghia. When I arrived home my precious dog was fitting repeatedly, so I ran back to where I had seen the car. The vet had me jump in beside him and we rushed home. Sadly, Rusty died of a subdural haematoma (a clot of blood on the brain) as a result of the trauma. I was very distressed but also curious about this development. I was only to understand the mechanism for it and the accompanying personality change when I became a clinical student years later. It can happen in people too and can and should be successfully treated.

Rusty's death meant that we were without a pet at home – Snoeky had died some time previously – so I decided, without consulting my family, to fill that gap. I purchased a Siamese kitten as a Christmas gift for my unsuspecting parents. My friend Jean and I managed to secrete it away somehow until Christmas morning, when I released the enchanting though energetic kitten on poor Mum and Dad. They were amazingly tolerant of this gesture and of the ball of fur that could circumnavigate their entire living room without touching the floor!

Around this time, my parents were able to purchase 11 Wembley Avenue as sitting tenants, and although it was a major decision, it was worth the financial burden. Dad was an excellent DIY man and restored the bungalow to a high standard, so they were able to sell it at a profit and eventually move to a rather larger house. I was not involved in the decision and was quite shocked to one day find myself in a new home on Westcliffe Drive in Layton. It was, however, a good move and eventually that house too was upgraded and sold on when they moved to Great Eccleston in the Fylde. During their married lives, my parents lived in a total of 18 different properties.

There was still no central heating in the Westcliffe Drive property, but the room in which I did my homework was adjacent to next door's chimney, so it was always warm and comfortable. Mum would encourage my efforts by bringing me a cup of tea or an apple. I used a table left behind by the previous owners – in fact, I still have that 'homework' table in my house today.

During my teens, my social life largely revolved around the church and music. This was in part because I went to a girls' school, so the annual school dance was a dull affair. It was organised with dance cards, which we had to fill in at the start of the evening. On one occasion I had to ask the head for a dance, and when the moment came for me to take Mrs Robinson onto the dance floor, my arms encircled her waist and I found what felt like a ring of steel there. I had not encountered stays before and was shocked as well as puzzled by her corsets.

I was by now part of a group of teenaged boys and girls who did everything together. I still had to ask permission to go out with any of them and I well remember us all going to a dance at the Blackpool Tower Ballroom. Beforehand, Dad had made me promise not to go to the bar. When all the other members of the group immediately did exactly that, what was I to do? So I joined them. It was busy with a lively atmosphere, and I remember feeling anxious and wondering what I should order, as I had no experience whatsoever to guide me. We were all 16, so of course we didn't consume any alcohol, but even going to the bar felt like seriously stepping out of line.

When I returned home, Dad was waiting up, as I knew he would be. My first words to him were, 'Dad, I'm so sorry. I went to the bar.' He forgave me. I never wanted to hurt him and was well aware of how important I was to him and how much he cared for me. Discipline in my father's hands was simply a look of disappointment, which I never wanted to see.

Surprisingly, for someone so protective, he did not seem to have any objection to my heading off to the Lake District to climb fells with this same group of teenagers. We stayed in youth hostels, and over the course of several trips, went up all the major peaks. I loved – and indeed still love today – the wild emptiness of the area. It was always a place of great solace, no matter what the weather. We travelled by bus and I have no idea who planned these expeditions and booked the youth hostels. Perhaps we simply turned up and worked it all out as we went.

In those days wearing trousers as a girl was fairly risqué, so my request for a pair of shorts to wear on these trips was nothing short of shocking. My argument was that if trousers got wet, it was very difficult to get them dry for the next day. If I wore shorts, however, I would only need a towel to dry my legs. I did eventually get my pair of shorts; they were very short indeed and made of beige corduroy. I remember the boys telling me that people followed me around in order to see if I was wearing anything under my anorak.

My surname was Dring and they gave me the nickname Gunga Dring the Water Carrier because I was never without a suitable supply. My anorak was not very robust and kept out neither the wind nor the rain. However, what the anorak lacked was made up for by my brilliant boots. They were tough army-style boots, with metal studs to provide grip. Of course, grip on soft ground translated into slipperiness on wet rocks. And the rocks were always wet! My shoes made a very distinct sound when we walked along the roads. They needed cleaning at the end of each day or there would be a flat surface of dried mud to walk on the following morning.

One of the downsides of staying in youth hostels was the

requirement to do jobs before leaving in the morning; for example, you might have to peel a sack of potatoes for the evening meal. There were no vehicles and rarely any bicycles around, so it was strictly walkers at the hostel. We slept in unisex dorms in our sleeping bags, and considering that our hormones must have been raging at that time, we were very chaste. I remember feeling embarrassed by some of the songs the boys sang. It was pretty innocent stuff by today's standards, such as 'She'll Be Coming Round the Mountain when She Comes' and 'Oh, Sir Jasper', but to me the songs were quite wicked.

I had my own Ward Lock Guide to the Lake District. There was no Wainwright Guide to follow then, but we were competent with a map and a compass. I was quite a keen botanist and enjoyed discovering my first carnivorous plants on one walking trip. My early experience of the Lake District and of walking was to develop into a lifelong love of mountains and the countryside in general. I have often remarked that my soul resides in the Lake District and the region has certainly been of great importance to me throughout my life.

Although I had plenty of extracurricular activities, I was nevertheless a dedicated student and I had long ago decided that I would become a doctor, and indeed a surgeon. The lack of careers advice at school did not hamper me, but when it came to actually applying to university, I really was in the dark. It never even crossed my mind to apply for Oxford or Cambridge. My ambition ranged only as far as Liverpool and Manchester.

I was offered interviews by both, so I took the train from Blackpool and found my way alone to my destinations. It was hard enough to find the money for one such train journey, let alone two, so there was no way that I could be accompanied. I still have a vivid recollection of walking along Oxford Road in Manchester and up Brownlow Hill in Liverpool. I wore a coat and matching hat, gloves and shoes and presented myself for the first interviews of my life, having done no formal preparation for them whatsoever.

I was delighted when both universities offered me a place; I chose Liverpool. Happily I passed my A Levels; I was amazed to achieve a sufficient standard to be accepted into medical school. I was granted a bursary, which covered my tuition and gave me the full grant of £200 per annum. This had to cover everything: clothes, travel, accommodation, books. I had no extras from my parents, though in some respects I was better off than those with wealthy parents, who might be expected to contribute but sometimes did not. At least I knew precisely what I had to live on.

Clothes were perhaps the greatest defect in my preparation for university. Because we wore uniform at school, I had an extremely limited range of other clothes. At the end of my first term away, I set about making some clothes in order to fill that gap. Despite an early teacher's report that 'Averil will never learn to sew', I was quite handy with the needle and thread when making something of interest, and of course that was also to be helpful later, in the operating theatre.

So, in 1955 I had all the necessary qualifications for going to university, though no understanding of what it would involve in personal terms. There were so many unknowns. But it was exciting and I was embarking on the road to becoming a doctor. I thought that road would simply carry me along and I had no fear of failure. In truth, I had little idea of just how difficult I would find this new venture, and at that time, no understanding of my lack of preparedness.

3
Off to Liverpool

Finally, in September 1955, the big day arrived. I was to commence the next major episode of my life, as a university student. The summer had passed quickly at home, with me initially waiting for the results of my three A Level exams, then for confirmation that I would be supported financially with a bursary. To pass the time, along with friends who were in similar positions, I would wander into Blackpool and stroll along the promenade, or better still, take a bus to the Lake District to stay in a youth hostel and climb the Lakeland Fells.

Although I was just emerging from school, some of my friends had already started their university lives, so there was a hint of what was to come, but neither school nor home offered any real preparation for this adventure. Of course, no one in my family had ever taken the step of applying to university, and although there were a few others from my school class heading off for higher education, I was the only one going to Liverpool Medical School. My success was reported in the local newspaper. The school did not offer me any guidance and I admit I didn't think too deeply about the detail. It was simply a necessary step on my road to becoming a doctor. I packed what clothes I had, which were basically a couple of jumpers and skirts. The only other major item I took with me was my portable gramophone, given to me by my 'rich uncle' Albert.

My parents delivered me and my very few possessions in their Austin van to University Hall in Liverpool, although my father was not even allowed to help me carry my trunk to my room, as men could only enter the main hall and not beyond. I felt a mixture of emotions on the day. I was excited yet at the same time bewildered and overwhelmed, though I kept my concerns to myself. I was allocated a perfectly adequate though sparse and uninteresting room that I was to share with a fellow student called Penny. This arrangement did not last long, however, as it was on the top floor and Penny turned out to be a sleepwalker. She was quickly moved to the ground floor and I found myself alone again.

I was not used to being on my own, despite being an only child, but I remembered my piano teacher's words: 'You have never been away from home before and you may feel lonely. If you do, find a piano, play it, and you will soon have friends.'

The words struck me as good advice and so on the Sunday evening, I did exactly that. I found an old upright piano down a corridor somewhere, and in no time, people had gathered round, all complete strangers who no doubt were also feeling lonesome. Friendships began and music was responsible for bringing me some all-important human contact. From then on, the piano rather dominated my life. I had always enjoyed entertaining others with music or drama or dance. Music provided a means of expressing my emotions, a rhythm to dance to, songs to sing and the joy of making wonderful sounds and tunes. While at university, I discovered the great pleasure of being an accompanist, and this would prove to be a continuing pursuit throughout my life. When times are hard, I have always turned to music for solace. At the end of a long, tough or frustrating day at work, I would routinely take out those emotions on the piano. When my husband died in 2013, the vicar asked what was the most important aspect of the funeral for me, and I responded, 'The music.' But just as importantly, music has been there for celebrations. Having my grandchildren play for me at my eightieth birthday party a few years ago was simply perfect.

My mother was never much of a cook and she did not pass on her limited skills to her daughter, but the hall provided us with breakfast and dinner, so at least I was well fed at university. The majority of first-year students were in such accommodation and it was ideal for me. No shopping, no cooking, no washing up and precious little cleaning. We did, however, have to wash our clothing by hand, and I remember the shock of seeing the colour of the water when I washed my underwear for the first time in Liverpool. The water turned black almost instantly. It took me a moment to realise that this was caused by the smoke-laden atmosphere of the city, long before smokeless fuel and low-emission zones were introduced. I also remember the first time I saw the lungs of a resident of Merseyside; they, too, were completely black from the smoke. It was quite shocking.

We sang a Latin grace before dinner and the student head of music had to pitch the first note. Picking the wrong pitch could be disastrous and might end with the whole room screeching or growling quite tunelessly. In my second year, it became my job to set the pitch. I can still sing it today. There was a formal top table with the warden and other staff members, but it was far from an Oxbridge experience. However, dinner in the hall – which looked a lot like my school assembly hall – was probably the nearest to that collegiate atmosphere and it provided a great opportunity to sit down and converse with new friends. I especially appreciated the fact that we were from a diverse range of backgrounds and in diverse faculties; for me, this was the core of a good university experience. The fact that the hall was unisex, however, was a distinct disadvantage.

Because I had the necessary A Levels, I was placed without discussion straight into the second year of medical school. That was a mistake. Although the first year would have been largely a repetition of what I had learned for A Levels, I would have benefited greatly from having a year to adjust to this new life away from my home and family.

There was no guidance about how to find our lectures, or even the timetable, and I missed some classes out of sheer ignorance. I had not found any other medical students in my all-female hall of residence, though I learned that there was a tram from Edge Road, close to the hall, that took us to the university. I had been interviewed in the Medical School and eventually managed to find it again, at the centre of the red-brick university, with its Victorian building and clock tower.

The first lecture I attended was, I later discovered, on the subject of superficial and deep fascia (the connective tissue that surrounds organs and muscles). At the time, though, I had no idea what the lecturer was saying and could not even work out how the words were spelled, so I had no hope of looking them up afterwards. I was too shy to ask for help. I did not know a single person in my class at that stage and there still did not appear to be any women from the hall of residence among the new medical students. Women were greatly outnumbered by men and the male students seemed to have all the confidence that I was lacking. The men were also largely in groups, possibly of old school friends, and this gave them a great advantage when settling into this new life and learning the ropes.

The next hurdle in that first momentous week was the toughest: the dissecting room. Human bodies were laid out on dissecting tables in a vast room. Students from the second and third years were to work on bodies at the same time and of course, the third-year students knew the ropes, so they ran the show. They could spot an overwhelmed schoolgirl a mile off. Everybody was allocated a part of the body to dissect. Around each body there would be a group of eager (or was it terrified?) students, two to each body part. That meant two working on each arm, two on each leg, abdomen, chest, head and neck – at least a dozen working at each cadaver.

Back when I was at secondary school, I had asked my parents to give me a book about the human body for my Christmas present. They did so, but the pages about the reproductive systems were solidly glued together by my protective father. He would have been horrified had he known that the perineum was the part I was allocated in a male cadaver. I was pretty horrified myself.

I had enjoyed, indeed excelled at, dissecting a frog at school, but this was entirely different. It was overwhelming. The smell of formalin. The proximity of men. The enormous room. The embarrassment of the genitalia. I was quite simply out of my depth. Having dreamed of getting to medical school and even of learning human anatomy, the reality was shocking. I had – in fact, still have – a beautiful dissection kit in a black leather zip-up wallet. I so wanted to get on with the job, but the practicalities proved difficult and I struggled to keep up. I never truly recovered from that initial setback and was greatly in need of help and guidance. But you had to stand on your own two feet and absolutely not admit to feeling left behind. I did have a wonderful dissection partner called Gerry, but he was as lost as I was, so together we weren't able to make much progress.

One other early memory I have of medical school seems incredible from a modern perspective. In one of our pharmacology classes, we were divided into two halves and told we would be given an injection of the new drug penicillin. There were two types, so half the class received one type of injection and the rest had the other. No consent was sought. We were just guinea pigs. Happily, there were no anaphylactic reactions.

With my classes all proving extremely difficult, I found solace in music and did rather more musical activity than was sensible given my workload as a medical student. I was a good pianist by this point and set about becoming a good sight-reader. I came to be greatly in demand by my fellow students in all faculties, be it to accompany a choir, to play for dances or simply to provide entertainment, all of which I enjoyed enormously. Music was a refuge for me, something I could enjoy, while my classes in the likes of anatomy and physiology proved difficult.

The whole medical course was six years long, but I, of course, was starting at year two, having bypassed the first Professional Examination. The first major hurdle, known to all as 2nd MB (Bachelor of Medicine), was two thirds of the way through year three, my second year, so for me it fell five terms after I started at the Medical School. It was a major exam and required detailed knowledge of human anatomy and physiology. There were no preparatory exams and no mock exams you could take to judge how prepared you were. It was my very first experience of university-level examinations.

I failed. I had simply not done enough work. I was devastated. I recall sitting alone in the garden that surrounds the Anglican cathedral and weeping. After years of wanting to become a medical student, I was now in danger of being thrown out. Just one more chance and three months to do it in. Fortunately, by dint of much hard slog, I made up for lost time and was hugely relieved to pass at the second attempt.

Year four (my third year) was the start of three years of clinical teaching and the beginning of the real business of medical school: visiting hospitals, meeting patients and learning about diseases and how to diagnose and treat them. For this clinical teaching, we were placed into groups of eight, known as firms. The university, in its wisdom, labelled the students who had initially failed the 2nd MB as Group F, so we could not forget our narrow escape until we qualified. Of course, I did not let the same situation arise again and from then on passed everything. It had been a hard but useful lesson.

Unlike the years of pre-clinical teaching, I absolutely loved the next three years of clinical work. At last I was doing what I had set out to do. It all came easily to me, in complete contrast to learning anatomy and physiology. I was by this time used to being an independent student away from home and had a great thirst for the knowledge that I was there to acquire.

Each day would commence with a lecture at the university, then we would travel, usually by bus or tram, to our appointed hospital. The clinical teaching took place in our firms, overseen by the medical staff of the unit to which we were assigned. My first surgical firm was at the David Lewis Northern Hospital, which would many years later become my consultant patch. It was an old hospital on the northern end of the docks, with both Nightingale-style and round wards, where the nurses wore smart uniforms of starched aprons and frilly hats. The surgeons in charge of the firm to which I was allocated were Mr Hunter and Mr Hawe, and we were all in awe of them.

We were even more in awe of the ward sister, who ran the place with a rod of iron. Officially, us students were known as clerks on the medical units and as dressers on the surgical units. We were called dressers because one of our roles was to assist with the dressings that were deemed to be required daily. They were kept in a large round sterile drum and this drum accompanied us on the rounds. One day, it was my lot in life to pass the required dressing to the ward sister. I was meant to lift the lid without touching the inside of the drum and pass the dressing to the sister using a large pair of Cheadle forceps. But no one had told me that, of course, so I delved in and took out the required dressing with my bare and possibly grubby hands, thus rendering the whole lot unsterile and unusable.

What followed can only be described as an explosion. I immediately found myself on my way out of the ward and out of reach of the furious sister. Many years later, when I returned to that ward as a consultant, the same ward sister was in charge. She didn't allude to my unfortunate drum incident in any way, but I was sure she remembered.

Because we were on our feet for most of the day, we would often drop exhausted into a Lyons Corner House café after work, for a coffee or tea, and a sticky bun too, when we could afford it. The cafes were always warm and comfortable and provided refuge at the end of a sometimes tough shift. I recall becoming seriously worried by the pain I felt in my feet towards the end of each day. I had to resolve the issue; if I was to become a surgeon I would often be standing for many hours at a time. I knew that I had bigger-than-average feet; once, my mother had taken me to Manchester specially to buy shoes that would fit me. What I did not know was that the shoes she was able to purchase, the biggest available, were still one size too small for my feet. That explained the problem, but did not provide a solution, and buying shoes has remained a difficulty throughout my life in the UK. In truth, I was always most comfortable in theatre, where we wore clogs. They were unisex and so came in a wonderful array of large sizes.

As part of our clinical training, we were allocated patients. They would tell us their histories in response to our questions and we would learn how to examine them, what investigations to order and what treatment to give. Taking a patient's history was done according to a series of questions, including subheadings such as 'previous illnesses' and 'history of the present complaint'. We were, of course, feeling our way into the different manners in which people spoke about their anatomy and their complaints. We had to learn how to ask questions about personal things without causing embarrassment and in a way that every patient understood. The art of how to communicate – asking and explaining in a way that is readily understood – was not taught then, but it is undoubtedly an art form and it remains a vital part of a doctor's work.

The consultation was followed by a physical examination, which we were taught to make comprehensive. I never resorted to a shortcut examination of only the apparently relevant part. A patient might present with a hernia, for example, and it would be easy and quick to simply examine the hernia. But so often there is a backstory of chronic bronchitis, smoking or constipation, which are all highly relevant when it comes to the management of hernias. I stuck to this routine throughout my career. It took more time but, for me, it was an essential step in the care of the whole patient and it sometimes resulted in finding problems of relevance outside the main area of referral.

When Pam, a fellow student, fell ill and struggled to explain her own symptoms to us, we understood just how difficult it must be for patients with no medical background to find the right words. However, it was quite clear that Pam was seriously unwell, with what later turned out to be ulcerative colitis. She sought help from one of our teachers and, for the first time, I saw the additional burden that can be imposed on doctors when they know the patient they are treating well. We would not generally give treatment to or operate on a relative, and sometimes we need to extend that no-go zone to other people we are close to.

Pam became rapidly more sick. Even as a student I could understand the surgeon's obvious reluctance to propose a major and drastic operation to remove all of the diseased colon and give her an ileostomy, which is a stoma, or an opening, on the abdominal wall – an irreversible intervention. Instead she was given more and more medical treatment, which gave no remission, and she became increasingly frail. Sometimes we have to be dispassionate and pay no heed to the fact that a patient might be a young, attractive and promising student. We have to do the unthinkable that will save a life. Pam eventually had the surgery, but it was too late. That reluctance cost Pam her life. It was a heartbreaking lesson for us all.

As a budding surgeon, I could see the gravity of the decision-making that my chosen specialty would involve, but I was not deterred. I was keen to get into theatre whenever possible to assist with operations. I spent most of the summer holiday after 2nd MB assisting in theatre at Blackpool Victoria Hospital in my hometown. I learned to scrub up, to put on my gown and gloves and generally to be a useful pair of hands.

The first time you scrub up is pretty daunting. You are watched over by an experienced theatre sister who will not be shy to point out your errors and make you start all over again. In essence, you wash, and in those days scrub, for ten minutes up to the elbows and then, after drying your arms on a sterile towel, don a gown and gloves without letting your skin touch the outside of either. On the first occasion it took so many attempts to get it right that the patient was being wheeled back out of the theatre by the time I achieved the theatre sister's standards.

We wore dresses when I first started in theatre, though now most surgeons wear trousers and a V-necked top, known as scrubs, which I am sure are familiar to TV viewers. Over the scrub suit you wear a gown that has been washed and folded inside out, packed and sterilised. The folding is to enable the surgeon to put on the gown without touching the surface that would be in contact with the patient. The hands must never come into contact with the outside surface of the gown until the sterile gloves have been donned. Similarly, the gloves are presented to you in such a way that you can put them on without touching the outside surface. It can be quite a tricky performance when you are a beginner!

During my career, single-use disposable gowns were introduced. I remember being quite horrified at this development because of the waste that resulted, but it was justified as cost saving. Something similar occurred with the drapes that cover the patient during an operation. Originally these were washed and reused, until disposable drapes came into being. Even the method of attaching the drapes to the patient so they don't slip changed, from clips which attached them to the skin to holding them in place with an adhesive.

It was much easier to justify disposable gloves. As a student I was sometimes given the chore of mending used gloves after they had been cleaned and before they were resterilised. We had a cylinder of compressed air, patches of latex and an adhesive to stick the patches over the air leaks until the gloves were airtight. Before they were sterilised, the cuffs were turned back so that the surgeon could don the gloves by only touching the inside.

Syringes were made of glass then and were continuously used, washed and resterilised. Pretty much every item – apart from things that were destined to remain inside the patient – was reused. Even the needles for sutures were cleaned and reused; the theatre sister would thread catgut or silk through the eye of the needle. Ligatures were often served up to the surgeon on a bobbin. Nowadays a suture is attached to the needle, which is only ever used once.

Major changes came in terms of the materials available for us to work with throughout my career; this was particularly beneficial in catheters and cannulae, where the use of plastic enabled their wall thickness to become thinner and the channel through which fluids travelled (the lumen) to therefore become wider. In my early training, catheters were made from latex rubber and the wall thickness constituted much of the diameter. Here too, though, disposable became the byword.

During my time at Blackpool Victoria Hospital, I saw a wide variety of surgical operations and became familiar with surgical anatomy, as well as with the tools of the trade. I always loved the instruments and went on to become adept in their use. I learned all the names and functions, which stood me in good stead back in Liverpool. There was a huge emergency load at the hospital in Blackpool, often because people would ignore their symptoms so as not to spoil their family seaside holiday by seeking medical advice. Becoming a patient in a strange town was far more disruptive and it meant that the operating theatres were frequently overtaken by emergencies. My extra pair of hands was welcomed even if I was inexperienced.

I quickly found that I could see the difference between the truly skilful surgeons and the less good ones, and I was determined to be in the former category. The young student who is adept at doing practical tasks has a head start in surgery and is far more likely to enjoy the discipline. In later years I often took part in skills demonstrations on models at the Royal College of Surgeons. School students would come along and have a go at putting sutures into artificial skin. It was clear that some were naturally able, while others were far clumsier.

As a medical student I was continually encouraged to acquire good practical skills. That process begins with very small procedures, such as cutting the sutures inserted by a surgeon at exactly the correct length. Another part of the learning curve is the discovery that 'exactly correct' for one surgeon is not 'exactly correct' for another. You also learn how to ensure that the surgeon has a good view of the operative field at all times, using instruments called retractors. The inevitable bleeding must not be allowed to obscure the view and for this you learn how to use swabs and a mechanical sucker in an unobtrusive way.

After some time, students may progress to inserting a suture in the skin themselves and ensuring the correct alignment of the two sides of the incision in order to give a good scar. For me, that first suture took place in the Casualty Department (now A&E) in Liverpool when I was asked to sew up a small wound. I was nervous but excited; it felt like a giant leap into my surgical future.

The next level was using a scalpel. Plunging a knife into an abscess feels a major step indeed and, of course, is a mightily relieving one for the patient too. It requires almost no expertise. My next step was actual surgery, albeit a very minor one, when I was allowed to remove a small skin lesion. Even something so tiny requires good control of the scalpel, and a neat and tidy result for the patient is essential.

Slowly but surely, I was building up the repertoire of skills needed to be a proficient surgeon. Doing these kinds of minor procedures also allows others to appraise your potential, and for this, a good senior colleague whom you trust is essential. I thought it was important to have my potential assessed at an early stage, rather than risk discovering rather late in the day that I fundamentally lacked the skills for a career in surgery. Students are no longer able to undertake minor operations, so this appraisal of their technical potential is delayed – in my opinion, regrettably – until they are committed to a career in surgery.

One of the surgeons at the Northern Hospital during my first clinical term as a surgical student was a thyroid specialist. Removing part or all of the thyroid gland is a highly demanding exercise. Any surgery in the neck requires precision because so many vital structures, in particular nerves, pass though it on their way from the brain to a destination in the rest of the body. Add to that mix the blood vessels going to and from the brain, and you're in tiger country. The thyroid requires a good blood supply, even more so when it is overactive. An overactive thyroid can prove to be a challenge to remove, as there might be excessive blood loss. This blood is quickly removed from the operative field by the assistant, using a sucker and swabs, so that it does not obscure the surgeon's view.

A standard part of every operation is to count the swabs going into the operative field and coming out again. This ensures that swabs do not get lost inside the patient. It is highly unlikely that a swab could get lost in a very superficial wound such as that for thyroidectomy, but the rules are always followed.

When I was a student, these recovered swabs filled with blood were placed individually on a rack, where they were then counted. They stayed on display in the theatre until the conclusion of the operation. At that point the theatre sister would count all the swabs and check all the instruments to ensure that nothing was missing, then she would announce to the surgeon that all was correct. A rack could hold many swabs, but it was rare for more than one or two rows to be used.

The first thyroid operation I saw on that unit was exceptionally bloody and the first rack filled up quickly with swabs. To everyone's surprise, a second rack had to be brought in. The bleeding continued and, lo and behold, a *third* rack was required. I was amazed and shocked, but eventually the bleeding was controlled and the wound closed. Generally, surgeons intend to have a completely dry wound before they suture it, but sometimes they insert a drain to allow any blood to find its way out rather than risk it building up in the wound. Such a build-up in the neck could cause pressure on the trachea and lead to a compromised airway.

I had no yardstick by which to judge this operation, but it was certainly memorable. It impressed upon me the fact that surgery is unpredictable, that the surgeon must always find a solution to a difficult problem and can never simply walk away from it. In my opinion, this is why surgeons' working hours have to have flexibility and must allow for the unexpected.

There were some wonderful teachers in the medical school at Liverpool and their lessons accompanied me throughout my career. They wanted to teach and inspire, and I hope that I too was able to pass on the baton in this way when it came to my own time to teach. There is nothing more important in life than training the next generation, be that at school, at university or in the workplace. As Nelson Mandela said, 'What counts in life is not the mere fact that we have lived. It is what difference we have made to the lives of others.'

One such teacher was Mr Howell Hughes, an excellent surgeon with a great sense of humour and a distinct Welsh accent. Some of his comments were particularly memorable. To a patient who seemed to be exaggerating his symptoms, he once said, 'You've had this pain day in and day out for four years, and the wonder of it is, you're still alive!' And when delving deep in an abdominal operation, I recall him announcing, 'Tie a bit of string around my legs, I'm going in.'

Another teacher with a marked Welsh accent was Mr Thomas, an orthopaedic surgeon. Some orthopaedic conditions are well known for being self-limiting. In other words, no matter what we do, the condition persists until it has run its course and then it cures itself. If your treatment happens to coincide with that self-cure, you may be tempted to take the credit. For some such conditions, Mr Thomas would tell the patient to rub the affected part morning and evening with 'goose grease' and then return to see him in six months. When, on their return, they complained that the pain persisted, he would ask if they had applied the goose grease cold or if they had warmed it first. Whichever answer they gave, he would deride them for being so stupid and tell them to go away and do the opposite. Six months later they were pleased to tell him that his cure had worked.

Dr Baker Bates, known to us students as BB, was a physician, but really, first and foremost he was a teacher. It was clear that he simply loved imparting knowledge into the brains of his students. He would gather up a group, take us off to his hospital and make sure we could examine patients ourselves – properly. It is something I have never forgotten and it inspired me to do likewise later in my own career. Indeed, I truly always wanted to train the next generation of surgeons more than anything else. The nicest thing anyone ever said about my teaching was that I taught as though teaching students was the most important task I had to do that day.

When BB wanted to remind us to consider the most common diagnosis first, he would say, 'If you see a couple of birds in Pembroke Place [the street outside the Infirmary], they're probably sparrows, not canaries.' He regularly took part in a teaching session on a Friday afternoon that was known as 'the Circus', because the students in the hot seat were rather like circus animals, there for the entertainment of others. It was the scariest time for the 'performing' students – really it was more ritual humiliation than education. He was the 'good cop', and the 'bad cop' was Dr Robertson, who was skilled at reducing students to gibbering wrecks. 'Don't imagine for one second that that smile is going to get you through finals,' Dr Robertson once remarked to me. The Circus was a voluntary session yet it was always packed, which shows that, like it or not, we knew it was good for us.

Another important message from BB was to avoid admitting patients to hospital if at all possible, because 'if you put a patient in hospital, the skin will rub off their seat and the spirit will evaporate from their soul'. How sadly true that is.

But it was a gynaecologist called Harold Francis who provided me with the single best example of how to teach. His tutorials were always oversubscribed. He was even more popular than his wife Winnie, another gynaecologist, who was also greatly loved. He would ask a question of a student and consider their answer with care. If it wasn't correct, he would say something like, 'Well, you could be right, but the orthodox view is . . .' That kind of teaching allowed us to venture into new territory without fear of reprimand if we got something hopelessly wrong.

We are all teachers throughout our lives, no matter what career we follow, and understanding that and celebrating its importance is fundamental to progress. Yes, I was learning to become a surgeon, but at every level I was passing on my newly acquired skills and knowledge to those who were a step or two behind me. I always hoped that my teaching was of the BB or Harold Francis model, and that my students would never be afraid of me.

Later in life, I became a founder of the Women in Surgery group. I was thrilled to see their recent slogan: *Lift as you climb*. It is so important to offer a helping hand to those on the step below you. I was also greatly influenced by the view of Edgar Parry, who was to become my surgical trainer and mentor, that we should aim to ensure that at the conclusion of their training, our trainees are better than we are. No top-dog complex for him, but rather a willingness to see others come through training to take his place and perhaps to shine more brightly.

As a student, in the clinical years I benefitted greatly from the dedicated teachers of the Liverpool Medical School. Teaching and training continued throughout the year with almost no break. This meant that there was little time to take any paid employment; there were so many subjects to fit into the final three years that summer holidays were no more than a couple of weeks. I did, though, have one memorable holiday job as a 'Kleenex Girl'. I was home in Blackpool for a short break when I saw the job advertised in the local newspaper. It involved giving away a new luxury item, the paper handkerchief. The advert read: 'Preference will be given to those with personality and charm.'

Three of us were appointed. We were given smart uniforms and a tray to wear around our necks which was loaded with giveaway packs of Kleenex. We were each allocated different areas to visit and sometimes were photographed with celebrities as part of the job. There were always plenty of stage people, such as Terry-Thomas, in Blackpool for the summer season and, through my work for Kleenex, I met many of them. I also learned that summer just how hard it can be to give something away for free. Human nature always assumes there must be a catch!

Following the example set by my father, who had handed over his wages to my mother every week, I presented him with my first week's wage of eight crisp £1 notes. They were still untouched in his wallet when he died many years later. His maximum income towards the end of his working life was £20 a week, but my parents managed their finances very well and he never needed to spend the wages I gave him. They refused to buy anything unless they had the full sum available. No 'never-never', as hire purchase was then known, for them.

Most students had two years in a hall of residence, but if you were given an appointment in the hall, such as student president or, in my case, head of music, you were given a third year. This meant that I was still resident in University Hall in June of 1958, the month of my twenty-first birthday. My parents threw me a party and on the day, they arrived in a splendid car that had been loaned to Dad by his boss for the special occasion. We wore black tie and my dress was short, made of cotton and printed with vegetables. There is a small remnant of it in my possession to this day. The party was in Southport, at a hotel called the Prince of Wales, and a group of my friends was invited for dinner, dancing, cake and fun. About half of those in attendance were medical students, but music was the common theme of my friendship with most of them. My best friend Suzette, who was studying history, was among the group, and in a photograph taken that evening, I can see she is looking fondly at my friend Peter, a musical medical student who was a year or two ahead of me. She went on to marry him, but at that stage their romance had not yet kindled. Indeed, he referred to me then as 'Dringsy darling' and we wondered if he felt some interest in my direction.

I have simply no idea how my parents funded this splendid affair – it must have been very difficult for them. It is a prominent and especially happy memory for me. In other photographs from the day the men are posing to impress, just like the photographs we see nowadays of our prime ministers in their youth at the Bullingdon Club! One of them looks to be wearing white tie and tails and is smoking a pipe – all very grown-up. We went back to Blackpool after the party and returned the car to Dad's boss. Our funds were definitely insufficient to stay the night at the hotel.

Most of my student life had to be confined by the grant I received. No bank would have entertained a loan to a student and my parents only just got by on my father's wage, so my £200 annual grant was it. It meant that I could only travel back to Blackpool at the end of each term. My grant had to cover clothes, books, travel and accommodation. Present-day students would be astonished that I did not once encounter alcohol during my university years. At Christmas my parents would splash out and buy a bottle of port, and in my clinical years I remember an annual bottle of sherry being bought, but that was it. Indeed, I was a qualified doctor before I ever drank anything more than a glass of sherry at Christmas.

During the three years of clinical training, we encountered

all the main disciplines. Medicine (which is a specialty in its own right, covering chests, hearts, digestion and so on) and surgery made up the lion's share, but we also did obstetrics and gynaecology; paediatrics; ear, nose and throat; eyes and psychiatry. Everything had to be fitted in, for two good reasons. Firstly, we needed the basic knowledge for whatever future career we chose, and secondly, we needed to sample all the various disciplines in order to make that choice. I had gone to medical school with the intention of becoming a surgeon and that remained my goal, although I did have one brief detour into thinking I might become a neurologist. Diagnosis in neurology was at that time based on clinical tests and skilful examination – there were no brain scans then – and I was fascinated by that. But I changed my mind after working for a few days in such a unit and discovering that no matter how skilled you might become at diagnosis, the real problem was the lack of treatments available. So I returned to my first love.

I particularly enjoyed the fact that, as a surgeon, you took the patient on a journey during which your skills would form a major component of the treatment and which had the potential to provide a complete cure. It seemed so unlike medicine, where the most you could really do was prescribe pills. In surgery you actually took a hand in treating the patient and a great deal depended on your skills.

One of the specialties that might have attracted me later in my career was radiology. It was quite simple in those early days, without much to offer in the way of intervention. Little did I foresee the huge advances it would make in my lifetime. At that stage there were no ultrasounds, no CT scans, no MRIs and no major procedures. It was the area where I saw the greatest changes during the course of my working life.

I spent one summer term during my clinical years in Paris, working in a surgical unit at the Hôpital Cochin and living in student lodgings at the Cité Universitaire. Both the hospital and my lodgings were the definition of basic, with no frills of any kind. Paris as a city, however, was a revelation. As when I had stayed with the Chollet family almost a decade previously, I found it completely magical and I very much enjoyed my time there. I was accompanied by a fellow Liverpool student also called Avril, though her name was spelled the French way. I learned a lot about life and about France, but not so much about surgery.

Money, as always, was tight, so we walked everywhere. We had an evening meal in a different student restaurant each evening, so we quickly learned the best ways to move around Paris. The main department stores, such as Au Printemps and Galeries Lafeyette, advertised free teas if you took along the advertisement from the Cook's Tours travel brochure, so we were able to have tea and delicious cakes at least twice a week. We were careful to ensure that we found a new waitress each time.

I had a few near scrapes because of misunderstandings with the language. I will never forget the gales of laughter coming from one particular group of male patients while I tried to take a urological history in my idea of colloquial French. On another occasion, I found myself assisting with a post-mortem examination having expected to be helping in the operating theatre. Overall, it was a memorable and enjoyable summer term, after which I returned to Liverpool for the next clinical subject.

As part of our obstetrics training, we spent a week in residence, and despite seeing all the emergencies that arose, we had a lot of fun. We were expected to attend a number of home births and my first was in the circular tenement block known as the Bull Ring, which was, and indeed still is, close to the university. When I arrived, there was a lady on the doorstep who looked just like the grandma from the then famous Giles cartoons, complete with long black coat and black hat. She was the patient's grandmother.

'Are you the doctor?' she asked.

'Well, no, I'm actually the medical student.'

'Yes, yes, the doctor. Have you done this before?'

'No.'

'Don't worry, I've delivered many myself. It will be fine.'

And so it was. The baby turned out to be a girl and I was even promised that she would be named after me!

At the start of my fourth year, having had three years in University Hall, it was time to find a flat for my last two years as a student. Many of my friends had already completed their three-year degrees, among them my best friend Suzette, so they were not available to share with me. In the end I lived with the other Avril, who had been with me in Paris, and another girl called Rosemary, who was doing a master's in social science.

There was a shortage of accommodation in Liverpool at that time, so finding a flat was difficult. Once found, it had to be visited and deemed appropriate by the Director of Women's Lodgings, so one day, we all went along together to view the flat. When our delightful future landlady answered the door, she was greeted by the words, 'You do realise that this is in the heart of Liverpool's hareem?' I feared that Mrs Jones might slam the door in the Director's face. The flat admittedly was right in the middle of the red light area, but it had the big advantage of being close to the university, and most hospitals were within walking distance of it too. Also, importantly, it was affordable. The weekly rent was £4.10 shillings (10 shillings equals 50p). We each therefore contributed £1.10 shillings for the rent, and the same for food.

The houses in the area were all dilapidated Georgian terraces. One identical to ours on nearby Faulkner Street appeared on a recent TV series about the history of houses, in fact. Our flat was on the top floor and consisted of a living room, two bedrooms and a small kitchen. I learned from the TV series that these would originally have been the servants' quarters. The bathroom was shared with the other residents of the house. There was no running hot water; gas fires were needed to heat it and money in the slot meters was required to pay for the gas we used. When we asked about baths, the response was, 'Well, I suppose I could heat the water once a week if you really must have one.' I had heard a rumour that many Liverpudlians used their baths to store coal, so perhaps taking a bath regularly was deemed unusual.

Despite the rocky start, we had the good fortune to have a warm and welcoming landlady, and we loved her and her small children. She was having quite a hard time trying to make ends meet and when we first arrived, she was pregnant with her third child. There was a particularly difficult next-door neighbour who took to tossing her rubbish across the fence into our backyard. My landlady asked the neighbour to stop doing so, telling her, 'As you can see, I am having a baby and it makes my life difficult.' The response from next door was, 'And what do you suppose I'm having, a bleeding horse?'

The three of us shared the chores, in particular the cooking. As ever, the budget was tight, but we discovered that if we went to the large indoor market in the city centre at closing time, we could pick up bargains. We got on well together but were not particularly good cooks and rather missed the regular provision of meals in the hall of residence. There were no extra expenses then, as there was no TV, no phone, no refrigerator, no washing machine and, of course, no internet. None of us possessed a radio, but I had my gramophone. With other students, we owned between us about a dozen records and we wore them all out one by one by playing them so much. We learned about world affairs from newspapers, which were provided in the student union.

We did little in the way of entertaining because we were too busy and poor to contemplate it. If any male students visited us, they would often stand at the window, watching the antics of prostitutes in the street outside as they tried to pick up clients!

I do remember once that a boyfriend was to take me to a ball and I thought I would give him a meal at the flat beforehand, as we could not afford a restaurant. I decided to give him a steak with barbecue sauce made from green peppers. I mistakenly made the sauce with chilli peppers instead of the sweet capsicums I should have used. Fortunately, I tasted it just before the boyfriend arrived; there was an utter conflagration in my mouth, but at least I knew not to serve it to him. Saved by the bell!

There were then just two years left to reach the final hurdle and, with so many clinical topics to be covered, we nonetheless seemed to be hurtling towards the end. Final exams were looming and I measured the amount of reading I needed to do in feet and inches. I moved into the chilly attic space above our flat in Huskisson Street in order to have some isolation for studying. There was a roof light and I could hear the bells of the Anglican cathedral, though it was not in view. I purchased a small paraffin heater, which I placed as close to me as I dared. There was so much to learn and so little time in which to cover it.

My father and I had long before agreed that I would buy a cheap car when I qualified as a doctor. I had passed my driving test in my last year at school. I was very keen to learn and got a provisional licence on the first day that I was eligible. My father proved to be a very nervous tutor and eventually passed the job on to his friend. I remember coming home from school on the test day and changing out of my school uniform into something a bit more grown up, as I felt they were unlikely to pass a schoolgirl. I was driving my dad's friend's car, and when we returned to the house after my success, Mr Parkin threw the keys at me and said, 'Off you go, take it for a drive on your own!' My dad paled.

After I started at university, I realised that as a doctor, I would be too busy working to make much use of a car, but as a final-year student who needed to travel to many far-flung hospitals, a car would be wonderful. So with some persuasion I was able to advance the date of acquiring my own vehicle and I left an extremely anxious father behind me in Blackpool when I drove off to the big city in my bright blue Austin A40. Dad made sure I knew a lot about its maintenance so that I could be largely self-sufficient. It cost just £1 to fill its admittedly rather small tank.

My dad had heard terrible stories about cars in Liverpool. He was told that if you parked in certain areas, you would return to find that the car had no wheels. No such problems afflicted me, and my trusty car was truly a godsend. It was frequently overloaded with student friends and proved to be utterly reliable.

On one occasion, on leaving the Mersey Tunnel at night and heading alone to my flat in Liverpool, I realised that I was being followed. No matter what I did, the car behind stuck to my rear. It was clear that it would not be wise to drive alone to my flat, so I eventually drove up the ramp of the A&E department at the Royal Infirmary, at which point my tail vanished.

I was quite proud of my resilience and, happily, nothing like it ever happened again. That little car stayed with me until I set off to work in the USA some years later.

At the beginning of my final year, I was resident in the hospital to do my casualty (now A&E) training. On the first day, the consultant said to me, 'Go into that cubicle and assess that patient. He is supposed to have had a heart attack. Tell me what you think.' You might think that after all those years in medical school I would be able to diagnose a heart attack. Not so. I suddenly realised just how little I actually knew. It was a most valuable wake-up call and I settled down to consume my medical textbooks with a new and urgent intensity. I was soon to be a doctor. I would need that knowledge and patients would expect me to have it. I was well aware of the enormous responsibility that would land on my shoulders as soon as I qualified. I was responsible for people's lives. I was not afraid, but simply rather determined to be good at my job. Knowing that I would be expected to be competent in all the various aspects of the job from day one was a big incentive to prove my worth.

Towards the end of our studies, it was usual for students to arrange to do locum cover for the house officer on the unit in which they aspired to work. It was a way of getting experience of the job you wanted. I started my first locum on the surgical unit at Broadgreen Hospital, at the end of a day of exams. It had been the main operating day of the unit, so there were lots of post-operative patients. I knew none of them and had not seen their operations. It was the first time I had had any real responsibility for patient care, and I was acutely aware of my shortcomings and of the potential consequences my inexperience might have for the patients.

That same day, I heard my name being urgently called on the tannoy and I had to make my way with speed to one of the two wards I was responsible for. There I found a man on a theatre trolley with a bulging scar in his neck and a face that was navy blue from lack of oxygen. He had bled into his wound following a thyroidectomy earlier in the day and his trachea was seriously compressed. His life was in danger. Fortunately for him and for me, there was an experienced ward sister in charge. She told me exactly what was needed. 'Take out those skin clips with this,' she said, handing me the correct instrument. 'Now cut out those deeper sutures.' After I did as I was told, the blood was able to dramatically escape, the trachea was released and the crisis was over. Little did that patient know just how fortunate he was, but I certainly understood. Not for the last time in my career, I was grateful for the knowledge and skill of senior nurses.

Over the following two weeks, I learned what I was letting myself in for and worked pretty well round the clock. The registrar on that unit was also my final-year tutor, so I gained practical experience as well as factual knowledge. I still have the pay slip for my first week's work as a student locum: £1.12 shillings and 8 pence! My locum finished just in time for me to head home for Christmas and simply fall asleep.

My finals came along in 1960. They began with written papers, which we took in the original red brick part of the main university buildings, then there were oral exams and, finally, clinical exams taken on the wards in the teaching hospitals. After the written papers, I went climbing with a group of friends in Snowdonia in North Wales. There had been an unusual number of adder bites that year and we read reports in the newspaper of the medical consequences. We did not believe a word of these reports, so when we returned to

Liverpool, we consulted *Price's Textbook of the Practice of Medicine* and became experts on the subject. To my astonishment, two days later, in the oral exam for medicine, I was handed a preserved adder's head in a pot. I was asked if I knew what it was, then if I knew anything about it and its effects on those unfortunate enough to be bitten by one. After feigning shock about being asked about such a difficult topic, I then regurgitated all that I had learned only a couple of days before... which perhaps explains how I managed to pass and finally become a doctor!

I finished my final exams just prior to my twenty-third birthday. On 21 June I celebrated my birthday and also the longest day of the year by visiting the beach at Freshfield with student friends and taking a swim in the estuary of the Mersey, as had become a mini tradition. The next day, we were again seeking to pass the time while waiting for our results and decided to take tea in a department store in Liverpool. The choice was between Henderson's and George Henry Lee's, then a branch of John Lewis. One of the students wanted to buy something in G. H. Lee's, so that determined our choice. It may well have saved our lives.

While we were having our afternoon tea, we heard the sirens of fire engines, and when we emerged, Henderson's was ablaze. There were people stranded at an upper level where the cafeteria was and in total 11 lives were lost. It was a shocking scene and one I will never forget. I always carried a small camera with me then and I took some photographs, though I could not bring myself to have the film developed for about 15 years. I felt guilty that I had taken photographs of such a tragic event. Now, they serve as a reminder of that terrible day.

The results of my finals were as hoped for and I was duly awarded my MBChB (Bachelor of Medicine, Bachelor of

Surgery). I didn't, however, receive honours, which were awarded to just five students. My parents came to Liverpool that same evening to celebrate. My dad had made a name board for me but would not paint the letters on until I rang to say that I was indeed officially Dr Dring. He then completed his wonderful gift, and the paint was still wet when they arrived.

We dined at a seafood restaurant in the centre of the city, which was owned and run by a lady called Jenny. She was well known in the area and we would never normally have eaten at her very popular establishment, but of course this was a special occasion. Jenny joined in the celebratory mood and provided little gifts for all her 'clever students'. In among them were some Balkan Sobranie cigarettes. My father was a smoker, of course, but I had never taken up the habit. Nonetheless, we were pressed to try them, and so we did. Over the following couple of years, I joined the smokers at work but happily never became addicted. Eventually, I stopped smoking just as quickly as I had started.

Before us, a long summer holiday beckoned – the first for a while and the last for several years to come. My trusty car was to take the other Avril and myself to France and beyond. We had successfully climbed the mountain and could scarcely believe that we were now officially doctors. In a light-hearted mood and feeling ready for an adventure, we set off for Europe. We took a tent, some walking gear and a map, and off we went. The world of work could wait while we had some fun.

4
Life as a Doctor

After a carefree summer in 1960, it was back to reality, but I was looking forward to the next step. As a final-year student, I had discovered Broadgreen Hospital because my surgical tutor David Glenn was the registrar there, and it was where I had done a stint as a locum as a means of later hopefully getting a more permanent position. This proved to be worthwhile because I did subsequently become a house officer at Broadgreen Hospital. Although I had graduated as a doctor by gaining the necessary degrees, I was still not a registered medical practitioner with the General Medical Council (GMC). In order to become registered, all doctors were required to do a 12-month period of pre-registration posts, usually consisting of six months of medicine and six months of surgery. This acknowledged the fact that, in that first year following graduation, the new doctors had the theoretical knowledge but not yet the practical skills and experience to act independently. That period has now been extended to two foundation years for new doctors.

My first post at Broadgreen was on the Surgical Professorial Unit, where Professor Charles Wells would put in an occasional appearance. He was the revered head of the University Department of Surgery, a demanding boss and an excellent surgeon. The senior consultant was John Shepherd and his younger consultant colleague was Edgar Parry. My final-year tutor David Glenn was the trainee surgeon, or registrar, and I was to become the doctor responsible for the day-to-day medical care of about 60 in-patients, a huge undertaking – but very normal at that time. It was a happy, close-knit, supportive unit. Because it was the professorial unit, we also occasionally saw the senior lecturer in surgery, whose name was Laurie Tinkler. It was essentially a normal surgical unit, apart from the fact that, from time to time, the Professor would join us for rounds and operating.

I was allocated a room in the doctors' residency, which was spacious and situated over the front entrance to the hospital. That probably meant it was quite noisy, though I never had any trouble falling sleep as I worked so hard. Each morning, I was able to see the consultants arriving in their cars and I then knew to make a mad dash to be on the wards ahead of them. A lovely lady at the residency would come around early each morning with a cup of tea for each of us. She would sing 'Love Is Like a Violin' as she did her rounds, and if ever she suspected a liaison, she would call through the door, 'One cup or two today, Doctor?' I did have a boyfriend at the time, though not one who shared my room, so it was only ever the one cup of tea for me.

Our wards were the remnants of wartime buildings and mainly consisted of Nissen-type huts. I was totally responsible for two large Nightingale-style wards, one for men and one for women. There was never any mixing of the sexes in the wards – probably just as well, as there was precious little privacy. We were never short of beds because extra beds were simply brought from the store and placed down the middle of the ward when needed. There were never extra doctors or nurses just because there were extra patients, though.

The house surgeon's job was to care for all these patients. On admission I had to write down their story in the hospital record, then examine them and take notes on that too. Each admission would take about half an hour to complete, and at the end I would have at least two sides of A4 paper covered in neat and legible notes. The next task was to decide what needed to be done for that patient. Blood tests and X-rays were organised and a plan of management put together. If a major operation was needed, then blood would be cross-matched, ready for transfusion if required at the time of the surgery. The notes would be updated regularly as investigations and procedures occurred. Obtaining consent for operations was also one of my tasks and it involved a fairly sketchy outline of the procedure compared with the comprehensive consent process of today. The operation note would be written by whoever did the operation, but apart from that, all records were my responsibility. Finally, a discharge summary was written, ready for the patient's GP.

The hospital management staff was tiny by today's standards. There was a wonderful physician superintendent called Dr Findlay and a hospital secretary who was the equivalent of what would today be a CEO. Dr Findlay lived in a house in the grounds of the hospital and so was available almost all day and night when anything required his presence. Each unit had its own secretary who was an integral part of the action and who arranged admissions, as well as looking after all the letters.

Our unit had two days of operating a week, and on each day we had two big theatres for major cases and two smaller theatres for minor procedures. There was no closing time; we simply continued with the list until the operations were all done. There was no such thing as recovery wards or intensive care then, so following surgery, the patients returned to the ward whence they'd come, to the nurses who knew them but who generally had no special expertise in the care of the critically ill.

There was a wonderful theatre superintendent who ran the show at Broadgreen, and yet was equally ready to participate in the day-to-day work. It was always a special day when Betty Wilkinson scrubbed up for your case, as she knew all the surgical tricks and would readily share them with everyone. A quiet 'Mr P would . . .' from Betty was better than gold to me.

As well as looking after the two wards of surgical patients, on alternate evenings I would cover the casualty department too. The professional A&E doctors left at about 6pm and then it was over to us. There was always a first and second on call, and we worked well together and would always readily help out if casualty got busy. There were rarely ever more than one or two people waiting to be seen and no one turned up for any trivial reason. We had to deal with whatever appeared and we learned fast on the job.

I had various lists of 'What to do when . . .' in my May and Baker diary, which all new doctors carried in their pockets back then. I still have that original diary today. My lists covered subjects such as what to do for the unconscious patient, or the patient who is severely short of breath, or the patient with chest pain.

On one evening, an unconscious patient was brought in and I set about working through my list of things to do and check. After a few minutes, I was no wiser and had run out of ideas, so for no good reason I sent him to have a skull X-ray. Within minutes I was summoned to the X-ray department because the picture had revealed a bullet in the middle of his head. Horror! What had I missed? Could it be true? Surely it would be obvious if he had been shot. On closer inspection, I found the tiny entry wound behind his ear made by a homemade gun in a suicide attempt. Something else to add to the list in my diary.

Another time, I remember phoning a registrar when I had a patient with a fish bone stuck in their throat. He responded by asking what kind of fish it was. Consternation! I had no idea and did not realise that some fish bones will simply melt away while others require removal. I found it difficult to persuade the patient that this bone was of the harmless kind.

In those days, when we ordered an X-ray, we were the ones to interpret it. Although radiologists were on the consultant staff of the hospital, they did not expect to be called out simply to look at an X-ray. That was our job and we were pretty inexperienced at it. We had seen X-rays as students but now we were having to make real-life decisions based on our interpretation of them and I found it difficult and worrying. Was that a fracture? Was that a dislocation? Was that how pneumonia appears? Based on our interpretation of the wet film (rapid film driers had not yet been devised), we would decide the next step in management.

If a patient required an operation, we would have to call in the registrar, book an operating theatre, arrange an anaesthetist and do all the preliminaries. In this, we were hugely helped and guided by experienced and knowledgeable nursing staff. We would then assist in theatre, which often became a place of refuge from the cut and thrust of the casualty department. Every operation required both a surgeon and an assistant, and in complex cases more than one assistant. The assistant's job was to make sure the surgeon could always see the structures they were working on, by ensuring that they were not obscured by blood. I enjoyed, indeed relished, the opportunity to be up close to the action and to begin learning about the steps of operative surgery.

The night ward round at about 9 or 10pm was very worthwhile because we got to see all of our patients. We checked them over quickly and could agree with the nurse in charge whether, for example, a drip would need replacing if it failed.

Such decisions had the potential to save us a few precious moments of extra sleep later that same night.

Although there were many patients, most of them were recuperating uneventfully after surgery. Back then, a patient who had a hernia repair might be in hospital for a week, whereas today they would normally be a day case. Some patients were so well that they would even assist with taking round refreshments to other patients. They might also usefully spot when a fellow patient took a turn for the worse and alert the overworked couple of night nurses.

In addition to the rounds every morning and evening, once a week there was a big ward round which all the team were expected to attend. Decisions were made about investigations, operations were allocated to surgeons and theatres, and discharges were anticipated. As the house surgeon, I would present all the patients to the senior doctors, discuss any problems and plan next steps. I took care to be well-informed and organised, so the weekly round was always a pleasure.

There was a huge variety of surgical problems and, in the male ward, one of the commonest was retention of urine caused by an enlarged prostate. The rapid resolution of this involved the insertion of a catheter, with an operation at a later time, but our hospital's professor was of the opinion that it was better for the patient to have an emergency operation, a prostatectomy.

Today, most patients who need prostate surgery as the result of benign prostatic enlargement will get a relatively non-invasive transurethral resection, in which the prostate is approached via the urethra that runs through the penis and is 'cored out' with a special cutting device to make a wider passage for the urine to flow through. In those days, however, it was a major open operation involving a large abdominal incision. It often provoked untoward consequences and could mean a prolonged stay in hospital.

I remember one such patient was a Mr Harper, whose bed was halfway down the ward and whose stay was prolonged as a result of infection and delayed healing. I looked after him throughout his stay and he marvelled at my tolerance of lack of sleep. Eventually he recovered and was well enough to be discharged. When he returned for his clinic appointment, he decided to come in to see me on the ward and entered through the far end, thus walking the whole length of the long room in order to visit me in the office. He was carrying a huge bunch of chrysanthemums with blooms about a foot across and declared as he walked through the ward that they were for the 'lady doctor'. The result was that almost every patient present in the ward that day thought it was the required thing to present flowers to the 'lady doctor'. I was inundated, in the nicest possible way.

There were only two junior doctors on the unit, myself and the registrar, David Glenn. As he had been my final-year tutor, David knew of my long-term surgical ambitions (I wasn't simply there to do the mandatory six months in a surgical unit), so he guided me through the first steps of various simple surgical operations. To my amazement, one night I took out an appendix. I was so thrilled that I had to rush off to find a phone in order to tell my parents of this momentous step.

I did not fully appreciate then what a major event it is for the person teaching to allow a junior staff member to take on a first operation. Of course, the standard of care has to be as good as it would be if the teacher were performing the surgery themselves. It is always easier to do an operation than to guide a beginner through those steps. But it simply has to be done, because otherwise there is no future for surgery.

David patiently guided me through many such operations and determined that surgery was an appropriate ambition for me to have. We were to remain in contact for the rest of his life, and after a time, I came to feel like one of his family.

I remember learning an extremely valuable lesson during my time at Broadgreen. One day, I was told by the boss to go into Theatre 3 and operate on 'that big toe'. The patient was already asleep and 'that big toe' was prepped and draped, ready for the incision. I was, of course, young and inexperienced, so I was rather slow to take up the knife. Fortunately I had enough time to realise that the prepared toe looked perfectly healthy, so I wondered if the toe requiring surgery might possibly be on the other foot. Stopping to ask the senior consultant anaesthetist to see the consent form felt like a risky move, but my caution was vindicated. Today, the foot would have a large arrow on it pointing to the diseased site, and that arrow would have been placed there in the full knowledge and with the full agreement of the patient. At every step along the way, the consent form will be checked to ensure it matches the arrow. It was perhaps the most important lesson of my surgical life. Never again would I blindly accept the word of others. Instead, I would always check for myself.

The first six months were tremendously hard work, though they were also highly fulfilling. There was great camaraderie among the junior doctors. Because we were all resident at the hospital, with our meals provided, there were lots of opportunities to share concerns and problems with each other. Wherever we were in the hospital, we tried to get to the doctors' mess at 10pm, when the pot of tea was delivered. The mess was a place where we could seek advice and guidance from our peers: men and a few women. There was a hugely supportive atmosphere. Women were, of course, in the minority, but that was of no consequence to me, and we were always treated as equals. Everyone was learning, and although it was a steep learning curve, it was a very enjoyable one. Peer support was hugely valuable and I never felt isolated. It helped that I seemed to be able to manage with sleep deprivation, although I do remember one time when a ward sister took a needle from my hand when I could barely see for exhaustion, and put it in the patient's vein for me.

Alcohol is not permitted in hospitals now, but back then we had a bar in the doctors' mess. It was a place to relax when time permitted. Each year the consultants gave a Christmas party in the hospital for the junior doctors, and one such occasion provided me with my first experience of the surprising effects of alcohol. A party with freely flowing alcoholic drinks was a novel experience for me. I remember heading rather uncertainly to the bathroom, working my way around the edge of the room as my legs had developed a slight wobble. Party or no party, however, there were still patients to be cared for, and after the event I had to carry out – for the first time – a procedure that involved me making a small incision in the skin of the patient's lower abdomen and inserting a catheter. Thankfully, my observant registrar kindly accompanied me and lent a hand. All went well.

There was a huge volume of work to be done and I was often indebted to an experienced nurse who would remind me, for example, of the need to have cross-matched blood available for a major operation. I did not always get it right. On one occasion I forgot to order an X-ray in the operating theatre and had to admit the omission and try to remedy it with a phone call and an abject apology. The consultant radiologist was stern in his admonishment, but Mr Shepherd came to my rescue, explaining that it was his job to shoot the house surgeon, not the radiologist's.

Vascular surgery was in its infancy in the 1960s in the UK. Surgery for varicose veins is a small part of the discipline and was well established at that time, but arterial surgery was new. The arteries to all parts of the body can become diseased or even blocked, meaning that part of the body becomes seriously short of blood. A frequent presentation then was the femoral artery becoming blocked, which would make walking difficult and painful. It was possible to clear out blocked arteries or to replace them using either a vein or a prosthetic graft. Another common disease of the arteries is called an aneurysm, which is when the artery becomes ballooned and can burst. This is life-threatening if the main artery or aorta is the one affected, and ideally it is repaired before it ruptures. If rupture occurs, the patient's life is seriously at risk and urgent surgery can sometimes save a life. During this first job I was lucky enough to see and assist with an operation for an aortic aneurysm. It was the first operation of its kind to be done in Broadgreen and probably in Liverpool. Edgar Parry was to do the operation using skills that he had learned in the USA, but no one else present had any experience at all. I had never seen anything remotely like it. I was captivated and determined, there and then, that I would learn to conduct this fascinating new kind of surgery myself.

The operation was scheduled for a Sunday, in the correct expectation that we would need the whole day. The patient's ballooning aorta was at risk of rupture. It was to be replaced with a Dacron graft, which looked like a pair of trousers and was often referred to as a trouser graft. The aorta had to be clamped off, so there was no blood supply to the lower half of the body while the graft was inserted. I was completely amazed by the whole event, which was pulled off without a hitch. Afterwards, the boss and his wife kindly invited the whole team over for dinner to celebrate this major first and to express thanks for everyone's support. In so many ways that momentous day was responsible for the direction I was to take in my career.

I spent my second six months as a house officer on the medical wards. Of course, one huge chunk of work was missing – no days were taken up with operating – so I had a far calmer pace of life, helped by the fact that the turnover of patients was slower, as they stayed in for longer. I looked after a similar number of patients, but they often had chronic problems with the heart, chest or brain. As I did when working as house surgeon, I kept records, arranged investigations and prescribed drugs, but I missed what I saw as the opportunity for a real cure that surgery provided. It did, however, leave me time to enjoy an occasional game of tennis.

We still covered A&E out of hours, and occasionally that would lead to a court appearance to give evidence about an accident or on criminal proceedings. On one such occasion, a fellow house officer found herself called to give evidence when we were due to be in Europe on holiday, after our year had finished. The defendant's lawyers were more than happy to advise that it would be fine to go on holiday, knowing that it would result in a welcome delay of the court case. That advice resulted in a contempt of court accusation and a court appearance for my friend. Happily, the judge declared her to be 'ignorant but innocent'!

So concluded my first year as a doctor and one of the most demanding learning experiences of my life. I was often exhausted but never bored. I loved every moment and only wanted to do more. In particular, I loved the practical side of my job and knew that my choice of career had been the right one.

I had fulfilled the requirements for registration with the GMC, but decided to extend my experience to include obstetrics and gynaecology, which involved taking on a third house job. For this I travelled to Preston, in the mistaken belief that it would allow me to see my parents when I was off duty. The obstetrics unit was extremely busy and only really dealt with unusual or complex cases, so every single night was manic. I covered alternate nights as well as working every day, so basically I would work for 36 hours, take 12 hours off and then start again. When I went to visit my parents, I usually ended up falling asleep. My time in obstetrics and gynaecology did not persuade me to change tack, although there were some who thought that it would be a more appropriate choice of career for a woman than surgery.

Undaunted, I then applied for and was appointed to a senior house officer role in surgery back in Liverpool. As a woman I was an unusual candidate for surgery, but I never felt that my sex was in any way detrimental to my chances of getting the job.

The unit had both general and also open-heart surgery. I was familiar with general, but cardiac surgery was new to me and indeed to most people at that time. Cardiologists only referred the absolutely end-stage patients and, in consequence, many did not survive. I personally questioned the wisdom of undertaking cardiac surgery, which I thought was too risky and unlikely to continue. In fact, the technical aspects of cardiac surgery were not the problem. It was the preparation for surgery and the care afterwards that was lacking. The development of intensive care units (ICUs) would later change all of that.

My new role reminded me of the huge importance of anatomical knowledge, and I began to review information about the relevant anatomy prior to undertaking an operation. This was a habit I continued throughout my career, especially in cases where the anatomy was less familiar to me. Although anatomy can be distorted by disease, it remains the fundamental building block for a successful operation. There is no shame in brushing up on knowledge.

At this time I was dating a tall, blond and handsome surgical hopeful, though it wasn't to lead anywhere. We took our second skiing holiday together and then quite amicably parted company. I think we surprised our families, but the spark simply wasn't there. Hearing that I was newly available, an old boyfriend of mine, Jonathan Mansfield, an architect, came round to visit me. He explained that he had won a Harkness Fellowship to the USA and said – quite out of the blue – that he would like to take me with him as his wife.

The how and why of my acceptance remains something of a mystery to me to this day. I liked him a lot and I suppose I thought I loved him. The prospect of travelling to America was exciting, and we did marry. And so began the next phase of life and our careers: marriage and training in America. Most young surgical trainees did at some point or another spend time in the USA; we jokingly referred to it as getting the BTA (Been to America) diploma. It would normally have occurred somewhat later in my career – not that it mattered, really. One advantage of starting married life in the USA was that I did not have any night calls, so I could take time to adjust to my new life in a new country.

5
Becoming a Woman in Surgery

It simply never occurred to me that it might be difficult – or indeed impossible – to become a female surgeon. I had met women doctors in my childhood and had no doubt that they had chosen to follow the career of their choice, and so, I would do the same.

I liked practical things and enjoyed using my hands. Although I loved music and drama, in terms of my vocation in life, there was no real contender to surgery. I always knew what I was going to do.

I had kept my ambition fairly quiet until I'd graduated, when I'd confided in David Glenn, who had given me those invaluable firm foundations while I was a house surgeon. He formed the opinion over the first few months that I could indeed become a surgeon, so I eventually mentioned it to the consultants as well, and they too began to increase the amount of practical procedures that they would entrust to me. They did not express any surprise, nor indeed offer any opinion, but no doubt they were watching my progress with care. I never felt that there was any reluctance because I was a woman and I certainly didn't believe that it was of any consequence.

By now almost two years had passed since my graduation and I had spent more than half of that time involved with the specialty of surgery. I was ready and keen to progress further. However, I had accepted Jonathan's proposal of marriage, so I went to see the senior surgeon from my first post to inform him of my plans. He had always tacitly endorsed my wish to become a surgeon, and for that I was grateful. I wanted to keep him informed of my progress. However, I was not expecting his response when I informed him of my forthcoming wedding. He said, 'What a pity. You had such a promising career ahead of you.'

I informed him that my plans in that regard had not changed, but it was the first time I was made aware of some of the difficulties I might face. I was surprised and perhaps disappointed by his response, but in no way deterred.

My former flatmate Avril was to be my bridesmaid and we decided to have a trip to London together, to do some shopping for my trousseau. We stayed with my 'rich uncle' Albert in Chorleywood and were entertained by him and Aunt Phyllis in the local pub. They drank quite a few gin and tonics while we nursed just one each for the whole evening. We were mighty relieved when the bell eventually rang for 'Time, gentlemen, please', as was the tradition then. We made our way to Albert's Jaguar outside, but he didn't start the engine. 'Why are we not moving, Uncle Albert?' I asked after some time had passed. 'Oh,' he said, 'we're just waiting for the police to check the pub is empty before we go back in again!'

In September of 1962 I was married in a church in Poulton-le-Fylde, wearing a dress I had designed myself. My father gave me away, and at the reception he tried to make a speech, but he was overcome by emotion and gave up after a few words of thanks. Jonathan and I enjoyed a brief visit to the Lakes and then it was time to head off to America. We left Liverpool by train and my parents came to the station to see us off, knowing that we would have no face-to-face contact then for two years. The look of devastation on my father's face haunted me for months afterwards. We wrote to one another every week, but we only spoke at Christmas and had to book the phone call weeks in advance. Jonathan's parents were able to come and stay with us during our second year out there, but mine could not afford such a major trip.

We travelled by sea and met the tail end of a hurricane, with unfortunate consequences for all those on board (including my new husband) who were prone to seasickness. Dinner that particular evening was attended only by myself, the captain of a whaling factory ship and the composer Peter Maxwell Davies. We dressed smartly nonetheless and had the best of service. It was the start of a lifelong friendship between Max and myself.

We arrived in New York in the early morning and I was on deck to watch with amazement as the city and its imposing skyscrapers appeared. I had never seen anything like it. I was also amazed by the skill of those who manipulated our great vessel into its mooring. The passengers were gathered into a cinema for disembarkation instructions and as the process began, a man in a belted raincoat, looking for all the world like a member of the FBI, stood on the platform and asked if 'Mr and Mrs Mansfield and Mr Peter Maxwell Davies would follow me quietly, please'. It seemed clear that we were about to be locked up. But in fact he had been sent by the Harkness Fellowship programme to ease our path through the process and speed us on our way.

We were invited to dinner with the foundation that same evening, so to kill time beforehand and look around we took a stroll in Central Park. We found it almost deserted. At dinner, we expressed our surprise that this great amenity was so little used, and our hosts were horrified that we had risked our lives, as they saw it, by taking a walk in such a dangerous place.

The next day we set off by train to cross the country to California, where we would set up home in Berkeley. I spent quite a lot of the first year on the vascular unit of the University of

California San Francisco Medical Center, where I met some truly innovative surgeons who would remain my friends for many years, among them Jack Wylie, Bill Ehrenfeld and Ron Stoney. In the early 1960s, vascular surgery in the UK was a mere subset of general surgery, but these surgeons were already doing only vascular procedures. It would be the early part of the next century before vascular surgery became a recognised discipline in itself in the UK.

I initially worked as a lab technician in the pathology laboratory of Highland Hospital in Oakland, prior to obtaining my ECFMG (Educational Commission for Foreign Medical Graduates) exam, which would allow me to see patients. Dr Robert Parsons ran the department. He knew that I was a doctor and an aspiring surgeon too. He was always taking me to medical meetings in the hospital, to further my education and my enjoyment of my stay, all of which he achieved without appearing to favour me in the eyes of my fellow lab technicians. He was a true gentleman.

We discussed potential lines of future research, including the possible importance of introducing pulsatile flow during cardiopulmonary bypass. During cardiac surgery, blood circulation is maintained by a machine that provides a continuous flow, unlike the body's normal circulation, which has a regular pulse. We felt it would be interesting to carry out research to determine which was best. Dr Parsons was also responsible for a temporary deviation in my ambition from vascular to plastic surgery. He himself needed to have an operation that involved a pedicle graft, which meant moving a tube of skin from one area to another, in this case from the scalp to the nose, two completely visible areas. It was fascinating and resulted in me reading tomes on plastic surgery to learn more about such amazing procedures. It was a brief love affair, and my strongest motivation was really always to save lives and limbs and prevent strokes, but plastic-surgery techniques are useful in all branches of surgery.

The time I spent learning laboratory techniques in San Francisco was valuable in several ways. I learned exactly what went on when I made the request for a blood or other laboratory test. I learned how to work in partnership with and respect those unseen technicians who respond to doctors' and surgeons' requests. And I learned about the process of running a lab, which was to be useful at every stage of my career, particularly when I began to undertake my own research.

One of the least popular tasks among the lab technicians was looking at microscope slides that might have acid-fast bacilli in them, which indicated TB. It was regarded as a chore, only meant for a junior technician. The acid-fast bacilli were rendered red by the stain, so they stood out from the background, but they were rare, and after quite some time had passed, I had still never found one. Then one day, after hours of tedious searching, I saw one on the slide. In great excitement I went to show it to the boss, who simply responded by admitting that he had planted it there, in order to be sure I knew what I was doing and that I was concentrating.

I was also responsible for cross-matching blood. Whenever it is anticipated that a transfusion may be required, blood of the appropriate type is prepared for that individual patient. This was a normal preparation for major surgery then and it still is today. Occasionally, in the midst of such routine work, there would be an urgent request for blood to be cross-matched for an emergency case. On one occasion, an unusually large volume was requested and the accompanying request form simply said 'GSW'. I was perplexed. I asked my fellow technician what GSW stood for.

She looked at me in astonishment. 'You really don't know?'
'No,' I replied.

She turned to the other lab technicians and announced, 'She doesn't know what a GSW is!' They erupted into gales of laughter.

At that stage in my career, I had never seen a gunshot wound, apart from the attempted suicide that had foxed me a few years earlier. They were sadly not so rare in America. In this instance, an armed sheriff bringing prisoners for treatment to the hospital where I was working had apparently been told by voices in his head to shoot the first people he came across; afterwards, he gave himself up. It was mayhem in the hospital, with lots of demands for blood to give to the injured. The doctors involved were grateful to have the support of someone who knew first-hand how urgent the need was, and I worked hard to provide them with the blood they needed.

I took the ECFMG exam that would allow me to work as a doctor in the USA on the actual day of the Cuban Missile Crisis in 1962. I set off in my little car with a heavy winter coat in the boot in case of a nuclear fallout. My exam seemed of very little consequence in comparison to the threat we were facing. There were hundreds of candidates taking the test from all corners of the globe. Together with a couple of other British doctors, my main concern was to find a portable radio in order to establish if we were at war. Between the written papers there was an English test, and I remember thinking that they should have let me read out the questions, as the examiner's strong American accent proved difficult to understand. In the end there was no war and I even passed the exam too; good news on both counts.

Armed with my ECFMG certificate, I then spent time on the vascular surgical unit in San Francisco, which fostered my early love of the developing discipline. My experience was very limited but I loved the precise nature of the work. I found that I was particularly drawn to the more urgent procedures and I was always keen to provide good emergency care. Vascular surgeons are skilled at controlling bleeding and thus saving lives. In addition they can replace blocked, injured or diseased blood vessels, saving life or limb, and they can clear blocked arteries and again prevent death, preserve limbs and avert strokes. All of this was developing before my eyes, and I enjoyed the feeling of being on the advancing edge of a new specialty.

We lived in Berkeley, where Jonathan was a postgraduate student at the university, so there were lots of opportunities to meet new people and explore the area. The landscape was superb and there was much to see around San Francisco. I loved the city, with its steep hills and trolleybuses, and the Golden Gate Bridge often forming the backdrop to an impressive view. The surrounds were beautiful too, with hills and redwood trees dotted about the nearby countryside.

We were encouraged by the Harkness Fellowship to travel as much as possible and to learn about the USA. We soon realised that having a car was not a luxury but absolutely essential. At first we drove a VW, and later the fellowship provided us with a car so we could fully explore the country in the three months of travel which we were required to undertake. This vehicle was the biggest I had ever seen and certainly the biggest I have ever owned. It was a Chevrolet Bel Air, which did seem 'long enough to have a bowling alley in the back', as Eartha Kitt famously sang in 'Just an Old-Fashioned Girl'. I had to take a driving test, and as part of that test, I was required to park in a space that looked, as I explained to my examiner, about half the length of my car. His response was simply, 'Park!' Happily, I was somehow able to fit in the gap.

We moved to Philadelphia for our second year. To me it had a more European quality than San Francisco, though it was still a large, high-rise city built on a grid. I remember that many of the roads were named after trees: chestnut, spruce, pine. I was glad to get a good post working with Dr John Howard, a famous pancreatic surgeon at the Hahnemann Hospital. I flew there ahead of Jonathan, who took a few weeks to drive across America with our good friend Max from the voyage over. I enjoyed my first experience of flying and was amazed by the short amount of time it took to cross the country. I arrived in Philadelphia when the temperature was very high and the humidity around 95 per cent, so my first night spent in a YWCA was memorably uncomfortable. I rapidly endeavoured to find us an apartment.

The department was staffed by doctors from around the world and I made some very good and long-lasting friendships, as well as learning a huge amount. Among my cohort was a surgical trainee called Iain MacLaren, from Edinburgh. He was a superb raconteur and great company. He was a bachelor at the time and did not cook, so when he wanted to give a Burns Night supper, he asked if I would arrange it and host it in my flat. He was a very skilled piper and memorably piped in the haggis. My neighbours loved the experience and assured me they would never forget it.

I was carrying out research during my time at the Hahnemann Hospital and was in my lab on the day that John F. Kennedy was assassinated. Everyone went into a state of absolute shock. All work was abandoned and we mutely followed the developments in disbelief. No one had any idea what to do or what might happen next. Philadelphia simply fell silent.

I loved Philadelphia for many reasons, but mostly the people. Top of my list had to be the wonderful Mrs Romoser, who was my lab technician. She was appointed after her interview, to which she memorably wore a black suit and a large pink hat. She was about 30 years older than all the other contenders. After having a family she had returned to university to update her biochemistry degree. It must have been like starting from the beginning again, as so much had changed. But she became the backbone of the lab and the young lab techs always looked up to her. She was also the first person to instinctively realise that my marriage was not what it should have been, and she became a true friend.

My boss Dr Howard ran a happy and successful department and was generous to his overseas visitors. He often invited us to his home, where his wife and six children would entertain us. He once told me that he had two separate lots of children. I thought he was saying, 'Three, career, three', but it was actually 'Three, Korea [as in the Korean War], three'. He was quite a famous war surgeon and had developed some vascular techniques that were to benefit the profession for the long term. He and his wife were originally from the south and had wonderful, soft, lilting southern drawls and a relaxed outlook. He maintained his interest in my career from then onwards. He attended the ceremonies when I was honoured by the American College of Surgeons (I was to become their first female honorary fellow) and then by the American Surgical Association, and later even travelled to London for my retirement dinner.

I had found a flat for Jonathan and me over a grocer's store, which was probably the equivalent of the Harrods food hall for Philadelphia. It was a large ground-floor store with top-quality food and polished customer service. It was quite different from the supermarkets I had used in California! It was run by a Mr Costello, who was also our warm-hearted and generous landlord. On the day that I moved in, our fridge was full of goodies from the store, at no cost to me. I was making an effort to learn to cook at the time, so his advice and his shop were a great asset. I used to borrow a cookery book from the library every two weeks and use it to develop my skills. There were no night calls then, so I had much more time to practise. After a year, I purchased the book that had served me best and I still regard it as an essential component of my kitchen today: *The Joy of Cooking* by Rombauer and Becker.

On one occasion I decided to cook beef Wellington for some guests and I bought the beef fillet from Mr Costello. 'And what are you going to do with that?' he asked. When I told him my plans, he was horrified, insisting that I was 'gilding the lily'.

The flat was close to the Philadelphia Art Gallery and I had a delightful walk into work, passing the Rodin Museum en route. I usually had the 'sidewalk' to myself as walkers were a rarity. There had been no possibility of having a piano in California, but I decided to sort out that omission and managed to buy an old piano during our time in the flat. It was a very heavy, iron-framed upright piano, and the movers who had to carry it up three flights of stairs expressed their horror to me in quite a forthright way.

There were some good restaurants in Philadelphia and our favourite was one called Old Original Bookbinder's. The only way we could afford to eat there was to have just a starter and a pudding, and of course to eat every scrap of the bread roll that came with it. Clam chowder followed by cheesecake was our usual order. When the time came for us to leave Philadelphia, the department held a farewell dinner for me there, and at the end of the night, the only way the restaurant could get

My parents' wedding day, 1932.

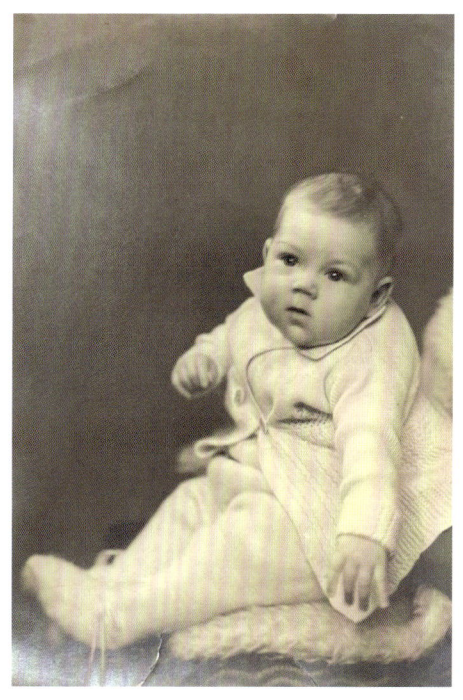

Me as a baby, 1937.

My first car!

With smart Aunt Olive, late 1930s.

With my parents, at home in Blackpool.

Ready to take on the world!

The terrible conditions in which my father worked throughout the 1940s. We were grateful though; he would have faced even more difficult circumstances had he been sent to war.

Looking quite scary in my gasmask.

With my much-loved red scooter, made for me by my father.

Celebrating my fourth birthday with friends, and holding my first musical instrument!

Posing in my ballet outfit.

I loved learning and was always delighted when I managed to come top of the class.

With my classmates at Layton Primary School (I am in the middle row, fourth from the left).

Evidence of an early interest in helping the 'sick and suffering'; my British Junior Red Cross certificate from 1948.

On holiday with the Chollet family in France, c.1952. Their very comfortable way of life was wildly different to my own, but that didn't stop us enjoying our time together.

At school in the early 1950s.

COUNTY BOROUGH OF BLACKPOOL.

BLACKPOOL COLLEGIATE SCHOOL FOR GIRLS.

RULES.

1. Talking in the corridors during school hours is forbidden except at Recreation.
   Girls must not run along the corridors.

2. No pupil is to be absent from class without permission from the Head Mistress.

3. An explanation in writing is required for each absence, and this must be addressed to the Headmistress.

4. Girls are absolutely forbidden to borrow books, slippers, school materials, etc., from one another without permission from the Form Mistress.

5. In Forms I. to IV. all girls must wear the school uniform, consisting of a navy blue serge tunic with a white blouse. Girls in Forms V. and VI. are permitted to wear simple navy blue dresses; only white or cream collars may be worn.
   Girls may wear, from Whitsun to the end of the Summer Term, the School Summer Dress.
   In both the School Winter and Summer Dresses a pocket must be provided.
   Only black, navy blue or white hair-ribbons may be worn.
   Pupils are forbidden to wear any jewellery except a brooch and a wristlet watch.

6. Pupils must wear the School Winter hat with the School Badge.

7. Each pupil must keep at School, in a bag provided for the purpose, two pairs of slippers—a pair of house-slippers and a pair of gymnasium shoes. It is advisable to keep an extra pair of stockings in School. Every pupil must change her shoes for slippers; permission not to change for any reason must be obtained from the Headmistress. Black gymnasium shoes must be worn for drill.

8. Coats, shoes, umbrellas, hats, stockings, school-bags, shoe-bags, slippers, etc., must be clearly marked with owner's name, and School Books must bear the owner's name and class. Fountain pens and "Eversharp," or similar pencils, are not to be used in School unless the owner's name is permanently engraved upon them.

9. Money must not be left in the dressing-rooms, desks, lockers, school-bags or attaché cases; it must be carried in the pocket of the School dress.

10. Permission for exemption from drill must be obtained from the Drill Mistress.

11. Girls are not allowed to remain in School or on the playing-fields after School hours unless permission has been obtained from a Mistress. Pupils who go home for dinner are requested not to return until 1-30 p.m. unless for special reasons.

12. Cooked dinners are provided at the cost of 6d. for each meal for those who wish to have them.

13. Outside Activities. In the interests of the girls' health, growth and progress, parents should limit their daughters' visits to places of amusement to the weekend or to Wednesday evening when no homework is set. Many school activities are of a recreational character; beyond these, no girl may on any day of the school week, take part in any dramatic performances, concerts, dancing displays, festivals or other entertainments, or any rehearsal in connection therewith, without previously having obtained permission so to do from the Headmistress.

The rules were strict!!!!

On the pier at Blackpool in my late teens.

Dressed up for my university entrance interview.

A pre-university studio photo, 1955.

us to leave was by turning off the air conditioning. Philadelphia was a hot and humid place during the summer months.

I was very sorry when my time in America came to a close. I had learned a great deal, in particular how to run a happy department from Robert Parsons and John Howard, two very different leaders but both with the knack of looking after their teams and making everyone feel important and cared for. There was a 'work hard, play hard' ethos to life in America, which was very different from the British scene at that time, where 'play' seemed of little importance.

By the time we left Philadelphia, we needed a U-Haul tow truck to get our accumulated goods to New York, where we were to board the RMS *Sylvania*, which was to take us home. I greatly entertained the New York dockers with my attempts at reversing the truck to the edge of the dock. On eventually arriving in Liverpool via the River Mersey, we felt as though we were entering a tiny toy town. But I was happy to be home. It was particularly good to be reunited with my parents; the separation had been very hard on them.

Towards the end of our stay, we had each received tempting job offers, but visa rules meant we had to return to the UK for two years before becoming eligible to work in the USA. When further job proposals arrived from America after the two years were up, though, I found I did not want to move away from home after all, as by then I had settled into a house and work.

Getting a BTA was all very well, but now came the serious business of getting formally trained and passing exams. The Royal College of Surgeons determines the requirements for becoming a fully fledged surgeon. The training culminates with exams, then, if successful, the candidate becomes a fellow of the college (FRCS). Most young trainees take about eight to ten years to complete this training. One of the required posts involved a stint in A&E, and for this I worked at the Royal Southern Hospital in Liverpool. It was close to the Mersey and served the older end of the docks and the large local residential zone, where there was considerable poverty and deprivation.

I was essentially the doctor in charge of the department. There was a consultant nominally in charge, but he was a general surgeon with little to no interest in what actually went on in A&E. I worked with a very experienced Irish nurse called Kitty O'Reilly, and she was a wonderful source of knowledge and advice for me, the novice. The patients were always polite and respectful. Only once in my year in the job did I feel threatened, when a drunken patient came stumbling towards me, but Kitty soon sorted him out.

We were occasionally expected to travel by ambulance to a serious case and would always have a kit of tools and drugs ready for emergency calls. On one occasion, we were responding to a man who had fallen into the hold of a grain ship and broken his leg. I was expected to go down a pole into the ship to administer analgesia (pain relief) before he could be rescued. The 'audience' of shipworkers delighted in telling me that there were rats the size of dogs down in the grain. The other problem was that this was the era of the miniskirt, and you can imagine what that meant. Following the incident, I instituted the purchase of some 'Casualty Officers' Emergency Dungarees' as an addition to the kit.

This was the only year of my UK career that did not involve night calls, and I made good use of it, studying hard for the first set of required exams. The exams that were the first and biggest hurdle were known as the Primary FRCS and mainly concerned anatomy and physiology. They had a very high failure rate, around 80 per cent. I initially found myself in that majority, and after a couple of attempts, I was close to giving up. I decided to take six weeks off and work non stop on my studies. To my great relief, I was successful at the next attempt. I later learned that most sensible trainees took a whole year off and taught anatomy in order to pass the hurdle. I determined to sit the next big exam, the final FRCS, as soon as possible, to get the stress of examinations out of the way.

My ambition was to become a surgical registrar and I knew that, if I succeeded, I was very likely to complete the training and become a consultant surgeon. In 1966 I applied for and was appointed to a registrar position working across a number of Liverpool hospitals, which involved moving between some of the different specialties of surgery. Landing the job was wonderful but also seriously scary, as I had no one between me and the consultants and I was very much expected to just get on with things.

During this time as a registrar, I did one year of paediatric surgery. I wonder if this was possibly a push from my superiors in the direction of a specialty deemed more suitable for a woman. Senior surgeons would decide and allocate these posts behind the scenes; I was not involved in the decision-making process. I was the only surgical registrar at the Children's Hospital, so was available for calls six nights every week. It was hard work, but the volume of experience that I gained was incredible and it proved to be a great start to my surgical career.

There was a superb group of paediatric surgeons in Liverpool and the most senior one was a woman called Miss Isabella Forshall. She was something of a *femme formidable*, who always carried a large handbag (or rather, made us carry it for her). I had met her previously, with considerable trepidation, during my student days. She used to give us a short tutorial at the start of her outpatient clinic. There were eight students in the 'firm' and one was a delightfully shy blond man called Pete, who blushed easily.

She introduced one tutorial, saying, 'Today I will talk to you about circumcision.'

Turning to Pete, she then said, 'Lend me your . . .'

By the end of the theatrically long pause, poor Pete was bright red with embarrassment. She then happily proceeded to demonstrate the operation on his . . . thumb. It could have been much worse.

Paediatric surgery was then based across two sites in Liverpool and I was registrar in the 'downtown' branch, the Royal Liverpool Children's Hospital. The other branch was Alder Hey, and Miss Forshall generally confined herself there. The surgeons at both sites were uniformly good and also great characters. Peter Rickham was the most senior of my bosses. He had a central European accent and frankly I found him quite scary. On my first day, one of the nurses in theatre said to me, 'You won't cry, will you?'

'No, I have never done before. Why do you ask?'

'Because all the previous registrars have.'

Mr Rickham delighted in trying to terrify me, but I am not easily perturbed. If we were slow in getting a child ready for theatre, he would always threaten to call an ambulance to take the child to Alder Hey, suggesting that they were more efficient there. I was pretty sure he said the opposite when in Alder Hey.

He could sometimes be difficult to prise from his bed when on call. One night, when I rang him and needed him to come, there was a long silence on the other end of the line. I assumed that he had gone back to sleep so gave a loud cough. 'I am not sleeping, I am thinking, sweetie,' he responded. He did eventually come to my and the patient's aid.

A difficult surgical problem in paediatrics then was oesophageal atresia, in which the gullet is incomplete at birth and so does not join up with the stomach. Peter Rickham was an expert in dealing with this abnormality. He tended to be single-minded about surgery, and his wife often found it difficult to get his attention, so she would slip the words 'oesophageal atresia' into her speech in order to galvanise his attention.

One of Mr Rickham's special interests was a condition called hypospadias, which is an abnormality of the penis that results in the child spraying urine all over the place when they urinate. His aim, he said, was always that they would be able to write their name in the snow after a good operation.

He was also interested in the surgical treatment of hydrocephalus and spina bifida. These were then relatively frequent congenital abnormalities, which have since been largely prevented by pregnant women taking folic acid, which prevents neural tube defects in offspring. Some babies with this condition were so deformed, with very large heads and abnormal spines, that their parents abandoned them. I found this very distressing and decided that I could not spend my life in such a specialty. My own mother would sometimes visit the abandoned children and I loved to hear them proudly say afterwards, 'My mummy's been to see me today.'

Neil Freeman was a South African paediatric surgeon at the hospital and one of the most skilled, gentle and precise operators I ever saw. He taught me a great deal. I always sought to emulate his beautiful surgical technique and to retain that ability when I later transitioned to working on adult patients again.

There was just one other female surgeon that I knew of in Liverpool. Her name was Irene Irving, and she was always so kind, gentle and smiling, and a truly exquisite surgeon to watch. She would go on to sacrifice progress in her chosen career to marry and have children, but later returned to work and reappeared in my life. Some years after I became a consultant in Liverpool, she asked me to teach her an operation that I was doing regularly, and which she needed to start practising. It was access surgery for dialysis and involved joining two small blood vessels together. As a paediatric surgeon, the blood vessels Irene had to join were even smaller than the adult ones I was used to. Teaching my former teacher was pretty daunting, but as always, she was kind, warm and welcoming. It was a memorable day.

Within paediatric surgery at that time, there was a newly developing specialty called urology. There were initially only two paediatric surgeons in the UK who treated just the kidneys, ureter and bladder (the other was at Great Ormond Street Hospital), but their excellent results supported the wisdom of such specialisation. Mr Johnston was one of those specialists. He worked in the two Liverpool Children's Hospitals and he loved to go to the football on Saturday afternoon, so we would do everything possible to avoid calling him at that time. But on one Saturday afternoon, I was confronted with a little girl with extensive trauma affecting all parts of the urinary tract, and I needed help. Mr Johnston was dragged reluctantly out of his seat and performed the most amazing feat of reconstruction. Apart from some scarring, the little girl was restored to normal.

There was a lot of trauma to be dealt with, and when, one evening, a five-year-old was admitted with a ruptured colon after a traffic accident at 10pm, I asked the mother how it had happened. She replied, 'He's not used to the roads, Doc.'

One of the most helpful doctors I knew then was the senior anaesthetist Dr Jackson Rees, who was a joy to work with. He had seen far more paediatric surgery than I ever would and his wisdom and advice felt heaven sent. If he was passing the hospital after an evening out and saw my MGB in the car park, he would often pop in just to see if all was well. He taught me a great deal about surgery and his presence was always enormously reassuring. I remember him scrubbing up to help me with my first baby tracheostomy, which involves inserting a tube directly into the windpipe. This is necessary if the airway is compromised in a child or adult and it is often urgent. It can be a particularly serious situation in a baby. Even though I was the one holding the knife, it was pretty clear who really knew what was going on. The operating field is normally exposed for the operating surgeon by the use of instruments called retractors. I can still picture Dr Rees now, holding his two tiny Langenbeck retractors and using them to direct me to the right spot.

When I was being tediously slow operating for the first time on a pyloric stenosis, which is when the outlet from the stomach in an infant is narrowed, he watched for a while and eventually said, 'You see that stuff coming out of the wound? Well, that's the omentum. Gently pull on that and the transverse colon will appear. Gently pull on that and the pylorus will appear.' And, lo and behold, it did.

One day, an eight-year-old girl was admitted with acute appendicitis. I met her and her parents and spoke with them about the problem. I explained that she needed an operation to remove the appendix. She was a wonderfully feisty little girl with a strong Liverpool accent.

'Who's going to do this operation, then?' she asked.

Fearing her response might be adverse, I replied somewhat meekly, 'Well, I am.'

'That's good,' she said, '''cos I don't want any of them man doctors to see me with me knicks off, do I?'

Although I decided not to become a paediatric surgeon, it was nevertheless superb training for my future career. The small size of the patients, and the precision and gentle handling required, were all excellent foundations from which I could progress.

During my year in paediatric surgery, I learned a great deal, performed many operations and developed a good technique, but by the end I was keen to return to my first love: adult general surgery and the developing specialty of vascular surgery. I returned to Broadgreen Hospital, where I had been a house officer back in 1960. Now, in 1967, I was a registrar, just as David Glenn had been, and this time around all the responsibilities would fall on my shoulders.

Roger Maudesley, the registrar I was replacing, was a very popular and talented man, so there was a lot to live up to. Everyone was sad to see him go. As luck would have it, at the same time an extremely popular secretary named Gladys left and her replacement, Elaine, was also well aware of the big shoes she was trying to fill. Not surprisingly, she and I, 'the new girls', became allies and friends. In time, we instead became, as we saw it, the 'the good girls', when comparisons with former members of the team ceased. I never felt at any time that I was treated differently because I was a woman. It was clear to me that the only thing that mattered was the quality of the work. I must acknowledge, though, that I was fortunate to have the stamina, as it was hard graft.

At that time when I was learning the basics of vascular surgery, there was a new gadget on the horizon that sounded as though it might be very helpful in diagnosis. The Doppler effect was discovered by Christian Doppler, an Austrian physicist, in 1842. In essence it is the change in pitch observed when, for instance, a train with its whistle blowing approaches and then leaves a station. This phenomenon was later used to develop a tool using ultrasound to measure blood flow, which eventually became an invaluable instrument for the vascular surgeon and cardiologist.

My first contact with this device was when a sales rep brought it to Broadgreen Hospital and I saw the potential for finding and measuring blood flow in both arteries and veins. In some ways, I was more impressed by its ability to detect flow in veins, because arteries have a pulse and veins do not, so it was much easier to detect blood flow in arteries by feeling the pulse. However, it was abundantly clear to me that the equipment could still revolutionise our understanding of blood flow in vessels. This was all very well, but its price tag (about £300, more than £4,000 in today's money) put it well out of reach and I sadly told the rep that we were both out of luck.

Following his amazing demonstration, I went for a late lunch in the dining room, where the only other occupants were a small group of hospital managers. They were discussing the fact that they had money left over in the budget – just a few hundred pounds – and no way of spending it in the given timeframe. They were reflecting that as a result, they would have to forfeit the sum of money. Summoning my courage, I wandered over to their table.

'I could not help hearing your conversation, and I have just seen . . .'

To my amazement, they were very happy to buy the gadget

rather than lose the sum back into the main coffers of the NHS. Such good fortune. That little black box gave years of excellent service and I have no doubt that it saved both legs and lives.

That year, I took and passed the FRCS examination in Edinburgh, which seemed to me to be as close to Liverpool as London was. Many of the consultant surgeons at my hospital (though not the Professor) were Fellows of the Edinburgh College. I had gone there to sit the first part of the exam, so it felt natural to complete it there. I took a short course in Edinburgh prior to sitting the exam as I was determined that I would pass on the first attempt. I lived in a bedsit and simply studied every hour of the day and much of the night. On passing the exam, candidates lose the title Doctor, so if you are a man you become Mr, while female surgeons become Miss, Mrs or Ms. I did pass at my first attempt as hoped, and so became 'Mrs'. I felt a great deal of pride in the change, which was an important symbol of my progression.

When I told Mr Shepherd, the senior consultant, that I had passed the Edinburgh Fellowship, his only response was, 'The trouble with the Edinburgh Fellowship is they are inclined to let the borderline candidates through.' I happened to know that I had actually achieved top marks, though I was too reticent to tell him so. The next friendly comment came from the Professor, who asked, 'And when are you going to take *the* Fellowship?', by which he meant the London FRCS. Without doubt my favourite response came from Helen Stewart, a rare female surgical trainee whom I had met in Scotland, in the form of a postcard that simply said, 'Hi, fellow fellow.' Nonetheless, I did take the hint from my superiors at the hospital and took the exam in London a few weeks later, becoming FRCS England as well.

One of the truly special and exceptional aspects of that unit was that everyone got on so well; we even did ward rounds together. At the time I thought that was how all units behaved, but sadly it is in fact a rarity. We would do a full round of all the patients, who numbered about 60, before sitting in the office with a cup of coffee to decide the operating lists and who would do what. Overseeing that process was an important skill for a registrar, which also made it a powerful position. In theory it allowed me to plan my training, although things did not always work out as envisaged.

One day the senior surgeon said to me, 'There is a gallbladder to be done. You have done gallbladders, I presume?'

'No, sir. I'm afraid not.'

'Ah well, a cholecystectomy is a difficult operation with many hazards, so I'll teach you how to do it. Indeed, I'll take you through your first 12. Put it on your list and I'll assist you.'

This was a very welcome offer.

The next morning, the patient was asleep and ready on the operating table, and I was scrubbed up, but where was the boss? I discovered that he was operating in the next theatre, so I sent a nurse through to tell him that the patient was on the table.

'Does she know what incision to make?' came the response.

So I told the nurse which incision I planned to make, and he approved and said, 'Tell her to make the incision.'

A few moments later I was in the peritoneal cavity, the sac in which all the abdominal organs are housed, so again I asked the nurse to kindly inform the boss.

This time the message was, 'Tell her to start looking for the cystic artery and the cystic duct.'

This is the crucial step in the operation and the place

where real problems can occur. Tiger country indeed. With great care, I started to explore as instructed and, after a few minutes, I found those two seriously important tubular structures.

I said to the nurse, 'Please would you go next door and say that I have found the cystic artery and the cystic duct?'

She returned with the message: 'He says, "Ask her what she is waiting for, then."'

So I proceeded, without incident, to remove a gallbladder for the first time. From then on, whenever a cholecystectomy was on the list, I would hear, 'She's done gallbladders, so that can go on her list.' I was never assisted once, let alone 12 times.

Luckily I didn't usually have to work in this way. Being in charge of organising the list as the duty registrar meant that if there was a case I thought would be best in the hands of a particular surgeon, I could arrange that. But if there was a case I hoped to be instructed on and a surgeon who was happy to teach me, then I could make sure my name was down for that procedure.

Edgar Parry was the younger consultant and an exceptionally good surgeon. He was to become my mentor. I have always hoped that I behaved and operated as well as he did. As with my father, his look of disappointment was all I needed to urge me on to do better. He was a calm and skilful surgeon, and no matter how difficult the operation, I always sensed that he would find the way to a successful outcome. The worst I ever heard him say when everything was falling apart was 'Damn', in his gentle Welsh accent. Few senior surgeons are as humble as Edgar was. My connection to him has continued down the generations with his family, much to my delight.

One of the difficulties resulting from working for someone as superb at surgery as Edgar was that, in my eyes, nothing that I was capable of could ever remotely measure up to the standard that he set. Feelings of embarrassment would flood over me as he watched me at work. I wanted him to teach me how to become like him, but paradoxically not to watch me failing to match up to his level of skill. Despite this, I routinely manipulated the operating lists in order to get the opportunity to be taught by him whenever possible, and thus to further punish my self-esteem. In truth, though, I was progressing well, gaining skills and growing in experience. I was very fortunate to have such a superb role model and seeking to emulate his skills stood me in good stead for the whole of my working life.

The areas dealt with on this unit encompassed what would now be several separate specialties. They included urology, head and neck, upper and lower gastrointestinal, breast, hepatobiliary (liver and gallbladder) and, of course, the newly developing field of vascular surgery. It was an amazingly comprehensive place to train, with a steady supply of emergencies to confront. I was the only trainee and so had very little time off, but that loss was more than compensated for by the experience that I gained so quickly. There were no rules about hours of work then, no European Working Time Directive. My logbook for those two years would be the equivalent of about a decade's training now. You needed resilience and energy, but benefited greatly from the workload. I could be called in every night and my car seemed to know its way from home to hospital with little help from me. Jonathan was proud that I was a surgeon and he accepted the disruptions to our social life.

LIFE IN HER HANDS

We were two people living together, enjoying our respective careers and sharing a love of music.

Possibly the most important care we give as surgeons is that which is due to the emergency who can present at any hour of the day or night. However, medical care in general is based on trying to avert emergencies by preventative management. For example, repairing a hernia is far safer that having to deal with a strangulated one. Removing a gallbladder before the stones have migrated into the bile ducts is a safer option. Finding the cancer of the colon before it blocks the bowel prevents far more dangerous emergency operations further down the line.

But there was no such thing as screening when I was a junior doctor and many diseases were diagnosed late, often too late. Thus the need to be competent at dealing with the unexpected – and the life-threatening – was hugely important as I trained. But there will always be emergencies, even today, when screening is so much more advanced. Emergencies do not always have a happy ending, and coping with death and its emotional impact is also a big part of any surgeon's development. When you have tried and failed to save a life, there is inevitably a lot of soul-searching. Could I have done more? Could someone else have done better? Are there lessons to be learned? Clearly the major impact is on the family and one of the toughest tasks a surgeon has to undertake when they are already feeling wretched is to talk to the next of kin and explain what has happened.

During my two years as a registrar on this unit, I became a competent surgeon in a very wide field, and although I later confined myself to vascular surgery, I was forever grateful that I felt comfortable dealing with all the other organs that might impinge on my chosen specialty. One operation I remember from my more senior years of practice – a vascular tumour lying in the back of the abdomen – involved urology, gynaecology and colorectal surgery in addition to vascular surgery. My early training enabled me to feel competent and comfortable in dealing with such a problem.

As a registrar I was not resident in the hospital. One evening, I was at home and getting ready to go to a concert at the Philharmonic Hall when I was phoned by the hospital and informed that I was needed at once. I urged Jonathan to hurry in the hope that we could fit it in and still make the concert. As a result, he nicked his skin while shaving and bled a little. As we drove around the ring road, he held a handkerchief to his chin. I was driving just a little over the speed limit and a police car pulled alongside us. I wound down my window and waved my stethoscope at them. They in turn waved their handcuffs at me. I shouted out that I was going to an emergency, and I think they assumed my bloodied husband *was* the emergency. They dutifully drove alongside us, providing an escort all the way into the hospital. In those days the telephonists sat at the main entrance and luckily, they were able to appraise the situation quickly. 'Thank goodness you are here, Doctor. They are waiting for you, go quickly . . .' My accompanying PCs left!

One area of vascular surgery that I was interested in early in my career was venous thrombosis. It so happened that the contraceptive pill had appeared on the horizon at about the time I was learning to be a surgeon. It was welcomed and widely used, but the dose of oestrogen thought to be needed was very high and was responsible for a number of women getting deep vein thrombosis of an extensive kind, which was a significant problem.

I had seen older patients getting such clots in leg veins

after major surgery, but these were young, healthy women. If all the veins in the leg thrombose, the consequences are serious. A clot might move and become a pulmonary embolus, which can be life-threatening. In addition, the leg becomes so swollen that its own blood supply is reduced, which can have serious consequences both at the time and in the future. Naturally, I wanted to be able to remove the clots and prevent these two worrying consequences.

In the 1950s, a young American medical student called Tom Fogarty had invented a balloon catheter for removing clots from arteries. This was something I was already familiar with. There was also a version of this device that could be used to remove clots from veins. The catheter was passed into the vein until it went past the clot, where the balloon was inflated. It then pulled out the clot as the catheter was removed.

I remember, in 1967, saying to the consultant radiologist that it would be wonderful if we were able to watch the catheter as it travelled along the vein during this operation. He volunteered to bring the 'X-ray image intensifier' to the theatre and show me on the screen where the catheter was. I devised the technique of inflating the balloon with contrast medium (a special dye used in some X-rays) and then following the progress of this balloon as it was withdrawn. We would then do an operative angiogram to check that we had completed the job. I operated on many young women using these techniques and published the results and method in the late 1960s.

One of the worst such cases that I treated was a young woman who was very seriously ill from thrombus in the leg and the resultant pulmonary embolism. Mysteriously, there did not appear to be a cause in her case, as she denied taking the pill. She was a very good-looking young lady, and it turned out that her mother had become concerned about the way she was attracting the opposite sex and had been slipping the pill into her morning tea. The girl happily made a good recovery.

It was quite by chance that I was a registrar at the time of this issue with the pill, but the development of the operation was important for my career as well as for the patients' lives. In publishing and presenting the results, I became a familiar face at various important meetings in the surgical world. It was a valuable opportunity which I grasped with both hands.

Progress in a surgical career depends on a number of factors. Ability in the operating theatre is clearly very important, but there are other attributes of similar significance – for instance, knowing when to operate and, just as crucially when *not to*; keeping a cool head when faced with difficult and sometimes life-threatening emergencies; and being able to communicate well with patients and their families, as well as with colleagues.

Alongside all of this is the need to participate in developing the specialty – being 'on the cutting edge', as I have often thought of it. In doing so, young doctors in all areas have the opportunity to present their work and research and thus to educate others, but also to become better known and advance up the training ladder. I was already doing such presentations, but I was to take a major step forward in the next phase of my surgical training when I became a lecturer in surgery.

6
End of Training

Throughout my early career, no sooner had I started one job than it was time to start thinking about the next. While I was training, finding the next position was very much a do-it-yourself situation and the modern run-through training had not yet been invented. So, as I progressed through my registrar's role, I was naturally considering my next move.

It needed to be a senior registrar job in general surgery, preferably with some vascular surgery included too, so I could work to make that my special interest. As a registrar, I had started to carry out some vascular operations, initially with the assistance of the boss and then with a more junior trainee giving me assistance. I could deal with a ruptured aortic aneurysm without the need to call in more senior help, I could carry out a bypass for a blocked artery, and I had developed and was using the technique to remove clots from deep veins – and giving papers on the subject.

The majority of the operations I did during my time as a registrar were in the field called general surgery; this included the removal of the stomach, or the bowel, or the gallbladder. The unit at Broadgreen did endocrine surgery (centred around the hormone-secreting thyroid, parathyroid and adrenal glands), so I was, for example, able to remove a thyroid. Urology was still a part of general surgery then, so operations to remove the prostate, and the kidney, if there was cancer, were common. Breast surgery was also in our remit, so I frequently removed tumours and carried out mastectomies too.

Lots of relatively minor operations, such as the repair of hernias, haemorrhoids, varicose veins and a whole variety of lumps and bumps, also had to be carried out. In my mind, these smaller procedures were just as important to the patient as the more major ones, and they had to be done well.

A lot of our work focused on the removal of cancers, which could involve a major operation when surgery was the best hope of a cure. The specialty of oncology was in its infancy back then, and although there would be some drug treatment, the core of care meant removing the cancer.

Emergency surgery in the 1960s could be best summarised as dealing with 'blocks, bursts and bleeding', and most nights would involve a call-out to deal with at least one of these. There was also a lot of trauma, and although the majority of trauma was in the field of the orthopaedic surgeon, there were a number of injuries that required a general surgeon instead. Seatbelts were not always used and airbags not yet invented at that time, so abdominal, chest, head and facial injuries as a result of car accidents were common.

This hugely wide spectrum of topics was normal then and provided a fascinating range of work for any surgeon. After such broad training, I was ready for the next step on the ladder, the last before I could apply for a consultant position.

In 1969 I decided to apply for the post of lecturer at Liverpool University. It was the equivalent of a senior registrar post but would allow me more flexibility of experience. I would have some choice in the areas I worked in, and as there was not a senior registrar post yet established in vascular surgery, it was the best route I could take in order to focus on my chosen discipline.

In addition, I had previously set up a small laboratory in Broadgreen Hospital, using my own funds, to study the clotting problems associated with deep vein thrombosis, but a lecturer job would allow me a proper laboratory and the possibility of collaborating with others and of writing my thesis for a higher degree: the Master of Surgery degree, known in Liverpool as ChM. I also loved teaching students, which was a central part of the job, as was arranging student exams. Academic units tend to have more medical staff than the normal ones and they have to deal with teaching, examining and research in addition to the surgical care of patients.

I applied, was interviewed and was successful. This was immensely reassuring for me because most people who became a senior registrar or equivalent were likely to eventually get a consultant job.

The other lecturer in the department was Alfred Cuschieri, now Professor Sir Alfred. He wanted an academic future and I did not. I was a jobbing practical surgeon through and through, and although I carried out research throughout my career, I did not want all the other tasks that came with the territory of being a professor, as I feared that they would reduce the amount of time I could devote to the surgical care of patients. We were therefore not in competition with each other. We became good friends and could, as it were, watch each other's backs and alert each other to possible jobs coming up.

Prior to starting the role in 1969, I presented myself to the professor for whom I would be working and spent half an hour with him learning the requirements of the job. As I started walking home afterwards, a secretary came running after me calling, 'But you have not been to see the senior lecturer!'

I hastily returned to the department and the man I had unknowingly neglected proceeded to give me precisely the opposite instructions to the professor. They were not best buddies, as I later discovered, and of course I had no choice but to do as the professor instructed, not his subordinate. It was my first experience of disagreement bordering on hostility between colleagues, though sadly it was not to be the last.

When I had been a registrar at Broadgreen, they had become used to my presence and skills in vascular surgery. On my first ward round with my professor at the Royal Infirmary, my new hospital, I was summoned to the phone and an anaesthetist from Broadgreen simply said, 'Come now, we need you.'

That was it – there were no more details. I felt anxious about attempting to explain this to my new boss, but I was in no doubt that I simply had to go. The reason for the summons turned out to be a patient who was bleeding following vascular surgery and there was no surgeon present with the experience to deal with it. The bleed was life-threatening but luckily we were able to intervene and the patient survived. My new boss was not at all amused, however, and made it plain that Broadgreen could no longer regard me as 'available'.

Professor Stock retired soon afterwards and his replacement started. Professor Shields was very young and looked even younger. He found it difficult at first to get people to believe that he was actually the professor. He was a good researcher with an excellent CV and he taught me a great deal about carrying out and presenting research. My main ambition was to be a good surgeon, though, and at that stage I might well have had more operating experience than he did.

The new professor and I sometimes disagreed about the management of patients. However, he was very helpful in ensuring I did all the extra things that would enable me to progress in my career – things like giving papers at surgical meetings and writing articles for the surgical literature. One major step I took was applying to become a Hunterian Professor at the Royal College of Surgeons of England. This award carried much prestige, but actually involved the delivery of just one lecture at the RCS in London.

I was successfully appointed a Hunterian Professor and my lecture, entitled 'Management of the Source of Pulmonary Embolism', was about clots in the deep veins and their propensity to move off to the heart as a pulmonary embolism. In preparation, I spent a day in the college going through the archives of John Hunter, looking for relevant examples of his teaching. Hunter's own, original handwritten records are available for study and in fact happened to contain material relevant to my lecture. Apart from exams, this was my first real connection to the College.

The final words of my lecture were from a poem by John Skelton: 'That when ye think all danger fore to pass / Ware ye the lizard lyeth lurking in the grass.'

Perhaps all politicians should have these words framed and hung on their walls! To me, they certainly summed up the situation of a clot lurking silently in the deep veins, ready to move off without warning. I was fortunate to have a good number of Liverpudlian supporters come to the lecture and we all dined together afterwards, before taking the train back to Liverpool.

The lecturer post involved working for the professor as his assistant but also included a lot of independent operating. This was based largely at the Liverpool Royal Infirmary but included the Professorial Unit at Broadgreen too, with which I had had a lot of experience as a house officer and registrar.

Although it was mostly a general surgical post, it gave me the opportunity to carry out some vascular surgery and advance my ambitions in the field. I had so far only carried out vascular procedures at Broadgreen, but I was now expected to cover emergencies at the Royal too.

My first was a tricky one and, of course, I felt I had to prove myself. A registrar at a hospital some twenty miles away had diagnosed appendicitis in a 70-year-old man, but when he'd operated, he'd found a normal appendix. He had, however, also found blood behind the peritoneum (the sac containing all the guts). Bleeding there is usually coming from the aorta, so he'd realised that the patient in fact had a leaking aneurysm. His boss had told him to 'pack it'. This is a technique designed to hold back the bleeding but not to correct the cause. His boss had not done any vascular surgery and probably expected that the patient would not survive, with or without an operation. In reality, few such patients did.

A day or so later, the patient was still alive and an operation needed at least to be considered, so he was referred to me. Infection is the dread of all surgeons who have to insert foreign material into a patient, and the idea of operating on a patient who had a pack in place – and therefore a potential source of infection – was something of a nightmare. It was far from the nice gentle start I could have hoped for in my new post. Happily, the man did not develop an infection, and both he and his anxious surgeon were mighty relieved.

Towards the end of my period as a lecturer, I was asked to be a locum consultant in Ormskirk District General Hospital for a few weeks, while the incumbent had his gallbladder removed. The main operating list started on Friday mornings at 9am and I was informed that it should ideally all be finished by soon after noon. There were normally six major cases on the list, which could include the removal of a colon, gallbladder or stomach, for example, so it was quite a lot of work to be completed in that small amount of time. In order to enable this, the theatre sister would have six trolleys laid up with the instruments required for all six operations when the list began at 9am. If I needed an instrument that was not on the trolley, she would delve under the drapes on later trolleys and produce the necessary instrument, something no one would do today because of the fear of losing an instrument or of cross-infection. Only later did I discover that, when carried out by the regular surgeon, the list normally continued well into the afternoon, thus delaying another surgeon's access to the theatre. I certainly never got a coffee break, but I did usually manage to complete my work by the end of the morning. Of course, I only discovered this plot towards the end of my time in the job.

On one occasion during the locum role, a registrar opened the abdomen of an emergency case and, on discovering a leaking aortic aneurysm, came to ask for my help. I explored the possibility of operating but discovered there was not even a clamp suitable for clamping the aorta in the hospital, and certainly no suitable instruments or materials for replacing it. At that time, arterial surgery was only carried out in major centres. Our sole option was to put the patient into the back of an ambulance and take him to Broadgreen Hospital to deal with the aneurysm there. So, the anaesthetised patient was put into an ambulance with an anaesthetist, and the police were contacted to enable a smooth ride from the first hospital to the second. I decided to follow the ambulance rather than ride in it, so that I would have my car with me once I had completed the operation. It was the hairiest ride across Liverpool I ever experienced. Driving so fast left me shaking by the time we arrived and I had to take a moment to recover before tackling the operation. Happily, the surgery was successful and the patient able to return home afterwards.

An important international event in 1972 was the moon landing. Jonathan and I did not possess a television, but I was very keen indeed to watch the events unfold, so I rushed off at the last minute to a store to buy a TV. The assistant initially thought I was joking and quite clearly believed that I could not afford one. I bought a small Sony black and white set and then sat up all night to watch the landing. I was enthralled.

Towards the end of the four years of a senior registrar's appointment comes the time to apply for a permanent job. My lecturer role had been the same grade as a senior registrar, but it turned out that the appointment was for only three years. This was something of a shock for me, as I was somehow unaware of this initially and so became anxious about what might happen if I failed in my quest for advancement. I was only too well aware that many surgeons were in their forties before they were successful in securing a consultant position. I would be only 32 at the time I needed to start applying, so it could be some time before I was successful.

And I was female. Did that matter? I did not think so, and was of the opinion that it had not in any way hampered my progress to date. On the other hand, I was also very aware of the fact that there were no other women consultant general surgeons in Merseyside and precious few in the country. I was well trained, experienced, competent and not afraid of hard work, so I concluded that no, my sex would not stand in my way. Indeed, to me, it was of no relevance at all.

My first application for a consultant appointment, at the

West Middlesex Hospital in London, was unsuccessful. I had spent the morning prior to the interview looking in estate agent windows and becoming more and more gloomy – property prices in London compared with Liverpool were shocking – and I am sure it showed at the interview. I was reminded of the life insurance salesman who once visited me when I was newly qualified. He had said, 'Get your next job in London, buy the most expensive property you can possibly afford, then move into a mansion in Liverpool when you get your consultant job.' *Wise but laughable advice*, I thought. There was no way that I could have bought a house in 1960 when I first qualified. The West Middlesex job went to the sitting senior registrar and I was delighted for him (and also relieved that I did not have to worry about trying to find an affordable property).

In an unexpected but encouraging move, a senior surgeon who had been on the appointment panel took it upon himself to phone me to say that I should not worry about my failure, as 'better things are in store for you'.

Surprisingly, my second application was successful. I say surprisingly because I knew of many senior registrars who had to make numerous applications before even being interviewed, let alone appointed. The post was general surgeon at two of the teaching hospitals in Liverpool: the Royal Southern Hospital and the David Lewis Northern Hospital. There were a number of local and other candidates, but my main competitor was a lovely man called Will Lloyd Jones, who was a superb surgeon and a good friend of mine. We apparently divided the committee into 'his' and 'her' camps. Unknown to them, we went out for lunch together during the long day of interviews and we would have gladly supported each other whatever the outcome.

It went my way and I was overjoyed. I had spent the ten years since qualifying as a doctor training for just this point in my life, and I had succeeded. In three months' time, I would be a consultant surgeon. It was all I had ever wanted to achieve and now it was a reality. I called in to the garage for fuel on my way home and they were giving away matchbox cars to customers. Feeling boosted by my new success, I enjoyed saying, 'I will take a Lamborghini, please', and I still have that little toy today. Jonathan was also delighted and we celebrated my, and indeed his, success together. The spouse of a surgeon has to be very tolerant! My parents were overjoyed for me too.

The next major event of 1972 was my successful appointment as a Moynihan Travelling Fellow. This was a highly sought-after fellowship, awarded in competition by the Association of Surgeons of Great Britain and Ireland. It was a huge opportunity for the successful candidate, as it involved several weeks of travel, usually in America, to centres of surgical excellence. It was particularly timely, as I was able to work the final three months of my post as lecturer travelling in the States.

The interview for the fellowship took place at the Royal College of Surgeons in Lincoln's Inn Fields in London, and the Council of the Association made the selection. I found it was a far more relaxed affair than the consultant interview. I was invited to sit next to the Chairman rather than as far away as the room would allow, which was always how it was when I went for consultant roles.

The candidates were given a room to wait in and refreshments were provided. We were all used to selection committees, where the outcome would be announced at the end of the meeting, so we sat in this little room and waited and waited. Eventually, the senior person among us was deputed to take a look outside. To our shock, the committee had gone home long ago and the College was virtually closed for the night. Arriving back in Liverpool on a much later train than intended, I learned that there had been multiple anxious phone calls from the Chairman of the Committee to my home during my journey back. The news was good.

Armed with £750, I was able to plan a ten-week tour of ten different vascular surgical centres in the USA. It was an amazing opportunity and a chance to establish my thoughts on my future practice and its conduct. I have always believed that it is tremendously important to witness for oneself how surgery is conducted and organised in other parts of the world.

One very useful piece of advice that I received from my professor before I embarked on the trip was that I should tell my hosts that I was leaving on Saturday and tell the next team that I was arriving on Sunday. This gave me a much-needed day of relaxation between visits. I was expected to give lectures and to teach on the wards wherever I went, but most of my time was spent learning from my hosts.

My itinerary took me from Boston, where I landed, down the eastern states, across the southern states, then up the western states, ending in San Francisco. I met most of the well-known vascular surgeons of those regions and watched them operate with great interest.

I rapidly became aware that my finances were at risk of running out earlier than planned, as hotels and meals were much more expensive than I had anticipated. There followed a couple of weeks of strict rationing and using only public transport to get to my destinations. I had no expectation of being paid a fee for my lectures, so it was a pleasant surprise when I received my first one, and occasionally the host hospitals would pick up the tab for my hotel too. I then realised with relief that I could in fact manage my finances easily.

I think it is fair to say that the specialty of vascular surgery in the USA was ahead of us in the UK at that time. Most of its experts were conducting only vascular operations, whereas in the UK for many years afterwards we were general surgeons primarily, with a special interest in vascular surgery. I realised, however, that British surgeons had a much broader base of skills resulting from the breadth of their training, experience and anatomical knowledge.

I was often something of a novelty for my American hosts. I did not meet a single female surgeon or trainee during my visits. Indeed, some of the units had never *had* a female trainee. I was not perturbed by this, as I was familiar with the lack of female colleagues at home, and my hosts largely took this strange experience in their stride. Women made up only about 2 per cent of the consultant surgeon workforce in the UK at the time and it was roughly the same in the States. The American residents, equivalent to our registrars, were less open-minded, however. I was once asked to take some residents on a ward round in Columbia Presbyterian Hospital in New York, where there had never been a female surgical trainee of any grade. They were overtly cynical, which I found amusing.

We came to the bedside of a sick man who had been subjected to all the modern investigations at their disposal, without a diagnosis being forthcoming. I said to the others, 'Where I come from, we rely heavily on history and examination.' So I sat down at the bedside and asked him a series of questions: 'When did the pain begin? Where did it start? Has it moved?' The answers pointed towards appendicitis. Then I asked him if I could examine his stomach, and revealed to all the mass in the right lower abdomen, which was an appendix abscess.

I was thus able to help the patient and also gain respect from the young trainees.

At every stop on my American travels, I learned something new. Bariatric surgery, for the morbidly obese patient, was in its infancy, and although it was of no particular relevance to a budding vascular surgeon, I was fascinated to see the challenges that taking on this new kind of surgery caused in the hospitals. They had to purchase bigger chairs, stronger operating tables and deeper instruments.

In Houston, Texas, I visited the world-famous surgeon Michael DeBakey and was astounded by the apparently unlimited facilities at his disposal. He was both a cardiac and a vascular surgeon and had featured in the media both in the USA and in Europe because of his progressive work. His centre had as many as eight operating rooms working at the same time and an enormous post-operative intensive care provision of about 40 beds. Back in Liverpool, my hospital had no intensive care facilities whatsoever.

My final stop in San Francisco meant I was able to return to some of the haunts of my younger years. I loved being accommodated in the homes of friends that I'd met during my first trip to the USA, rather than in hotels. Many of these friends now had teenage children and I was surprised by the strict instructions these children received when heading out to a party: that they should not drink out of a glass, only from a bottle that they had opened themselves, and they should never place it down until it was finished. I had never previously heard of such problems, and it was some years before similar precautions were deemed necessary in the UK.

I returned to the Vascular Unit in San Francisco and was reunited with many of the team I had first met in the early 1960s. Surgery there was still beautiful, but it was so slow. I have always taught my trainees that in complex surgery you need to be able to change gear. Some parts of the procedure have to be taken slowly and with extra care, while the routine and straightforward parts can be speeded up. There seemed to be only one speed in San Francisco!

Another important moment was to happen for me that year, when I became the first ever female member of the Vascular Surgical Society. It was a relatively small and young society that had been started by an elite group of teaching hospital surgeons who were taking on this new subject. There was a selection process to join and initially, it was difficult for any surgeon in a district general hospital to pass muster and be elected. By the time I joined in 1972, it was slightly more diverse, though entirely male until my arrival. It was not wholly their fault, though, as I was also the first woman to seek membership. I was a consultant in a teaching hospital, so I fulfilled the criteria. I rightly expected to be elected to the membership and so I was. There was much good-hearted teasing by members afterwards, who said that the whole of the business meeting had been taken up by the momentous decision of whether or not to let in a female member. None of that mattered to me so long as the result was as it should be. It was some years before I was joined by other women, but happily things have changed much since then.

So I was now working as a consultant surgeon and had fulfilled my life's greatest ambition. My working week was divided between the two hospitals and both of them gave me a wonderful and warm welcome. The surgeons in particular were superbly helpful and I was encouraged to seek advice and discuss any problems with them. As a new consultant there is always so much to learn, and it was my good fortune to have experienced and communicative colleagues who simply wanted me to be happy in my work and for my patients to receive the best care. John MacFarland was my closest colleague at the Southern. He gave me every encouragement and also showed some interest in my new and developing specialty of vascular surgery, often wandering into the theatre to see what I was doing. I remember John describing an aortic bifurcation graft, which he had never seen before, as a pantaloon graft, instead of the more usual trouser graft, which I found very funny.

The nurse in charge of theatres was a Miss Jones. She used to delight in bringing new nurses to my theatre and saying in a loud stage whisper, 'Mrs Mansfield is doing a difficult and da-a-a-angerous operation.' It was often nearly enough to make my hand shake.

We always welcomed our colleagues into theatre, which could be a learning experience for everyone. I have never watched another surgeon without becoming wiser as a result. Usually it is a new way of tackling an old problem and sometimes it is how not to do something, but there is always something to learn. It was no surprise that my new specialty would attract some surgical observers, and there were frequently quite a few.

My first aortic aneurysm operation as a consultant was to take place at the Royal Southern Hospital. It was a new venture for the hospital, so everything had to be carefully set up, including the purchase of some new instruments. The anaesthetist was John Crooke, who was a wonderful friend of mine. I had met him earlier in my training, so he had observed my early tentative steps and watched my progress. Now he was fascinated by this new area of surgery and keen to be involved.

That first aneurysm is a good example of the ways in which we have progressed since. In 1972 there was very little in the way of pre-operative imaging – no ultrasound, no CT and no MRI. The best we could do was to take an image of the kidneys and ureters using an intravenous urogram, which gave a pretty good idea of the size and position of the aorta, but we relied on palpation (feeling with the hands) to estimate its size. I was astonished when, on reviewing the intravenous urogram, I found that one of the kidneys was down in the pelvis instead of up in the loin area where they normally reside. The majority of aneurysms are below the arteries to the kidneys, so when you clamp the aorta, the circulation to the kidneys continues without interruption. The position of the kidney in the patient's pelvis meant that for some time the artery to that kidney would be without any blood flow and the kidney might be endangered. I obviously knew such quirks of anatomy existed, but I had never had to deal with this particular one in a patient before. And of course, it would be my first aneurysm in a new job at a new hospital. Overnight, I needed to work out my strategy to keep the time the kidney would be without circulation to the absolute minimum. It was a challenge, but surgery is full of challenges; indeed they are a big part of its attraction. I was very glad when the operation was a success.

One evening I learned that the team were taking a patient to theatre to drain an abscess in the groin, so I popped my head around the door of the theatre to see how things were progressing. They were about to start and I could see from the door that the large swelling was pulsating. This was when I first used a phrase which I later became known for among colleagues: 'pause for pulsation'. It is easy to miss the pulsation in a swelling if the examining hands are moving. They need to remain still and then the pulsation becomes apparent. It would have been a major error if they had 'drained' the swelling, as it was in fact a femoral artery aneurysm.

Medical Board meetings were held every month; all the consultants on the staff would gather for the meeting and then have dinner together afterwards. The commonest agenda item was car parking. So nothing changes in hospitals, as you see! Board meetings would sometimes be an evening-dress affair and my first Royal Southern formal event was to be held at the Adelphi Hotel. I decided that it called for a new dress and I set about making one, in the belief that I could put it together in about the time it took to operate on an aneurysm. Easier access, no bleeding and a sewing machine. I found four hours on the Sunday prior to the event and made the dress successfully. It was just as I had hoped – long, simple and elegant.

My senior colleague at the David Lewis Northern Hospital was Bill Beattie, a highly experienced and reliable surgeon who was generous with his support towards me, the new surgeon. I could always ask his advice and be sure of good, helpful responses. There was never a hint of denigration. When he had been appointed many years before, he'd had the choice of two jobs. He chose the one that was offering a new hospital, which was anticipated to open in a couple of years' time. As it happened, the hospital was completed after he retired.

In those days, the wards were usually pretty full at Christmas. It was tradition for the hospital kitchen to prepare a turkey, which was then carved on Christmas morning on the ward by one of the surgeons. The honour of carving the turkey was mine in 1972, and dressed in appropriate surgical gear, I began. I had no idea how to go about it and my ignorance soon became apparent. A senior and much-loved physician called Dr Sanderson wandered into the ward at that time and announced, 'What a good job the patients did not see you carve the turkey before they let you operate on them.'

Thus, my first few months as a consultant and the momentous year of 1972 came to an end. I was aware that I had reached my goal, but I also knew that there would, indeed should, be further goals, and that really this was just the beginning.

7
Early Years of Consultant Practice

I settled quickly into my new responsibilities as a consultant. The two hospitals were of similar size and situated on either side of the city centre, close to the docks. I had excellent colleagues in both hospitals and the staff were more than willing to see vascular surgery, which was completely new to one of the hospitals, get up and running.

New consultants have patients referred to them by other colleagues and also by local GPs. There was the possibility of some private practice too, and I was allocated two regular spare 'sessions' for this. The week was divided into 11 segments, or half-days, and if you were appointed to be 'maximum part-time', as I was, you were expected to work for the NHS for nine of those segments, though in truth we always did far more. The salary reflected the reduction in sessions and I was paid 9/11ths of the full-time consultant salary. My annual income had leapt to somewhere between £4,000 and £5,000. Emergencies were included in my expected week's work with no extra pay, and most surgeons were working 'one in two', which meant we would be on call every second night and every second weekend. If you happened to have a specialty that was not otherwise covered, then you were always available for that specialty. I was the only consultant with expertise in vascular surgery, so was virtually always required to be available. In addition, as the new girl, I was given responsibility for the casualty department at the Southern, and although that did not mean I was actually working in A&E, I was in charge of it. I set up various new initiatives, for example, the first 'major incident protocol' in case of need. That need happily never arose during my time at the Southern, but we did rehearse our roles and ensured we were prepared. There was no allowance in the working week for travel between hospitals and most days involved work at both. My responsibilities included two outpatient clinics, where I would see new patients and also follow up on previous ones. I also did two full days of operating and, in addition, ward rounds and teaching.

The area around the Southern Hospital was pretty deprived. From one of my wards, I could see into the tenement block of flats adjacent to the hospital. I was shocked to observe small children being dispatched to get a slice of toast and a 'scrape' of margarine from the corner shop on their way to school.

Some of those same children would appear in the hospital's open car park and offer to 'mind your car, Miss'. Some of the doctors would pay just for the peace of mind. My approach was to remind the children of the fact I was a surgeon. I hoped they would associate that with sharp tools and leave my car alone. It seemed to have the desired effect.

There were neither mobile phones nor bleepers when I started consultant practice in 1972, and it was not unusual for me to arrive at one hospital only to find that the other urgently required my presence. I used to employ a lady to take my phone calls when I was not at home, and she had details of every move I made, including my seat number whenever I was at a concert at the Philharmonic Hall. From time to time, I would get a quiet tap on the shoulder in the middle of a symphony. I had always known and accepted that my work would be a huge commitment, but it was what I wanted to do and I did not question the situation nor seek to change it. I felt happy to have reached my goal and was keen to fulfil it to the utmost.

As vascular surgery was in its infancy then, it was not uncommon for another hospital to seek my help if a vascular emergency arose. I always kept a small supply of the essential sutures in the boot of my car and would readily head off to various destinations to tackle vascular procedures as needed.

Another requirement was to do 'domiciliary visits' if requested by a local GP. The idea was to assist GPs with the management of their patients who had surgical problems and were perhaps too sick to visit out patient clinics. This often entailed driving to a strange area, locating the flat or house in question and doing an assessment. I generally tried to take a student with me on such trips, to help with the navigating and for some additional security. It was good practice for the student and they were always keen to take part. One such outing involved a visit to the home of an elderly man who had lost both of his legs to vascular disease and was in bed. Everywhere I looked, I saw overflowing ashtrays filled with cigarette ends. He was covered in bedding bearing the name 'Royal Southern Hospital' and spread over that were several copies of a certain newspaper opened at page three. I could hardly blame him for that. Smoking was pretty universal in those days, and it often caused arteries to be blocked and, in consequence, limbs to be lost. Progress in vascular surgery would, in time, reduce the number of patients who reached this advanced and depressing stage of the disease. Clearly that came too late for this man, however.

I had my own 'firm' of students to teach, and as it was back in my own student days, there were usually groups of eight. At the end of term, the tradition was for those students to arrange a dinner and invite the staff, and of course the consultants would dig deeply into their pockets to support such events. At one dinner, the lead organising student sat next to me. He seemed rather agitated and from time to time would abruptly go outside. I thought perhaps he was a smoker and he didn't want me to see him with a cigarette. Eventually I asked if there was a problem and he admitted that he had taken on a wager. It seemed he had been dared to give me a kiss, but his courage had failed him. There was a simple solution to that. I asked him to stand up in front of everyone and the deed was done! There were cheers all round.

I often found it irritating to hear politicians or journalists alleging that consultants were always on the golf course or doing private practice instead of health service work. That was not my experience at all. I was available for private work but did not even rent consulting rooms initially, because no one wanted to consult me. As a new consultant you had to simply hope that the word would get around that you were available and good at your job. This took time and there was no advertising, so you relied on colleagues, usually general practitioners, to refer patients to you. I remember my first ever private patient. I operated on him the morning of New Year's Day with the New Year Concert from Vienna playing quietly in the background. Nobody had told me how much to charge and I sent him a ridiculously small bill.

I recall one occasion when a newly appointed surgeon asked a very senior colleague how much he should charge for a particular operation. The answer was so small a sum that the junior surgeon responded with shock, '*You* wouldn't do the operation for that much, would you?'

'No, but that was not the question.'

The partnership between surgeon and anaesthetist is central to the safety and success of an operation. Few patients understand that their life will really be in the hands of the anaesthetist. For me, the best anaesthetists are the ones who peer over the drapes to see what the surgeon is doing and are prepared for the consequences, whatever they may be. They are not fooled by the eternal optimism of surgeons, and are always well aware of the state of surgical activity. There is no need to tell them that, for example, the clamp is on or off the aorta. They keep an eye on the progress.

At the David Lewis Northern Hospital I was allocated a senior and highly experienced anaesthetist called John Hargreaves to work with. He was disinclined to use modern technology. By then, most anaesthetists were continuously monitoring the blood pressure in a major case via a cannula inserted directly into an artery. I saw no sign of that or even the regular blood pressure monitor, a sphygmomanometer, when I was operating with him for the first time on an aorta.

As part of such an operation, a clamp has to be placed on the aorta in order to insert a new graft. Once inserted, there is a moment of truth when the blood flow is restored. That moment can be accompanied by some bleeding and there is always a fall in the blood pressure as the legs fill up with blood again. Anticipation and preparation for these events are crucial.

I turned to John and asked, 'How is the blood pressure?'

'Why do you ask? You have done nothing whatsoever to make it fall.'

'Well,' I said, 'I am about to take the clamp off the aorta and that sometimes results in a big fall in the pressure.'

There came a squeaking sound from the top of the table, and John announced, 'I am taking the blood pressure with one of those newfangled gadgets.'

I quickly learned that John was a very safe pair of hands and that he was well able to balance a patient's physiological needs, even if relying only on a finger on the pulse.

Generally, the operating theatre is a relaxed place of work, and when all is progressing well, there is quite a lot of chat. John loved to try to teach me about vegetable gardening while we were operating together. I remember him once educating me on the fertilisation of my unproductive courgette plants. He was quite shocked that I did not know how to distinguish male from female flowers. 'Oh dear,' he said. 'Well you see, the males have this thing that sticks out.' When I spoke at his retirement dinner a few years later, I presented him with a bouquet made up of vegetables in addition to a gift of skis for his other favourite hobby.

John was one of four anaesthetists with whom I regularly worked and all of them were keen to be involved in vascular surgery. The collaboration between surgeon and anaesthetist is the closest of partnerships, and they all gave me huge support at a time when I was still feeling my way in the field. At the start of my consultant job, I introduced standard vascular operations, such as bypass grafts, endarterectomy (the removal of obstructing atheroma, which is the material that builds up on the wall of an artery and contains cholesterol and calcium) from blocked or narrowed arteries and the repair of aortic aneurysms. I also wanted to include carotid endarterectomy, an operation designed to prevent stroke by unblocking the main artery to the brain, the carotid artery, which is situated in the neck.

The first recorded operation of this kind, although others have claimed to have previously undertaken something similar, was carried out at St Mary's Hospital in London in 1954 by a surgeon called Felix Eastcott (coincidentally, I was to become his successor there in 1982). However, when I became a consultant surgeon in Liverpool in 1972, I had never performed this operation. The only surgeon doing them in Liverpool was Edgar Parry, and although he taught me to do every other current vascular surgical procedure in his repertoire, this one was different. The consequences of error were simply too great for him to contemplate letting a trainee carry out the procedure. The operation was done with the patient under hypothermia, as it was thought that this would enable the brain to continue to function even when the main artery supplying it, the internal carotid, was clamped off. I assisted him several times but had not even been allowed to do the preliminaries, such as exposing the carotid artery.

As part of my Moynihan Fellowship, I had observed in the USA a number of new approaches to vascular operations. Among these was carotid endarterectomy, which had taken off in a big way in the States – many more were being carried out there than in the UK. To my astonishment, they had abandoned the use of hypothermia, and even more surprisingly, there were no adverse consequences. It made the whole operation far shorter and meant it had none of the serious, particularly cardiac, problems associated with induced hypothermia.

The result was that when I became a consultant and wanted to perform this operation myself, I was not only doing it for the first time, but I also decided to do it without the addition of hypothermia. I felt that the eyes of the surgical world were upon me. Happily, everything went to plan, there were no complications, and I went on to do many more. The use of hypothermia was eventually universally abandoned, as surgeons realised that although the theory behind its use was sound, in practice it was unnecessary and came with its own complications.

It had taken quite some organisation to undertake that first case. A necessary preliminary was a carotid angiogram, in which a dye is inserted into the artery to help visualise it.

This couldn't be done until the hospital's new radiologist was appointed. Austin Carty was that radiologist and he was willing to perform such angiography, which cleared a path forward. In those days, the dye was injected directly into the carotid artery in the neck, which carried some risk. Nowadays, when this is required, a catheter is passed from a remote artery into the area to be visualised, and the risks are far smaller. I was in attendance when Austin Carty did that first carotid angiogram; I wanted to give him support and also to show my gratitude that he had been happy to take it on.

Then there was the question of anaesthesia. Liverpool had a proud history of developments in anaesthesia and a very strong academic department. In addition to John Hargreaves, I worked with John Crooke and Raymond Ahearn, who were wonderful, progressive colleagues. Dr Crooke at the Southern was happy to give the anaesthetic for that first case and also accepted that we should proceed without the use of hypothermia.

Finally, we needed a theatre nurse who could cope with a completely new procedure and who would ensure that all the required instruments were obtained and ready.

Having sorted out all the preliminaries, we were eventually ready to operate when a suitable patient presented to us. It took courage to undertake such an operation for the first time, and I well remember feeling quite anxious about it.

The blockage was situated at the bifurcation, or division, of the common carotid into its two branches: the internal, supplying blood to the brain, and the external, to the face. The first challenge came when, for a moment or two, I wondered how to tell which was which, but as usual, anatomical knowledge came to the rescue. The external carotid has several branches and the internal does not. Problem solved. The next step was the most daunting one: clamping off the carotid artery to stem the blood flow so I could open it up and remove the blockage.

This first operation went well; there were no adverse consequences from operating at normal body temperature and, most importantly, the imminent threat of a stroke was averted. I was delighted. For me, it was the door to many other such operations, and I often contemplate how differently things might have progressed if that first one had not been a success. It was a prime example of the importance of teamwork in medicine. For a successful outcome, the collaboration of neurologists, radiologists, surgeons, anaesthetists and nurses was essential.

Stroke prevention via carotid endarterectomy became one of my major interests. Indeed, I have no doubt that operations designed to prevent strokes are the most valuable ones I ever undertook. I remember how my father worried about the prospect of a stroke, although he never did have one, and I saw many patients for whom this threat was a huge anxiety. A successful operation removes that stress, but patients always have to be warned that the commonest complication of the procedure is the very stroke you are trying to prevent. Our job was to minimise that risk and to make it a rarity.

In Liverpool, the neurologist at the Royal Southern was unsure of the wisdom of this particular operation, and I felt the lack of support from a close physician colleague keenly. In later years, when I moved to St Mary's in London, I worked with Dr Dafydd Thomas, who was referred to with great affection as 'the surgeon's neurologist', because he understood and supported the concept of the operation. He would see all the patients both before and after surgery. At St Mary's we also discussed all our potential patients in a meeting, which was the forerunner of the now well-established multidisciplinary team meeting. In Liverpool I was making these decisions on my own without such valuable support, which added to the stress I felt.

It is quite a short operation by vascular surgical standards, but it requires technical perfection. I always wanted to be there when the patient recovered from anaesthesia, in order to reassure myself that they had not suffered that rare stroke complication. I remember one time when the patient in recovery started talking what sounded to me like gibberish. I feared the worst, but it turned out that Welsh was his first language, and so it certainly wasn't gibberish! On another occasion a patient's first words were, 'Put your money on Mustard and Cress.' Again, I worried that I had caused him to have a stroke but no, he simply wanted me to place a bet on a particular horse in the Grand National. After such operations, as soon as the patient was awake and well, I would go to meet their relatives. It became my habit to always try to speak to the next of kin both before and after a major operation; establishing that relationship was, for me, a vital component of good patient care. I am aware of just how hard it is to be awaiting news when your nearest and dearest has to undergo surgery.

Carotid endarterectomy could not be carried out if the hardening of the arteries had progressed to the point where the carotid artery was totally blocked. There was a potential remedy for such advanced disease, whereby the blocked artery was bypassed in a procedure called the 'extracranial to intracranial bypass'. This involved making a hole in the skull, known as a burr hole or trephine, and through it, attaching an artery from the surface of the skull (the superficial temporal artery) – the bypass – to a vessel within the skull on the surface of the brain. Skill in microvascular surgery was required. I had learned such techniques by visiting a Professor Yaşargil in Zurich. I knew that I would have to fight for the hospital budget to fund my new microvascular tools, and could see no point in learning a new skill but being unable to use it for lack of the correct instruments, so while I was in Zurich, I took the unusual step of buying my own. The suture material was nylon, finer than human hair, attached to a minute curved needle. One of the instruments I purchased was a rather expensive holder specially designed for such tiny needles, though the forceps that I held in the other hand were an impressively cheap addition to my tool cabinet. They were watchmaker forceps, which were of course readily available in the watch capital of the world.

When it came to the extracranial to intracranial bypass itself, I visited St Bartholomew's Hospital in London in 1980 in order to learn from Professor John Lumley, who was an expert in the procedure. There is a great camaraderie among surgeons who willingly teach others to carry out new procedures. I subsequently returned to Liverpool and carried out my first such operation at the Northern. I think that today an experienced surgeon would typically accompany the novice for that first attempt, but it was different then. You simply got on with it.

One of the patients on whom I did the EC/IC bypass was referred to me after he had completely lost his speech because of the blocked artery. One morning a couple of days after the operation, I walked into his room and he started singing, 'If you were the only girl in the world, and I was the only boy . . .' I was astonished, but it seems that sometimes songs that were learned long ago can be recalled even after speech itself has been lost. It proved to be a new means of communicating for him.

The history of the development of carotid surgery was lacking the rigour of a surgical trial in all aspects. Many operations were carried out without precedent and without the statistical certainty that is required today. Someone had to be first, and that applied to both patient and surgeon. Reading about those all-important first steps in surgery in the library books I had borrowed as a child had been largely responsible for my ambition to become a surgeon, and so when the time came, I was not afraid to lead.

Subsequent clinical trials led by neurologists, along with myself and other surgical colleagues, ultimately demonstrated the efficacy of carotid endarterectomy. Professor Charles Warlow was a neurologist in Oxford and then Edinburgh. He was generally believed to be somewhat cynical about the value of the carotid endarterectomy, so his leadership in the first trial was crucial. When the result was a clear demonstration of the value of the operation in preventing stroke, his participation made the result even more significant.

So that first operation was eventually proven to have been fully vindicated. I carried out many such operations and continued my involvement in trials throughout my career and even into retirement. Having decided to cease operating in 2002, I was very happy to become Chair of the Council of the Stroke Association.

Another major area of change in surgical care in the 1970s was the development of high-quality post-operative management. After massive surgery, patients may well be unstable and need support for several hours, sometimes for days. Intensive care is now routine after major procedures but was in its infancy then, and consultants dedicated to the area had not yet materialised. At the Southern we had a small unit run by an anaesthetist called Tony Gilbertson, with the support of a physician, Ronnie Finn, and me as the surgeon. We formed a good team. We met to discuss the management of patients, contributed our own expertise and began to observe the great benefit such teamwork brought to patients. Eventually this type of unit came to be run by anaesthetists and nursing staff who could give their whole time to these complex cases.

Critically ill patients might also be admitted to that unit to be assessed. I was called in to see such a patient one evening. I had been playing a piano quartet in a concert and we, the musicians, all doctors, were wearing evening dress. Immediately after it concluded, I was asked to go to the hospital for a patient who it was thought had a leaking aneurysm. I arrived in the intensive care unit wearing quite a smart dress and assessed the patient, agreed with the diagnosis and explained to him the need for immediate surgery. I told him what was involved and he consented. I made my way to theatre, changed into my scrub suit and carried out the operation. Fortunately he survived and, after a period of recovery, went home.

Some weeks later, my good friend and solicitor Derek Morris was in his barber's when this same man arrived. He told the proprietor, 'I've just been in hospital and had a major operation. There I was, at death's door, and along comes this bit of a girl who says, "I am going to operate on you and hope to save your life."'

Derek enjoyed relating this to me and I admit to enjoying the idea of being a 'bit of a girl', even if I was in my mid-thirties by then.

My surgical practice included most of the usual general surgical operations. Stomachs, colons, gall bladders and thyroids all came my way. At the same time, I was gaining in experience and reputation as a vascular surgeon and was still in awe of the aorta, which had so impressed me at my first encounter with it.

As I already explained, most aneurysms are situated below the arteries to the gut and the kidneys, but we had no way of establishing the actual location of an aneurysm until we were in the midst of an operation. The detailed imaging we now have simply did not exist back then. I operated on one patient with an aortic aneurysm only to find that it involved the arteries to the gut and the kidneys. That meant it was inoperable and I had no option but to close the abdomen. I later explained to the patient that his aneurysm could not be dealt with as it was too complex.

During his recovery from this unfortunately quite open and shut procedure, I began to wonder if someone elsewhere might in fact be able to deal with such a complex case. I therefore phoned the most senior vascular surgeon in the country, Felix Eastcott, and asked if I could send the patient to him. He declined, but encouraged me to read the reports of such operations being carried out in Houston, Texas. He suggested that as a competent vascular surgeon – he had been to watch me operate – I should do the operation myself after reading the reports.

My discussion with the patient was frank. I said that we could do nothing, or I could send him to Houston, or I could do the operation myself. I told him that I had never done or seen it done before. I also told him that it would be a hazardous operation, whoever undertook it. He was adamant that he wanted me to do it. He had no wish to travel to America and equally no wish to simply wait for the inevitable rupture and death to occur.

So we set about it, with John Crooke in charge of the complex anaesthesia and me as the surgeon, and in this instance the novice too. It may well have been beginner's luck, but all went well and the man recovered completely. Many complications can arise from such an operation, including paraplegia and even death, and over the subsequent years I would see most of them, but on this occasion there was a good outcome.

I knew that both of us had been fortunate and I determined that, as soon as possible, I would get myself to Houston in order to learn from the expert there, Dr Stanley Crawford. It took a few years for me to do so and meanwhile, whenever discussions arose at medical meetings about the condition, which is known as the thoraco-abdominal aneurysm, Felix would point me out as the one person present who had operated on it. Of course, it had only been the once.

Throughout this time, the new Royal Liverpool Hospital was making its stop-start progress towards taking over from the old and crumbling teaching hospitals around the city. From the time of my consultant appointment, I had been aware that I would eventually move into the new hospital, but there had been such slow progress with the building that we thought it might never be completed. At one point building work stopped entirely as a result of industrial action and the costs escalated.

Now we learned that there was finally a date in sight for its completion, so it was time to start planning suitable events to mark the closure of not only my two but in total seven hospitals, which would amalgamate into the new Royal Liverpool Hospital. All of them had long and proud histories. They had given service through two world wars and had preceded the NHS, so it was important to mark the occasions of their individual closures. There was excitement about the new mingled with real sadness about the demise of these much-loved institutions. Religious services and parties were to be organised and detailed plans put in place for the much awaited transition into the new Royal.

8
Jack Appears in My Life

My beloved father died in the middle of 1977. He developed coronary artery disease, likely as a result of his many years of smoking. At that time there was no operation or other intervention available, and his angina was untreated. He had a heart attack at his brother Harold's funeral and died 48 hours later, in Aldershot in the Cambridge Military Hospital, which had the only available nearby bed. His death was my first experience of the loss of a loved one. As a consultant surgeon, I was familiar with death, but this was up close and personal and I found it totally shocking. My father was without doubt the single most important influence on my life. I loved him unreservedly, and his unexpected death was a huge blow. I can only hope that I have somehow mirrored his character, but in truth I am unlikely to measure up to him.

Although I was heartbroken, life had to continue with hardly a pause. I had many responsibilities, an additional one now being my mother, who was left alone, unable to drive and without her partner of over 50 years. Fortunately, they had moved to Liverpool by then and lived reasonably close to me, so I took on the role of teaching her how to look after the garden and the greenhouse, which had been my father's hobby. She would later follow me to London too.

My marriage was by this point also under considerable strain. From the very beginning, it had been clear to me that all was not well. I had sought advice from a confidante after about six months and her advice was to 'soldier on'. Jonathan and I happily supported each other's ambitions without any rancour; he was very proud of my career and we shared a love of music. But it was a fraternal relationship. Somehow, the removal of the prop of my father caused me to question afresh the wisdom of remaining married to Jonathan.

Sometime towards the end of 1977, I received an entirely unexpected invitation to a meeting of European vascular surgeons, which was to be held in the Val Thorens ski resort in France. I remember asking, 'Why me?', but equally it was too good an offer to refuse, and I accepted. I was a keen skier and had taken a skiing holiday every year since I'd qualified as a doctor. Attending meetings without Jonathan was not unusual for me, but little did I know that this one was to change my life completely.

On 25 January 1978 I joined David Gifford, who had organised the event, and a party of vascular surgeons, some of whom I knew and others who were strangers to me, on a flight to Geneva. There we boarded a bus for Val Thorens. It had been a particularly cold winter and there were huge snowdrifts piled high to one side of the road. As the bus negotiated hairpin bend after hairpin bend, the surgeons who occupied it fell fearfully silent. That silence was eventually interrupted by a crashing sound when some of the overhanging snow fell and smashed a window in the bus. Thankfully, no one was hurt. The bus stopped in its tracks while the driver got out to examine the damage, and among the passengers, the initial shock was followed by a relieved buzz of conversation.

Then came those words that are now so famous to me: 'I think this calls for a drop of the duty-free.' Who *was* that handsome man administering gin and French in thimble-sized portable glasses to my fellow passengers? I was sitting with a friend, but neither of us had previously met him. He turned out to be called Jack Bradley. He walked down the bus and I too received a drink from this man who had a warm, twinkly smile and a great head of white hair. I was intrigued.

Suitably fortified, we were soon on our way again, and in the days that followed, a nascent friendship developed between Jack and myself. In later months, it would grow into the love of our lives. We were to become soul mates, until death did us part on 30 September 2013. But back then we were just enjoying each other's company on the ski slopes, with no thoughts of romance. Every day was a mix of academic papers and skiing. Val Thorens had a wonderfully extensive ski area which we explored together, and somehow my group always seemed to include Jack.

On 29 January we parted ways as friends with a brief kiss and returned to the UK and our work. I went back to Liverpool and the embers of a dying relationship, and Jack returned to London, to his family and his deeply troubled marriage. There was then silence until I received a phone call on 4 April, in which he asked, 'Are you by any chance going to the Association of Surgeons meeting in Sheffield?'

My mother was at home with me at the time and immediately asked, 'Who was that? You look like a cat who has got the cream.' How observant. And so, Jack and I met in Sheffield and his first gift to me was the romantic present of a wastepaper basket so that I would remember his initials, which were JWPB (WPB for wastepaper basket). 'So you won't forget me,' he said. I still have that basket in my home today.

I was giving a talk at the meeting, which was the main event in the year for the Association of Surgeons of Great Britain and Ireland. The majority of general surgeons working in the UK would try to get to at least some if not all of the three-day gathering. Jack and I spent most of those days together and even managed to rearrange the table plan for a dinner one evening so that we could sit side by side. We were just drawn to each other. He was a friendly, fun and loveable character who exuded integrity and warmth, and altruism was a value we both always cherished. I famously and truthfully told the world on *Desert Island Discs* many years later that there was no 'hanky panky' between us in Val Thorens. That very proper behaviour could no longer restrain our mutual feelings when we were in Sheffield after several weeks apart. In no time we had become *the* Association of Surgeons (with just two members) and we were to remain so for the rest of our days. But initially, I am certain that we had no idea of the profound changes we were embarking on.

My newfound friend showed no signs of going away and we frequently sought opportunities to meet. Of course, we lived 200 miles apart and were hardworking surgeons, so it wasn't easy. On the 8 May at the Northern Hospital I carried out for the first time an extracranial to intracranial bypass, and it just so happened that there was a surgeon called Jack in theatre visiting from Hillingdon that day too!

Later that week, we visited the Lake District together for the first time. Jack drove me there in his car, a yellow Triumph TR7 that he called the Flying Banana, and we lunched at the Sharrow Bay hotel. Then came the 'love me, love my wreck in the Lake District' moment when I took him to see my wonderful if ancient house there, Highgate. On seeing it he probably decided that I was mad, but at least managed to keep such thoughts to himself. Highgate, a house dating back to 1702 that I had purchased a couple of years earlier, was at that time without a roof, road access, water and electricity. It was essentially a ruin in a field. It was to become my restoration project for many years and I needed to know he might see the attraction of it.

Over the next few months, life continued at a busy pace as usual, but with the added urgency of the desire to meet up with Jack whenever I could. We saw each other at another surgical meeting in July, the Surgical Research Society in Dundee. A colleague, Philip Stell, admonished me there for appearing to care for Jack. Philip and I had often worked together on complex cases and had developed a mutual professional respect for each other. He had clearly become concerned for my reputation. He was the first person to whom I confessed that it was no mere flirtation.

Even phone calls were difficult before the days of mobile phones, and I was still busy gearing up for the closure of the old hospitals and getting ready for the move into the new Royal Liverpool Hospital. A producer at the BBC, Gerald Harrison, approached me to feature in a documentary about the opening of the new hospital as part of a series called *A Diary of Britain*, so in addition to my emotional turmoil, there really was a lot going on. The hospital events included dances on a Mersey Ferry called the *Royal Iris*, several after-dinner speeches and playing the organ for the closing service of the chapel in the Northern Hospital, and each of these occasions was to be filmed.

The closing events at the hospital came to a peak in September, when I was especially closely followed by Gerald and his TV crew. The centrepiece of the filming was to be a patient arriving at the Northern and then having major surgery to replace his aorta, and I was to conduct the operation. As a surgeon you become used to the need to isolate your mind from the many activities going on around you in an operating theatre, so happily I was able to forget the presence of TV cameras and simply do my job. It was a straightforward – if major – operation and all went well.

Dances, dinners, board meetings and services in the hospital chapels were all competing for my time. Little did the team from the BBC know that there was an even bigger turmoil going on in my heart. TV crews can be quite invasive, but somehow I kept my secret. They even once turned up at my home, where they found me washing my MGB in the street outside.

I decided against informing the BBC team when Raymond Ahearn, the anaesthetist who had taken part in the televised aortic operation, quite dramatically developed appendicitis just a couple of days later. My night's sleep was disturbed by an urgent call from his GP.

'Would you believe me if I said that Raymond Ahearn has appendicitis?' he said.

'Yes,' I replied.

'Would you believe me sufficiently for me to arrange his admission to hospital?'

'Yes,' I replied.

'Would you trust me enough for me to arrange theatre?'

'No,' I admitted.

The GP was correct and it soon became clear that Raymond had been working all that day despite appendicitis raging inside him. His name appeared twice in quick succession in the theatre log book – first as anaesthetist, then as patient. Gerald Harrison, despite our excellent relationship, was not best pleased that I had omitted to call in the TV crew when it all kicked off at around 2am.

On 2 October, the Northern moved officially into the new Royal Liverpool Hospital. The building of the new premises had suffered many setbacks, and right up to the opening there were problems and uncertainties with which to contend. It was, however, nice to see my patient who had been operated on in the Northern and filmed by the BBC make a full recovery and be discharged, though not before being transferred to the new hospital to complete his stay in the company of quite a few television cameras.

I was also local secretary for the annual meeting of the Vascular Surgical Society. Raymond Helsby, a senior surgeon, was our president. My role involved booking venues for all the meetings, social events and the formal dinner. Raymond was no easy taskmaster, and I must admit that my mind was not always focused on the society but rather on my seriously troubled domestic situation. I was trying to come to terms with the consequences of falling in love with Jack and the enormous repercussions of a divorce from Jonathan.

At this time, I was a tutor for the Royal College of Surgeons, which largely involved arranging teaching and lectures for trainees. I would often invite surgeons to deliver lectures at the Liverpool Medical Institution.

I used to meet them at Lime Street Station, drive them to the institution, sort out their slides and then give them dinner prior to the lecture. It never occurred to me that for some senior surgeons, getting into my rather low-slung MGB might be difficult. On one occasion the surgeon preferred to meet me directly at the institution, and when I arrived at the appointed time, he was in the bar with a gin and tonic already in hand. He then ordered a further double G&T, which he consumed before we went for dinner. Most speakers would have at the most a glass of wine with dinner, but he wanted rather more, and a brandy to follow too.

He gave an immaculate lecture with no sign of being under the influence. I noticed that, unusually, the librarian came onto the balcony to listen to the lecture. I later asked him why. He responded that prior to my arrival the speaker had consumed several G&Ts and he simply could not believe that he would be capable of standing up for his lecture, let alone speaking. Clearly he was used to it.

Somehow, during this incredibly busy period, I once managed to drive to Hillingdon Hospital in Uxbridge and back in a day, to give a certain someone a hand with his first and only carotid endarterectomy. Jack had a very good reputation as a surgeon, but this was the first time I'd had the opportunity to watch him and indeed to help with a case. It went well, but he never did another carotid after that, preferring to refer them all to me.

In November, the Vascular Society meeting took place in Liverpool. There was some seriously difficult juggling to be done. Jack was a delegate. Jonathan was still – just about – a spouse and also an entertainer. He had long ago been booked with some friends to sing barbershop songs after the dinner. Throughout this period I was operating, consulting, lecturing, going to meetings with groups like the Liverpool and Northwest Surgical Society and the college tutors' meeting in London, and all the while my personal life was in serious danger of exploding.

Into my diary, already bursting at the seams, had crept or perhaps galloped the love of my life, who by this time was living an independent existence in a small flat. And so, along with my work and duties, I also had a new family and new friends to meet. We were now openly spending time together and adding each other's family and professional commitments to our already bulging individual lives, so there was a lot of commuting back and forward to be done.

The die had by this time been cast as far as my first marriage was concerned, and on 12 January 1979 I met with a divorce lawyer. She proved to be kind and efficient, and before long I was single again. Fortunately, it was not an acrimonious parting of ways for me and Jonathan. Our marriage had been teetering since its very first week and the revelation of my love for Jack meant that we regretfully accepted its inevitable demise.

On 10 February, after an enormously busy week in Liverpool, I found myself hosting a dinner party in London. Guests included an anaesthetist who worked with Jack, her husband and two long-standing and valued family friends of Jack's. They were very important for our future happiness, but I had no idea how they would view our situation and that uncertainty added greatly to my stress. I wanted to be liked by Jack's friends and family, and of course to be forgiven for precipitating the family breakup.

As if that were not enough, the next day we visited Jack's mother, Danny, with two of his three children – Russell, the eldest, and Jason, the youngest (the middle child Lesley was not with us) – and one of Jack's sisters, June. Danny came to be very important to me and a good friend. I had met her previously when she'd invited me to lunch (just the two of us!) after Jack had first told her of his hopes for our relationship. She later told me that she had felt unease prior to his first marriage, so had wanted to meet me in order to form an opinion about my suitability and no doubt to tell him, this time, if she had any doubts. I later described that meeting as my interview! Fortunately, she approved and became a strong support. I came to love her dearly.

By midday on 12 February, I was back and lecturing in Liverpool. Looking back now, I can only observe that I must have had huge reserves of energy. It was an incredibly busy year, with travel between London and Liverpool on a regular basis and holidays that included the children for the first time. My house in Liverpool was very close to a sailing lake, so Jack and the two boys would come there and sail, or on other occasions we would visit the Lake District and climb the fells.

Of course, we both had ongoing and demanding work commitments. I was maintaining a practice in Liverpool; I loved my job and had no wish to give it up. I was greatly enjoying the new hospital and looking forward to the opportunities it would provide; I was also visiting my widowed mother most days, and I was trying to get to know Jack's children and at the same time work out our future. That future would have a very serious impact on the children, a fact that caused me considerable emotional strain.

During this period I was also secretary to the Liverpool Medical Institution, which is an independent library and postgraduate education centre. Its bicentenary fell in 1979, so we decided to entertain about two hundred guests to mark the occasion — quite an undertaking, which was simply another addition to my already heavy load. A committee of women cooked coronation chicken, all the trimmings and a mountain of desserts. Somehow, it all seemed to work out in the end.

One thing that did manage to draw my attention during that exceptionally busy time was the fact that the Vascular Surgical Society (of which I was still also secretary) did not, unlike most other such groups, have a tie. I decided to run a competition for the design of one and invited submissions. Most of the offerings were of the traditional type, based around a coat of arms. I made slides of all the submissions and showed them as a fun conclusion of the year's AGM, and we took a vote on which design to choose.

The outright winner was based on a postcard that had been sent to Felix Eastcott from Arthur Dickson Wright, a well-known general surgeon at St Mary's and father of the celebrity cook Clarissa Dickson Wright. The postcard was a painting he had done of a scene at the seaside with two figures dancing on the shoreline, based on the aorta and the vena cava.

Ties were made to this design for the men, and as the group's only female member, I had a brooch created. Jack was responsible for sourcing both the silk for the ties and the silversmith to make the brooch in gold and silver. In the belief that it could not be long before some other women joined the society, we had more than just one brooch made, and at a dinner a few years later, I was very happy to present the next four female members with their gifts. When we were deciding on the design, I asked the then president, who had a good private practice in varicose veins, whether he thought the aorta or the vena cava should be gold, with the other in silver. 'Well, there's gold in veins,' he replied.

As a woman with a good work ethic and no children, I had always managed to take on these extra roles, but by this point life was a little overcrowded. In early 1980, Jack and I were still living apart though we were very much a couple. Jack was staying in a rather frugal flat owned by close colleagues of his and we were both immensely grateful for this generous gesture. I was determined not to leave my job in Liverpool until I had one to go to in the south. Jack had previously tried to move to be near to me, but his heart was not really in it because he wanted to stay close to his children.

In an effort to resolve our dilemma, I applied for a consultant surgeon position in west London, and 16 May was to become a momentous date for us, as I was officially appointed to Hillingdon Hospital. So much would have to change. We owe a great deal to John Sales, the senior surgeon there, and I was to spend two very happy years working with him, during which we shared ward rounds and generally got on very well indeed. Without doubt he was the best work partner of my career, and the hospital had one of the happiest, most collaborative atmospheres of anywhere I ever worked.

However, this appointment meant that I had to leave my super job at the new Royal Liverpool Hospital, sell my house, leave my friends and make new ones. I had to explain to those who had appointed and supported me that, much as I loved my work, I loved Jack even more. We were 'living in sin' at that time, which left me feeling slightly insecure, however. I was giving up so much and wondered how I could possibly be certain of the success of this new relationship. I was also sufficiently old-fashioned to feel troubled by the lack of marriage vows. But like all good surgeons, I was used to making decisions sometimes based on fairly flimsy evidence. So the die was cast and I would have to bear the consequences.

I well remember giving my final presentation at 'Grand Rounds' in Liverpool. This was a weekly meeting of the hospital medical staff of all disciplines, where we would take it in turns to present an interesting case for discussion and our collective education. I told the story of a recent operation I had conducted for a large retroperitoneal sarcoma. I was a general surgeon in those days, but a large part of my work was in vascular surgery, so a tumour in the back of the abdomen, in close proximity to all the major blood vessels, was right up my street. It was enormous. The patient appeared almost as an appendage to the tumour. There were some major problems to be expected, including access, circulatory changes and blood loss.

My presentation was apparently memorable for others because in it I remarked, 'At this point I realised I couldn't get the tumour out, but what was worse, I could not get it back in either!' In that sense it was rather like a Champagne cork. Unlike a Champagne cork, however, it had major vascular attachment to the patient and finding a way to gain access to and divide those vessels was fraught with difficulty. There was no option other than to continue and attempt to succeed with the removal, and that of course is what I did.

I sold my house in Liverpool and bought a new one in Fulmer in Buckinghamshire, where Jack and I were to set up home. Of course I was a consultant surgeon with a job and a reasonable salary, but just to help with the move, I needed a bridging loan. *Not a problem*, I thought, and organised a meeting with my bank manager. He, it turned out, thought otherwise: 'You have no idea, young lady, what you would be taking on, and I simply cannot support this.'

I was shocked by his response and was being ushered out of his office when he suddenly asked, as he held the door open for me, if he might have seen me on BBC TV a week or two earlier. I said that I had been on TV and so yes, maybe he had seen me. This seemed to be the reassurance he needed and he let me have the loan after all. I found this quite staggering, and if I had not needed it so badly, I might have told him what he could do with his money!

I had a pet cat then and she howled in my car all the way from Liverpool to our new house in Fulmer. She had appeared as a tiny kitten in my garage one day and my cleaning lady had left a note saying, 'There is a kitten in the garage, presume it is yours, have fed it.' Tiki (she was named after a Māori mythological creature) became part of the family and did eventually settle in well to her new surroundings in the south.

I did not start work immediately and had a break of a few weeks between jobs. It was to be my only period of unemployment in the whole of my career, and it was a sensible move. It was not an easy time with so many changes in my life: new job, new house, new friends, new man and, most important of all, children. Of course they were not new children, but the first children in my life. It is often difficult to be a stepparent, but when you are inexperienced and only feeling your way, it can be especially tough.

Most people recognise that moving house is one of life's biggest challenges. That challenge is greater if the move is to a different area, and even more so if it is to a completely unfamiliar city. We had also moved just a couple of miles from the old family home, where Jack's wife still lived. The prospect of bumping into her in the local supermarket was highly undesirable. Similarly, we lived in an area where the friends of the now parted couple were still our neighbours and I had no idea whether they would be supportive or highly critical of our new relationship. But the proximity to work, friends and their former home worked very well for Jack and for the children, and it lessened the upheaval that separation and divorce can create, particularly when there are children involved.

Jason was then 11 and the two older children, Lesley and Russell, in their teens. The impact of our decision was clearly going to be huge for them and I was deeply concerned that we might be causing them harm. It was difficult getting to know the children while treading a line where I acknowledged that I was not their parent, but was often their guardian. We all want to be liked and, even better, loved, and I could not be certain of either of those responses from them.

Christmas and divorce can be uncomfortable bedfellows. Something that should be a wonderful family occasion can instead become a stressful event, with loyalties pulling in at least two different directions. My first Christmas came within a few months of my move south. Jack had two sisters, both of whom had been widowed at an early age and still had small children. He was, to a considerable extent, the lynchpin for them all and we extended a welcome to both their families for the Christmas festivities. Add to that Jack's mother, her siblings and my mother, who had also moved south by this point, and of course the children, and I was confronted with having to prepare a Christmas meal on a scale that I had simply never dealt with previously.

Jack and I would always visit our patients on Christmas morning, which meant travelling around the several different hospitals that made up our practice. All this while the turkey was cooking at home, of course. Our house was small, so it was quite a squeeze, but the day came together in the end and everyone was fed and happy. It was wonderful to see the family gathered and having a good time, and it gave me hope for our future.

The boys seemed to be, outwardly at least, relatively understanding and accepting of the disruption to their lives, but there was no way of knowing their innermost feelings. Lesley had understandably taken her mother's side in the breakup. Her love for her father was never in doubt, though, and as time passed she was able to display it again. Over the years she and I also grew to love each other. But it took time for the relationships between me and the children to develop. I was not their parent, though I took on many of the responsibilities of one. Trying to find a balance that worked for everyone was not always straightforward.

I must mention a neighbour of mine in Fulmer called Kate, who was close to Lesley. She befriended me as the result of us both going to a local night-school guitar class. She was instinctively supportive and mature beyond her years. I was very grateful and she was a good friend. We never discussed my situation or the family, but her friendship undoubtedly gave me hope that, in time, Lesley and I would become friends too.

As an only child with many cousins, I had never been short of playmates and company in general when I was growing up. It was only much later in life that I realised that through not having siblings, I had missed the opportunity to observe and participate in the development of another human being. I had never witnessed and marvelled at that creative process. My cousins and friends were generally around my own age, but the only other age group I met was my parents' generation.

I reflect on this because I have often wondered why it was that I did not see my childless first marriage as a disaster. My first husband and I were unable to have children and I just accepted that that was the way it was. I had never witnessed the arrival of babies and the development of young children as a child myself, so I did not see their absence from my adult life as a major problem. There was no one I could discuss it with and certainly no professional consultation was available or even deemed appropriate. How times have changed since. I simply accepted the status quo and also the disappointment that was evident, though never spoken of, by our parents.

Of course, many of my friends and family had children, the closest person to me being my first husband's sister, who had three. I loved those children but just accepted the fact that it was not to be my experience. Jonathan and I had got on with our careers and hobbies and friends and family instead. Eventually we parted and each of us went on to acquire three stepchildren.

Being a stepparent is challenging, possibly even more so if you are not already a parent. I was lacking the fundamental experience of bringing up children, though admittedly I did not have to face any conflict of loyalty, which I imagine could also be a problem.

I well remember the moment when Jack said, 'I have three children.' Little did I know then just how central they were to become in my life, how important and valuable. Imagine if your first contact with your children was when they were in their teens. In addition, imagine it being your first contact with any children for whom you are responsible. Of course, they were not and are not my biological children, but I cannot imagine feeling a stronger love for them if they carried my own genes. After all, no one thinks it odd when parents love adopted children. Why should the love one feels for one's adopted children be any different from love for one's stepchildren?

I had so much to learn. Of course, being a stepparent is not like being an adoptive parent in that you are effectively the 'third man'. Your presence may have been responsible for a huge upheaval in the children's lives. Resistance and resentment are common and understandable.

Jack had the perhaps quite simplistic view that, as he loved me and I made his life far happier, the children would also learn to love me. But there are no guarantees. It was a steep learning curve and required a huge investment of time and energy. It is difficult enough to learn to live with a new partner, let alone coping with that partner's teenage children.

Over time my bond with the children became stronger. I grew to love them and eventually had the courage to tell them so. I hoped that in time they too would come to love me and I know now that they do. All three went on to become parents and I am now the only grandparent left, so I have a very privileged position, which I value and enjoy. They and their spouses are all excellent parents, so it is a joy to watch my grandchildren progressing into adult life and becoming wonderful human beings, all of them.

Another important feature of this new life was that my partner was, of course, a surgeon. You might expect that a fellow surgeon would be the most understanding person when their partner failed to arrive on time for an event, or sometimes did not turn up at all. Not so. Through my relationship with Jack, I came to realise for the first time just how tolerant the spouse or partner of a surgeon has to be.

A particular difficulty was that one or other of us would be on duty at all times. Arranging leave was difficult. Previously I had always avoided the school holidays for my annual leave, as I wanted my colleagues with children to be able to have that time with their families. Now we both needed time off together, and during the school holidays.

Jack was a very good surgeon and much admired. He did

almost all of the general surgical repertoire, including standard vascular operations. On one occasion when I was operating on an aorta in Hillingdon, I asked for a different instrument from the one on the theatre nurse's trolley, and therefore different from the one that Jack would have normally used in that particular situation. When she asked someone to get it for her, the response from the theatre superintendent was, 'If it's good enough for him, it is good enough for her.' Jack was king!

We eventually realised that we needed two phone lines so that only the appropriate surgeon was disturbed during the night: one phone on his side of the bed and one on mine. One night Jack's phone rang after he had already been called out to one of the three hospitals he covered. I answered his phone and the registrar on the other end was in some difficulty. He hadn't known that I was also a surgeon but reluctantly gave me some details when I asked what the problem was, and rather surprisingly even took the advice that I offered.

My job left me with a couple of spare sessions each week, and eventually I looked to fill those at the Royal Postgraduate Hospital in Hammersmith. The Professor of Surgery there was Les Blumgart and the other vascular surgeon was Crawford Jamieson. There were 20 miles and a lot of traffic between my two hospitals, so it was never an easy arrangement.

On my first day at the Hammersmith hospital, I went to the ward to do a round and a team of trainees was awaiting my visit. I put my head into the ward office, where I could see a young doctor seated at the desk, and when he attempted to stand, his chair rose with him. He was tied to it.

'What is the problem?' I asked, bemused.

From within the office a female and very Yorkshire voice replied, 'He's not getting off that chair until he's done his discharge summaries.'

Pat was the super-efficient ward clerk and she ran that ward like clockwork. She was to become a lifelong friend of mine.

Professor Blumgart's specialty was liver and pancreatic surgery. I would join him from time to time on his ward rounds, and we saw our first ultrasound scan of the gallbladder together in the early 1980s. I well remember him commenting that it was not a helpful investigation and that no one would be able to detect the presence of gall stones from such pictures. The scans were indeed simply shades of grey and from that first example it would indeed have been difficult to predict just how important ultrasound was to become. Those inadequate grainy images have translated now into precise detail, from which essential information can be ascertained.

Les was sometimes a slightly difficult boss. On one occasion when I needed to have a discussion with him, I prefaced this by asking him to give me 20 minutes of his time and not to look at the clock once. He conceded with the words, 'Are you telling me that you are busy too?'

Together, Crawford and I had to take care of all the vascular problems in that hospital, despite the fact that we had only four sessions between us to fit them all in. Eventually, we both quit our roles, first Crawford and then me, as it proved to be an impossible load. I had a particularly tough time after Crawford left because by then I had started working mainly at St Mary's Hospital and in just a couple of sessions at the Hammersmith I was meant to look after all of their vascular problems and, worse still, their emergencies too.

One night I was called into A&E by Professor Blumgart himself, with the words, 'I have just seen an emergency in A&E and his problem is right up your street. He has a leaking abdominal aortic aneurysm.' I sped to the hospital and found quite a young man who had hung his motorcycle helmet on the hook behind the door. No ruptured or leaking aneurysm ever travelled by motorbike, nor were they likely to be so young. However, he did have a large, pulsating and tender swelling in his abdomen. He showed no sign of collapse, though, and it just did not add up.

There is an old-fashioned test that I made use of on this occasion. If there is a swelling in the abdomen, such as a large cyst lying on the aorta, it will appear to pulsate but is in fact simply transmitting the pulsation. If the patient then turns over so they are prone in what is called the knee-elbow position, the cyst falls forward and can no longer transmit the pulse, so you simply feel the cyst. Most such cysts in women arise from the ovaries and in men from the pancreas. Professor Blumgart's specialty was the pancreas and I was able to demonstrate that the patient in fact had a problem in his own special field, rather than in mine. I so enjoyed simply walking out and leaving the professor to resolve the situation.

At that time there was a superb vascular radiologist at the Hammersmith called David Allison, and I spent many hours in the X-ray department with him discussing interventions and then watching him carry them out. This period in the 1980s was the time when catheter interventions were beginning to replace some open operations. David was able to place a catheter in any blood vessel and to then carry out procedures on that blood vessel. It was clear to me that this was the way forward. Together we developed a particular interest and expertise in the care of patients with arteriovenous malformations. These are abnormal tangles of blood vessels, like the ones that cause birthmarks, but can involve vital organs too and can sometimes even pose a risk to life.

On the domestic front, Jack and I eventually decided to sell our home in Fulmer and moved into a bigger house in

Gerrards Cross, though we were still unmarried. Jack knew that I found it uncomfortable being in a partnership and not a marriage, so in 1987 he secretly arranged a wedding for us.

I was travelling to Toronto and then Boston with a very talented young Australian surgeon called Michael Grigg, to speak at a number of conferences. En route to the airport, Jack announced to me very casually, 'Oh, by the way, I have arranged for us to get married when you get back.'

He had told just two people of this plan, his secretary Sue Brain and Pat Young, that famous Yorkshire ward clerk who was now my secretary, and only in order to ensure that neither of us was working on the day in question. Both were sworn to secrecy and I later learned that he'd originally had no intention of telling me of his plan until the actual wedding day arrived. Fortunately, Sue firmly told him that he simply could not do that to me. 'She will want to buy a dress,' she insisted. Too true! I could not even pretend to be upset by Jack's presumption of my willingness to marry, though. I had already taken major steps to be his partner, and for me this was the final brick in the wall.

So it was that I became Mrs Bradley. We had a wonderful four-day wedding celebration in London and Cumbria, with all our friends and family around us. I wore a blue silk dress that I had bought in Boston and carried a posy of flowers provided by Clive, Jack's best friend, and his wife. Our wedding cake was made and decorated by Pat, and we had a beautiful church blessing at St John's in the Vale.

The effect of the wedding on me was profoundly good and I felt secure, supported and content. We were undoubtedly soulmates, and in my view, our relationship deserved the recognition that tying the knot provided. Neither of us ever felt a moment of regret.

Jack and I each recognised the importance of both our family and our careers, and we tried to provide a stable platform for both. I used to say that I would write the word 'tolerant' on Jack's tombstone. I did not do so in the end, but he was without doubt the most tolerant of human beings.

My busy and successful career owes a great deal to Jack's willingness to be the supportive spouse, and he would attend and participate in all the various functions associated with my work. He continued to work as he had done before we had met. He was a superb surgeon, providing expertise to three NHS hospitals on the outskirts of London and, in addition, running a busy private practice. To be regarded as the surgeon's surgeon is a coveted acknowledgement of special skills – and he held that place. He was much loved by his friends, colleagues and patients, and his trainees always greatly appreciated his teaching. If the need arose, we would sometimes operate together on a particularly demanding surgical problem, but that occurred only rarely.

Jack was ten years my senior, so his retirement came when I was in the midst of a very demanding job, which by then was as Professor of Surgery. I feared this might create problems, but it wasn't to be the case. He took on some of my domestic roles, in particular becoming a very good cook. He developed his practical hobbies around the house and the garden, and he really was my rock. He must have found my huge workload irksome at times, but you would never have known it.

Except on one occasion, that is. It was a Saturday and it seemed that every vascular surgeon in the vicinity of London had gone on their summer holiday. I had operated all day on a succession of vascular emergencies, and just when I thought I could finally escape home, a doctor was brought in with a blocked artery that had to be fixed at once. I phoned Jack and said, 'It won't take long. It will just be this last case and then I'll be home.' His frustrated response – 'You cannot operate on every artery in Greater London!' – showed his irritation that, on a day when we might have expected to be relaxing together, I was still busy at work. But it was only the once, and I had already learned myself just how hard it can be to be waiting at home for an in-demand surgeon to return.

Jack was to develop some health issues, which in his later years reduced his ability to enjoy gardening and walking. As a result we eventually moved from our house in the suburbs to a mews in central London and immediately found ourselves surrounded by a caring community of friends. It was and indeed still is like living in a village full of supportive neighbours.

9
And Now for St Mary's

In 1982 Felix Eastcott was to retire from the staff of St Mary's in Paddington. He was a famous and distinguished vascular surgeon and his was a job I had always wanted, at a premier vascular unit in a university teaching hospital. I applied, was shortlisted and then arranged to meet the members of the consultant staff with whom, if appointed, I might end up working in some way.

On 20 July that year, I was based in the morning at the Hammersmith hospital and was due to visit St Mary's in the afternoon. I vividly recall jumping into my car, in a rush as always, switching on the engine and the radio automatically starting with the words, 'There has been an IRA bomb in Hyde Park and the casualties are being taken to St Mary's.' It was clearly not the day for me to spend visiting potential future colleagues and it seemed unlikely that they would welcome assistance from a complete stranger. Instead, I watched the horrors of the day's events unfold from afar.

Eventually I met all the people I needed to see regarding the job, and most of them simply talked about the role and skirted around the question of why I wanted to move consultant job at that stage. I had been a consultant for ten years by then, but was still only in my forties, about the same age as some candidates who were still in senior registrar posts. There was a tendency in London then to stick in a job in the hope, or possibly the expectation, of eventually becoming the consultant on that unit. Of course, such highly experienced senior registrars were very valuable when it came to running those units. It was unusual to find a consultant wanting to move, so perhaps there were some unspoken questions regarding my motives. I was keen to work at St Mary's because it was an established referral centre for vascular problems, and although I was still doing general surgery, I was ready to concentrate more and more on vascular operations. And I had personal reasons too. Jack and I would find it far easier to work at different hospitals. We might be able to coordinate our on-call rotas and even plan some time off together!

My interest in stroke prevention surgery meant that I met the consultant neurologists at St Mary's, and one of them was Sir Roger Bannister. I had not previously met him but was well aware of his prowess and was somewhat in awe of the great man. As I was a well-established consultant already, generally the people I met were polite and friendly and there were no uncomfortable questions. It was not to be so with Roger Bannister, however. He wanted to interrogate deeply into the way I would treat his patients, were I to be appointed. I actually enjoyed this more probing enquiry and we would later become good colleagues when I successfully got the job.

Some months after my appointment, I was amused to experience his questioning nature once more, this time at a meeting at Imperial College. I had walked to the meeting from St Mary's across Hyde Park, rushing because I was running late, and it was a hot day.

'You look a bit hot and bothered,' remarked Roger.

'Yes, I was rushing a bit.'

'Why, where did you come from?'

'St Mary's.'

'How long did it take?'

'Oh, about twenty minutes.'
'It's only a mile!'

There was a strange habit back then of having an event on the evening prior to a consultant interview, to which the candidates and the consultant staff of the hospital were all invited. It was referred to as the 'trial by sherry' and was an entirely new experience for me. As I have often since reminded my family, no one can refill a full glass. So, I accepted the sherry but did not drink it, and wandered around with my full glass hoping to make a good impression on those I met. There were six candidates in competition for the role. Eventually we were dismissed and no doubt the consultant staff then discussed our relative merits.

A couple of hours later that same evening, I received a phone call at home from one of the consultants, a surgeon, suggesting that I would be wise to withdraw from the interview as I was not going to be appointed. 'It will look bad on your CV if you attend an interview but are not appointed,' he warned.

I was profoundly shocked by such an unexpected intervention. 'Thank you, I will sleep on it,' I replied politely. I had absolutely no intention of withdrawing from the race; indeed, quite the opposite. I could only guess at the motivation of such a call.

After our interviews, the candidates were sent to the pub opposite the hospital to await the verdict. I was candidate number four. When I came out of the interview and candidate number five went in, only number six was left, so I sat and chatted to him until it was his turn to be interviewed. As such I only spent a short time in the pub until I was invited back and offered the post. I was overjoyed and so happy to be back in a teaching environment, and with such a prestigious unit too. I was also delighted that I'd resolved to ignore the 'advice' of the night before and to this day can only wonder at what motives were behind it. I made sure that the 'trial by sherry' was discontinued as soon as I was in a position of influence at the hospital.

Just before I started my new job at St Mary's, Jack and I, along with Jason, decided to take a holiday on a canal boat. We collected the barge in Uxbridge and slowly, very slowly in fact, made our way to the Paddington Basin, where we turned round and returned. We had a unique view of the backstreets of west London, as well as the filthy state of the canal, which was right at the feet of the major teaching hospital that was soon to be my base. It was nonetheless a gentle, relaxing holiday, and a new experience for all three of us.

Starting a new job is always stressful and the tension was compounded by being the relatively unknown successor to an internationally very well-known and respected surgeon. I even went along to watch Mr Eastcott's last carotid endarterectomy. I was pleased to have had ten years of experience as a consultant at that stage, because my predecessor never actually left, and even after his retirement, would come to ward rounds and meetings most days of the week. My experience allowed me to listen to his words of wisdom but also to have the courage to do things differently when I felt it necessary. Two of the unsuccessful candidates for my post were senior registrars on the same unit, so I made sure to treat them with care until they each moved on to their own new jobs.

My first operating list was at the Harrow Road branch of the hospital, and when I arrived there, I had to drive round and round looking for the parking spot with Mr Eastcott's name on it. I did eventually find it, attached to the bike shed.

Doing my first arterial bypass operation in the main hospital was stressful, as I did things rather differently from my predecessor. The first time you operate in a new environment, with unfamiliar assistants and equipment, it is always somewhat daunting. As a surgeon you become familiar with and have preferences for particular instruments, and it makes life more comfortable if you know they will be provided. When the operation was finished, a nurse came up to me and said with compassion, 'I bet you're glad that's over.' I was, and I was also grateful for her thoughtful empathy.

Next morning on the ward round, I asked the patient how he was getting on with walking about. The quite direct Australian ward sister looked at me fiercely in reply and said, 'Actually, we don't get them out of bed for a week.'

'We do, sister,' was my firm response. I can still picture her horrified face now as I helped him to stand. I feel sure she thought that the bypass would fall to pieces on the spot. It was a change I needed to make, and in time, the sister came to see that it would in fact not result in immediate disaster.

I am a 'make haste slowly' sort of person, but there seemed to be an endless list of things that I needed to change in that role, and there was no time to waste. One element that needed no revision, however, was the student experience. I had always felt that the clinical teaching in Liverpool could not be bettered, but the standard at St Mary's proved to be very much at the same level. The staff all wanted to teach and to know the students as individuals. It was a small medical school, similar in size to Liverpool, and a really wonderful environment for learning clinical medicine.

In Liverpool, the anaesthetists and I had known each other in training and had great respect for each other. My new anaesthetic colleagues were somewhat cautious with me initially. No doubt they were thinking I was 'some woman from up north', but I knew my job and they were very skilled in theirs, so the ice was quickly broken.

The then Professor of Surgery at St Mary's could occasionally be somewhat dismissive, and following an especially and unpleasantly tense surgical division meeting one day, I chose to go up to his office to speak to him about it. He was surprised to see me there and invited me in. He was even more surprised when I expressed my displeasure at the rather curt exchange which had taken place.

His response was to pull out the drawer of his desk, where a bottle of whisky was lurking along with two glasses, and to pour two shots. I do not like whisky, but I drank that shot and happily he was never so abrupt in my presence again.

Throughout my career I have always tried to deal with difficult situations and behaviour in a direct fashion and, whenever possible, in private. Fortunately, I never had to deal with inappropriate behaviour of a sexual nature. It is not easy to call out bad behaviour and I admit that, on occasion, I should have done so but regrettably failed to speak up.

I should mention, however, that I am grateful to that professor for two things. Firstly, he could see that the future was in specialisation and that it was time for me to take the lead and become purely a vascular surgeon. I did so with some level of reluctance, because I enjoyed the breadth of surgery that my general practice encompassed, but it was the right move. Secondly, he was very supportive of me when I later became a professor myself. It was a pleasant surprise for me when he got in touch to say he felt it was a good move and an appropriate one.

My decision to follow his advice and become a purely vascular surgeon allowed me to increase the range of vascular surgery that our unit could deal with. There were some

My trusty dissection kit, which I have owned since I was at secondary school.

Studying anatomy at university, 1956.

With my university clinical 'firm'.

Snaps from the very special twenty-first birthday party my parents threw for me at the Prince of Wales Hotel in Southport, 1958.

With my brilliantly reliable Austin A40, 1959.

Visiting my mother at home with Jonathan.

Officially a doctor! 1960.

Some fantastic early 1960s fashion for an old girls' dinner back at school.

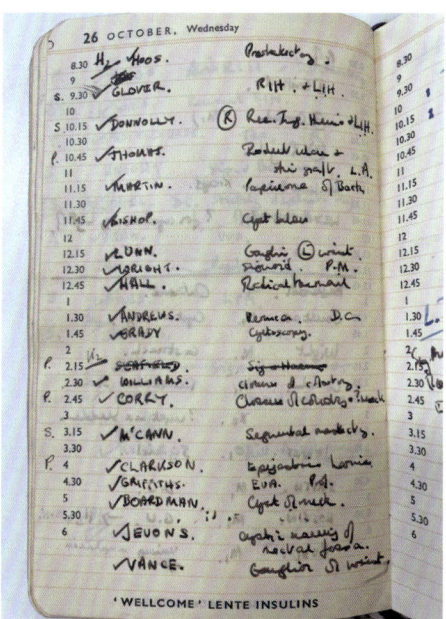

Notes from my work diary, 1960.

My wedding to Jonathan, 1962.

Celebrating my FRCS with my parents, 1967.

Not the first time I was the only woman in the room during my career!
A medical board meeting at the Royal Southern Hospital, 1972.

My parents.

Highgate, my much-loved Lake District home, 1985. It needed just a little work when I first bought it.

My marriage to Jack, 1987. A very happy day.

St Mary's Hospital in London; at work in the operating theatre with the team.

Volunteering at a 'Sing for Stroke' event, 1993.

Meeting Prince Philip at the Royal College of Surgeons. I only wish I could remember what he said to make me look so alarmed.

Receiving my CBE from the Queen, 1999.

With Jack at the Royal College of Surgeons.

Marking my last ever operation with colleagues, 2002.

Speaking as president of the BMA, 2009.

Jack and I celebrating our silver wedding anniversary at home with our family, 2012. I am wearing my wedding dress!

Music has always been a most important part of my life, and I have loved taking up the cello in retirement.

amazing referrals coming to the unit and there were huge opportunities to further develop the specialty by being dedicated to it. When other surgeons want to refer difficult cases to you, it is both a compliment and a responsibility. Prior to my move to London, I had of course tried unsuccessfully to refer a difficult case to Mr Eastcott from my practice in Liverpool. I determined that I would try to provide that sort of referral service for more complex cases, and in order to improve my ability to take care of certain difficult problems, I visited various experts in the field. Initially, my vascular colleagues were Ian Kenyon and Andrew Nicolaides. Ian was President of the Vascular Society and I acted as his local organiser for the annual meeting, which was being held in London. Soon afterwards he retired and, unlike Felix Eastcott, he did not linger. John Wolfe was appointed to replace him and he proved to be a hardworking colleague who cared deeply about the standard of care given to his patients. We had very different personalities and my hopes for combined ward rounds, which I had greatly enjoyed in Liverpool and Hillingdon, were not realistic, but that did not prevent us from forming an excellent unit together. We were never short of young trainees wanting to come and work with us. Those trainees, such as Simon Smith, David Reilly and many others, taught us as much as we taught them and were able to share with us some of the techniques they had witnessed on other units. Learning is always a two-way process.

Another task which my new job involved was setting up a private practice. As in Liverpool, I was appointed to be 'maximum part-time', which means that you have two sessions every week that are unpaid and in which you can carry out private consultations and operations. London is well provided for in terms of facilities for complex surgery. I rented rooms in Harley Street in conjunction with colleagues and I operated at private hospitals in the vicinity too. We began what would now be seen as a group practice: doctors with closely related specialties working in a building together and able to seek advice and help from each other when needed. The rooms were quite grand and traditional and needed a considerable amount of renovating to bring them up to modern standards. We were able to organise some investigations on the premises and this was very helpful for patients. I enjoyed the freedom from bureaucracy, as well as the range of referrals that came my way and the interesting people who were to cross my threshold.

As I've said, one surgeon can always learn something from watching another at work, and I visited one or two colleagues specially in order to see them operate. One was David Charlesworth in Manchester, who had the reputation for being the fastest vascular surgeon in the country, or even the world. While speed is not the aim of the job, wasting time is certainly to be avoided. That visit helped me to establish ways of becoming more efficient and removing certain unnecessary, non-productive moves.

One particularly difficult problem that I wanted to get better at dealing with was the thoraco-abdominal aneurysm. Someone in the UK needed to be offering the service to care for such a condition. By the time I became a consultant in Liverpool, I was competent at infrarenal aneurysms and determined to extend that to the more extensive and complex cases. The surgeon with the greatest relevant experience was Stanley Crawford from Houston, Texas. He had a huge referral practice for thoraco-abdominal aortic aneurysms. I asked if I could visit him at work and he warmly agreed.

So, in 1982 I travelled to Houston for the second time and stayed for ten days. During my visit, Stanley undertook nine such complex aneurysms, so I had a wonderful opportunity to learn how to deal with them. He was a gentle, polite man with a wonderful sense of humour. He tended to shun publicity, in contrast to some of his colleagues. When I asked if I could take photographs during the operations, he replied, 'Sure, just as long as you don't send them to the newspapers.'

Once, on an early morning ward round, we entered the room of a female patient who was recovering after an operation on her aortic aneurysm. Stanley murmured, 'It was a Duke 1 aneurysm, Averil.'

I failed to understand. I was familiar with the Dukes classification of cancer of the colon, but clearly this was something different. It turned out that the duke in this context was the Duke of Windsor, who had recently had surgery for an aortic aneurysm in Houston. Decisions about the need for an operation are usually based on the size of the aneurysm, as this is associated with the risk of rupture. Stanley explained that some people were of the opinion that the Duke's aneurysm might have been a bit on the small side.

Overhearing this explanation, the patient said, 'Dr Crawford, did I hear you say that I had a very small aneurysm?'

'Yes, and those are the really dangerous ones,' he replied.

Again, I didn't understand. But as we walked away along the corridor, he continued, for my ears only, 'Because if you don't do them, someone else will!'

During my time in Houston, the days were very long. I was staying in a local hotel where many patients also stayed before and after their operations. Stanley would often call in on his way to the hospital and leave me a chapter of the book he was in the process of writing. Then at 8am I would join him in theatre and he would ask what I had thought of the chapter. When I once admitted that I had not yet finished it, he exclaimed, 'Then you had better stay for a month so you can get through my book!'

The facilities at his disposal were amazing to me. As had been the case when I visited Michael DeBakey in 1972, I found that Stanley was also equipped with eight operating theatres, a 40-bed intensive care unit, a haematologist in theatre during operations, a team of surgeons who were themselves skilled in these difficult cases and, of course, the highly capable anaesthetists, known in America as 'anesthesiologists', who coped with the extreme physiological changes that can occur during complex procedures.

There was a huge amount to learn and it was a wonderful opportunity for me. Stanley had lots of visitors, but for some reason I got special treatment, and during surgery he always made sure I could see everything clearly.

I spent as much time with the anaesthetists as I did with the surgeons. The operation involves quite dramatic changes in the haemodynamics (the dynamics of blood circulation) of the patient and massive changes in blood chemistry and blood clotting too. This is why a haematologist was kept on hand. My greatest concern was whether it would be at all possible to replicate such conditions back in London.

During my time in Houston, I learned a very useful trick. At the end of a long operation, all any surgeon wants is a cup of tea and a rest. Visitors can be a nuisance in that they want to ask questions and so the surgeon gets little peace. I was a 'cat napper' for most of my working life, by which I mean that I often got about five, at most ten, minutes of real sleep, usually while sitting in a chair, in the middle of the working day. Stanley was the same. In order to achieve this, he would pull his theatre cap down until it covered his eyes and no one would dare to disturb him. This was a habit I gratefully went on to copy from Stanley.

In London I frequently struggled to book intensive care beds, and without that provision it is simply not possible to take on cases like these. In Houston the supply of these beds seemed infinite, though I do recall that one day, a nurse came and said, 'Dr Crawford, you cannot do the third case.' He was shocked and disbelieving and asked why.

'The intensive care unit is full.'

Clearly he lived in a different world from mine, as this was a rare, and perhaps even unique, situation for him to confront.

On my return to London, I had the task of organising all that was required for us to take on such difficult cases. I realised that I should have taken an anaesthetist to Houston with me because it would have been far easier for them to see it all for themselves. I had to take a fairly robust stance with all concerned, but particularly with Dr Knight, the senior anaesthetist with whom I worked then, in order to make progress. That was not, and is not, my normal behaviour – usually I prefer to be rather more persuasive. Peter was a superb anaesthetist and a very safe pair of hands. It certainly would have been better had we travelled to the US together, but we did not, so here I was, having the audacity to tell him how to do his own job. After some initial reluctance he did respond superbly to the challenge.

Before long we were set up and ready to take on our first case. Peter and I were not the only ones taking our first steps into this new territory – so too was the whole team, and tribute must be paid to the wonderful theatre nurses who seized the new challenge with both hands and made it work. The relationship between surgeon and scrub nurse is a very special and important one. Over the years I have been blessed with some quite superb nurses in theatre – Tricia, Gloria, Miriam, Di, Madge and others – with whom I have enjoyed a close bond, and I am immensely grateful to them all. Of course, that first operation at St Mary's was my second such case, as I had taken a leap of faith along with that very sick patient in Liverpool a few years earlier.

In general, the size of an aneurysm (and the associated risk of death if it is left untreated) determines whether surgery is necessary, but size is not the only consideration. The patient's fitness to undergo such a massive operation is a very important component of the decision-making process. The surgery to treat some of these most complex aneurysms was in itself dangerous and prone to complications. It can be difficult to ensure that the balance of risks is decidedly in favour of surgery and to only embark on an operation if there is a good chance of success.

On one occasion I was asked to see a lady in her eighties who had a thoraco-abdominal aneurysm. In my mind I had already decided that the risks in someone of that age would not justify taking it on. I arrived at the hospital and found a fit-looking lady dressed in a very regal purple velvet dressing gown. I completed the consultation and was about to tell her the news when she said, 'Well, young lady, I am prepared to take the gamble if you are.' Some patients simply find that to live with the threat of a rupture is so undesirable that they prefer to take the risk of surgery. I accepted the challenge and it turned out that she had made the right choice. It is important to remember that there is always a choice and that it is our job to explain it coherently, in words that the patient can understand.

In recent times, an additional choice has been thrown into the mix, as some vascular problems can now be dealt with in a less invasive way, by threading a graft into the affected part via a remote artery. It is essentially like putting in a new inner tube. However, it is relatively new and less well tried, and not always a straightforward decision. I remember sending one such patient away to think about that choice, so he could decide for himself. He returned two weeks later, saying, 'I have spent two weeks trying to research this on the internet. I am exhausted. Please just tell me what I should do.'

Such discussions can take time and should also involve the next of kin, so keeping a clinic on schedule can be challenging. I once took a friend to a clinic to support her in a difficult decision. The lady on the reception desk apologised, as they were running late. I said, 'Not to worry, that's good.'

'No one has ever said that before!' exclaimed the receptionist.

'Well, perhaps it means that the doctor is giving the patients as much time as is needed,' I replied.

To some surgeons the outpatient clinic is more of a chore than a pleasure, but I usually enjoyed mine. I liked the fact that you would meet a variety of people with an assortment of pathologies. No two clinics were the same and indeed no two patients.

In one such clinic I saw a man with a very large aortic aneurysm. He was referred to St Mary's from somewhere in south Wales and had a distinct Welsh accent. I explained what his problem was, and that urgent surgery was required. I went into some detail about what it involved and some of the risks related to the operation.

'Who exactly is going to do this operation?' he asked doubtfully.

'Well, I am,' I responded somewhat diffidently.

'Bloody hell, a woman!'

I smiled and we established a rapport despite his initial shock. It simply stemmed from unfamiliarity, which I understood. I can myself remember the feeling of surprise when at the start of a flight a female voice announced over the intercom, 'This is your pilot speaking.' Hopefully, such experiences are no longer a rarity either in flying or surgery.

The fact that I was a woman continued to cause occasional comment. One day, I was waiting for the staff lift in the hospital, and when it arrived, I invited a patient to step inside with me rather than leaving him to wait for the patient lift. He said, 'How come you're using the staff lift?'

'I work here,' I said.

'What sort of work do you do?' he asked.

'I am a surgeon.'

'A woman cannot be a surgeon!'

'Well, I am indeed a surgeon.'

'Then you must be bloody good.'

It is not always bad to be in the minority and I rarely took offence. I usually tried to defuse what might be an awkward situation by injecting a little humour. In my opinion, that works far better than climbing up on a high horse, and you even sometimes end up with a new friend.

Another example of my attempts to make light of situations was when a surgeon (who was well known to me, though we had never worked together) wrote in a national newspaper that women could not be surgeons, because when in difficulties they would 'get their knickers in a twist'.

In response, I found a haberdashery shop and asked if they still stocked old-fashioned ladies' knickers with long legs. They did! I bought a pair and threaded Christmas ribbon (it was December) through the frills on the legs, then tied the legs in a loose knot. I included a note 'from Mother Christmas', wrapped the parcel and posted it to the surgeon in question, ensuring that it was opened in a public place where he would be surrounded by doctors and nurses. Of course, he guessed where it had come from and sweet vengeance was mine!

In my early years at St Mary's, I was approached by the BBC again, this time to be part of a film about operating on aortic aneurysms for their series *Your Life in Their Hands*. I did not find the decision to take part easy. I have always felt unsure of the wisdom of showing operations to an audience. Although we call it an operating theatre, we are not there to entertain. Even instances of filming for a medical audience have sometimes caused me concern. We need to be absolutely certain that our behaviour will be exactly as it would if there were no onlookers. Difficulties and problems can arise in any operation and we have to ensure that we will cope with those difficulties in exactly the same way that we would in our normal private world. Filming is generally justified on the grounds of its educational merit, and in this case, it was education of the public.

I admit to feeling a little flattered to have been asked, but my absolute priority was to ensure that the filming would not be detrimental to the patient. In the end, I did decide to go ahead. I then needed to select a suitable patient and to discuss it with him. He was very willing and suggested, 'Perhaps it would be an idea to speak to my son. He is a lawyer.' Of course I agreed, and our conversation went well.

Professor Robert Winston, later Lord Winston but then in the early days of his media career, was to be the commentator. The rich timbre of his voice in my ear asking an occasional question was in fact enormously helpful. I simply got on with the job while he prompted me to speak and explain.

The BBC team were a delight to work with and even the patient seemed to enjoy himself. Jack and I had a party at home for everyone involved a few weeks later, and the patient and his wife were the centre of attention. Happily, he lived for many years after the operation. There are some patients who, for one reason or another, prove to be memorable, and he was one of them.

Another fomer patient whose treatment remains memorable for me is a lady called Linda, who was suffering as a result of Marfan syndrome. This is a very serious inherited disorder of the aorta, which in Linda's case had become life-threatening. Professor Sir Magdi Yacoub had previously dealt with her cardiac problems, before referring her to me for the rest of her aortic problem. The aorta begins at the aortic valve in the heart, then travels through the chest and the abdomen. Of course I was a vascular surgeon, not a cardiac surgeon. In the USA some surgeons are trained to do both specialties, but in the UK they are separate. This means that when the whole length of the aorta, from the valve to where it divides in the lower abdomen, is diseased, the two necessary operations will be done by two different surgeons.

Professor Yacoub let me know in advance that Linda would bring a tape recorder to the consultation, simply so that she could review the discussion later. A very wise move in my opinion. When we met, she was seriously disabled by the extensive aneurysm, which was affecting the whole of her aorta. The aneurysm in turn caused serious problems for her spine, which was being pounded by the huge pulsating artery and causing her extreme pain. She was young and, clearly, the situation needed to be dealt with if at all possible. Happily, she survived the very extensive surgery and she remains alive and well today.

We have a special relationship that has endured since that first operation and she contributed a lot to my team's research efforts. On one occasion I was walking the nearly 200-mile Coast to Coast Path, from St Bees in Cumbria to Robin Hood's Bay in Yorkshire, to raise money for the Royal College of

Surgeons. She joined me for a morning and walked a mile of the route with me. That was a momentous achievement for her, which would have been impossible without the surgery, and it proved quite an emotional experience for me too.

One of the constant stresses of my working life back in the 1980s, and indeed through to my retirement, was the uncertainty of being able to secure intensive care beds for patients like Linda who would certainly need one following surgery. By this period it was well recognised that intensive post-operative care saved lives, and we often simply could not operate until there was a vacant bed. I and others tried hard to increase the availability of such beds, but there never seemed to be sufficient funds or staff to do so. Not infrequently, there would be more than one surgeon fighting their patient's corner in the hope of securing the one available bed. I hated this process and admit to sometimes letting the anaesthetist with whom I worked do the fighting in my place. It was stressful and wasteful because if you failed in your attempt to get the bed, you and your team were left without any opportunity to operate. Of course we could not magic up a less complex case at the last moment. It would be inhumane to make a reserve patient fast ahead of surgery just in case it proved impossible to undertake the major operation.

The incisions required for vascular surgery tend to be extensive and can stretch from upper chest to lower abdomen. If the heart has to be exposed, then a common route is to incise straight down the sternum, or breastbone, which is called a median sternotomy. I remember one patient on whom I operated had an enormous tattoo of a crucifix filling his chest. It felt completely sacrilegious to make the required incision straight through Jesus on the cross. It simply had to be done, however, and afterwards came the added worry of ensuring that at the end of the operation, it was precisely realigned. I did not delegate the skin suturing to an assistant on that particular occasion.

Another memorable patient was a young man called Steve, who had been irradiated for a testicular tumour when he was in his early teens. He had been cured so far as the tumour was concerned, but a major side effect had been serious damage to his aorta. Radiation does have an effect on the arteries, but this was extreme. The aorta had essentially shut down and blood was only able to get to the lower half of the body via collaterals, small vessels that circumvent a blockage, which help but cannot completely resolve such a problem. It was not just his legs that were affected, as the circulation to his other organs, including his kidneys, pancreas and gut, was also seriously reduced. He was only 36 years old.

The surgery was unusually complex and multiple operations were required. For one of these, I was joined by Jack, and following the procedure, which initially seemed to go well, Steve needed many days of intensive care. There came a point when I feared he was not going to survive, and on one memorable early Saturday morning, I received a call from the ICU asking me to stick around as they thought I was going to be required to sign a death certificate. I felt I had no other tricks up my sleeve to help him, so I hung around and awaited the inevitable. By 11am no call had come and my thinking was that if he had endured three hours, just maybe he might stay alive for much longer. I went straight to the ICU and, with the team there, did every manoeuvre I could think of that might have some effect, and I tentatively began to feel some hope. Slowly, slowly, we saw some response. His blood pressure very gradually responded and he survived.

Steve taught me how important it is to keep on trying if there is reasonable hope of a good outcome. All new doctors are taught, as part of the Hippocratic oath, 'Thou shalt not strive officiously to keep alive', which reminds us to think primarily of the wellbeing of the patient, and not just how clever we can be. But Steve was young, had been cured of his cancer and had everything to live for, and live he did for a further 26 years. He was even able to join me at my retirement celebration. Such patients really do leave an indelible mark, and I remain a friend of his widow.

My practice also occasionally brought me into contact with some well-known people. I am fairly ignorant about celebrities and I used to have a secretary who so despaired of my lack of knowledge of film stars and the like, that she would buy videos of recent films for me so I could become better informed!

One such celebrity was John Mortimer, who I naturally failed to recognise initially. I was a creature of habit and always did a thorough history and examination with my patients. On this occasion, I asked what he did for a living.

'Oh, I write.'

'How interesting. What sort of things do you write, Mr Mortimer?'

'*Rumpole of the Bailey.*'

That was enough for even me to realise who I was speaking with.

'Oh, you're *the* Mr Mortimer!'

When, on a seperate occasion, I needed to admit another famous face to hospital, I asked if he had any preferences in terms of the choice of hospital. The answer was that it entirely depended on the wine list! I also recall Estée Lauder arriving for a consultation accompanied by a security guard, who stayed in the waiting room. After the consultation I walked her back to the waiting room, and en route she turned the tables and told me all that I should be doing for my complexion.

'Say, who is having the consultation with whom?' asked her security man. The next day, a big bag of the necessary cosmetics was delivered to my consulting room. Definitely a perk of the job!

At this time in my career, I began to have more involvement with the Royal College of Surgeons. The next phase of my work with the college arose when Felix Eastcott suggested that I should apply to become an examiner. Initially I rejected the idea, as I was fairly newly appointed at St Mary's, where I had lots to do and not much time for any extras. 'They never appoint you when you first apply,' said Felix, 'so don't be disappointed.' But for some reason, in my case they did. Perhaps my rarity as a female surgeon made me stand out from the crowd, but whatever the reason, I was surprised and in the end delighted too.

In 1986, I was duly inducted as a member of the Court of Examiners. It was a very formal affair. James Thomson – the other new member of this ancient and august body – and I were sworn in at a council meeting, photographs were taken and warm greetings extended. Unfortunately, the camera turned out to have been on strike that day, so we had to return a month later for a repeat performance.

The Court of Examiners was a central and vital component of my college work. It was entrusted with examining would-be surgeons and maintaining standards. It was made up of a small, hardworking group of surgeons from all specialties and from across the country. We set and marked examination papers and conducted oral and clinical examinations. There was great camaraderie among us and a determination to be fair.

The main defect of the exam system, in my view, was that the clinical examinations took place in a hall in Queen Square,

London. This was where I had taken my own exam many years previously. It meant that patients had to be transported from hospitals around London to the square, which was a huge logistical exercise, and of course only patients who could and who agreed to be moved were available for the exam. There was a group of patients with mobile conditions – for example, a ganglion of the hand – who would be very willing to turn up regularly in return for a fee and some food. Most patients enjoyed the experience and were pretty perceptive about the candidates. Nonetheless, examiners who worked in the London area had the added burden of constantly needing to provide such cases for the candidates.

The Chairman (or woman) of the Court was the senior examiner and the role was always held for a short period of a few months only. We felt it was time for the examiners to have a greater say in the workings of the college, and for that we needed to have an elected chair who would stay in post for two years. To my astonishment I was elected into the role for the first two-year period. It was a very special feeling knowing that I was supported by my colleagues. The most pressing task, in my opinion, was to make the clinical exam more 'real' by taking the candidates to the patients, rather than the long-standing tradition of doing the opposite. Other examiners contributed much time and effort in order to enact these changes, no one more so than Mike Pietroni, a surgeon at Whipps Cross who was very hard-working and forward-looking.

We set about instigating the new system, which meant finding willing hospitals and getting consent from managers. Not surprisingly, my own hospital ended up as the guinea pig, and the first clinical FRCS exam ever to take place in a hospital was held at St Mary's. There was complete agreement that this was the way forward, and from then on, the examination hall in Queen Square was relegated to history.

I had the good fortune to work with a wonderful team at St Mary's. The managers thought it a great idea, the ward sister was brilliant and the doctors enjoyed being on the other side of the fence for once. One enterprising candidate came along to the ward the evening before the exam, in the hope of chatting up the ward sister and getting a preview of the patients. He met his match in Sister May Herd! May deserves a special mention because she was truly a superb nurse whose only concern was for the wellbeing of her patients. She avoided any promotion that risked her being removed from patient care and I completely empathised with that sentiment.

Taking a quite traditional examination and lifting it out of its long-established setting of course entailed a risk of adverse change. We were convinced that the change was needed and did our best to maintain some aspects of the old exam. For example, we wore gowns for the presentation of the successful candidates, and we always gave them a glass of sherry or something similar at the end of the day (this had nothing in common with the infamous 'trial by sherry' I had previously encountered at St Mary's, however). Another long-established tradition that we preserved, the origin of which I must confess to simply not knowing, was the provision of a jam doughnut for the examiners to enjoy with their morning coffee. New examiners, wearing pristine white coats, always had to navigate the risk of a jam-stained coat for the day.

Having achieved a successful start, we went on to take the exam around the country, visiting the base hospitals of most of the regional examiners and ensuring that the exam was no longer only a London event. It was a wonderful opportunity for the surgeons on the court, as we were able to learn about a vast range of clinical problems.

General surgeons based in the British Isles have an association called the Association of Surgeons of Great Britain and Ireland. It was started by Lord Moynihan of Leeds in 1920, and although he was not their first president, he was certainly the inspiration. He expressed great concern that surgeons in one place often knew little of what surgeons elsewhere were doing. The Association enabled that levelling-up process to begin. In our small way we, the examiners, were contributing to that. My northern roots gave me an added incentive. I had seen for myself the high-quality work that was being done in the provinces and which was certainly not confined to London.

In 1990 I was having dinner at home with Jack in London when I received a phone call. It was from a colleague called Malcolm Gough and was to tell me that I had just been elected as President of the Association of Surgeons. I had no idea that I was even in the running for it and was completely shocked and delighted. I had always felt an affection for the Association, having been the grateful recipient of its Moynihan Fellowship some years previously in 1972. I had attended its meetings regularly, and of course, one such meeting in Sheffield back in the seventies had been especially memorable, as it was where Jack and I had first got together. The Association achieved some things that the colleges could not – in particular, it brought together surgeons from all corners of the British Isles and included the whole of the island of Ireland too. My presidency was a joy for me and I had the advantage of being president prior to the departure of several individual specialties, which later went on to form separate societies of their own.

The ceremonial medal was placed around my neck at the conclusion of the annual meeting, which was held on that occasion in Jersey. It is a beautiful gold medallion and chain, and of considerable value. My flight home was not until after lunch the next day and clearly, I could not risk leaving the chain in my luggage while I went out for the morning. My solution was to wear it sandwiched between two T-shirts while taking a brisk hike around the island.

My first event was a meeting in Dublin, to be organised by Professor Tom Hennessy. I expected that it would be a fun event and it did prove to be so. However, one problem arose when, on the first night in our hotel, I was woken by Jack at about 3am. He was suddenly in agony because of a raging infection that had developed in his elbow joint, as a consequence of a recent skiing injury. I called the night porter and asked where the nearest A&E department was. He was horrified. 'Oh you can't go there, you'll be there for hours,' he said. 'I'll get you a doctor to come here.'

I responded by asking if I could speak to the GP before he came. When I did, it turned out that the 'GP' was a locum, and in his normal life was actually an orthopaedic senior registrar. It could not have been better. In no time he had taken Jack in hand and admitted him to hospital. Poor Jack missed the whole event, but he thankfully received good treatment for his infection.

My main meeting for the association in 1993 was the big annual gathering, rather like the one in Sheffield all those years previously. Mine was to be held in Birmingham, at the new Conference Centre. It so happened that around the same time, a patient with a complex condition had been referred to me from Birmingham for an aortic operation. By the time he was discharged, he had learned that I would soon be responsible for a meeting in his home city, and he offered me his chauffeur-driven car for all my journeys around Birmingham. Such luxury!

Meetings such as that one are an important source of continuing education, because we doctors want – and are of course obliged – to ensure our knowledge is up to date. But organising or attending such events is always an add-on to the normal work of being a surgeon. It was essential for some members of the team to carry on with day-to-day work, so we shared out the opportunities to attend meetings equally. Despite this, whenever I returned to base there would always be a pile of work awaiting my return, and I tended to have to put in extra hours to get on top of it.

My professional life revolved around patients, but I was well aware that the profession required guidance and governance, and that came from the College of Surgeons, where I was already an examiner.

I had become an invited member of the Council of the Royal College of Surgeons when I first took on the Chair of the Court of Examiners. I was elected as a full member of the council in 1990 and took up the new position in July of that year. Previously, there had only ever been one female council member, Phyllis George, a surgeon at the Royal Free Hospital, and it was she who prompted me to allow my name to go into the ballot.

The council has an unusual tradition that is designed to introduce new members to the existing ones. Three times a year, a dinner is held and each new member has to speak after dinner at one of these events. The idea is to tell the others about yourself in whatever way you wish, and you have exactly 20 minutes to do so. It is amazingly revealing, both in terms of the stories told and also of the character of the individual.

I decided to accompany my talk with music and took along an electric keyboard so I could play snippets of various pieces of music that had played an important part in my life. I had pre-recorded the first two in case I was too nervous to play, and in the event I needed those recordings! I suppose it was in a way a mini *Desert Island Discs*.

I very much enjoyed my time as part of the council and I chaired a number of its boards and committees. I eventually rose to the rank of vice-president, the second ever woman to do so. I admit that I hoped I might progress even further to become the first ever woman president, but it was not to be. I was delighted some years later when Clare Marx, who subsequently became Dame Clare, achieved that honour.

Council meetings were quite formal; we wore gowns and would always stand to speak. The meetings lasted a full day and the London-based surgeons would then head back to base, in my case St Mary's, to catch up on our 'real' work. There was always something that required my attention.

The college had to be represented on other bodies too; I served as our representative on the Council of the Royal College of Anaesthetists and also on the General Medical Council. As a result of the latter, I became increasingly aware of our failure as a college to have any responsibility for the ongoing standard of care given by our fellows throughout their working lives. We were totally involved and took responsibility for the trainees and their examinations, and we would offer some courses for them beyond the FRCS, but we were not directly concerned with the standard of care after that point. Events that took place in Bristol cardiac surgery between 1984 and 1995 resulted in a public inquiry and there were some important lessons to be learned. We could, in my opinion, no longer cease our concern for the standard of surgical care once examinations had been passed. We needed to continue to take responsibility for surgical standards throughout the career of a surgeon.

If a member wanted to introduce a new topic to the council, they had to present what was called a 'pink paper' and be prepared to argue its merits. I proposed a Standards Board, and my pink paper was eventually accepted and developed. From then on, we were involved in the maintenance of high standards of surgical care throughout the life of a surgeon. It was the change I felt most proud of during my time with the council.

My other main contribution was in setting up a scheme called Women in Surgical Training. This began just prior to my becoming a full member of the council. It seems that whenever I reach a comfortable plateau in my life, I manage to find another challenge lurking around the corner. I felt that I had been fairly treated at every stage of my career progression and was consistently of the opinion that if I could do it, then so could every other woman who wished to do so. But I recognised that there were other issues at play.

The background to this initiative was the rapid increase in the percentage of women in medical schools. If 50 per cent of medical graduates were to be women, we needed to encourage those women to at least see surgery as a career option and not simply a job for the boys, as it was then widely supposed to be.

The Department of Health created a working party to consider the issues raised by Isobel Allen, who was a senior fellow at the Policy Studies Institute and who had researched issues affecting women doctors and their careers across all specialties. It was clear that there was a particular problem in surgery, and the fact that only 2 per cent of consultant surgeons were women meant we were well below the numbers needed to sustain the specialty, let alone to ensure that women were being treated fairly.

I was called in to join the working party, and as a result, the College of Surgeons accepted that something needed to be done. Virginia Bottomley MP, Health Secretary at that time, Dr Diana Walford, Deputy Chief Medical Officer for England (and a fellow Liverpool graduate) and Dame Rosemary Rue, Oxford Regional Medical Officer, were particularly influential in persuading the college. Its then president Sir Terence English, a well-known cardiac surgeon, was also very supportive.

Rosemary Rue was quite outspoken in her view that the College of Surgeons was neglectful, even saying its members should be ashamed about its treatment of women doctors who wished to become surgeons. She felt that much more could and very definitely should be done to encourage women into the profession. Rosemary was a remarkable lady, and I admired and was influenced by her. She was born in 1928, and when she married, was obliged to quit her medical school. Undaunted, she managed to move to another school and successfully qualified as a doctor. She had also faced more than her fair share of illnesses, the most persistent of these being polio. Initially she was unable to walk and indeed she was once told that she would never walk again. In recognition of all her contributions to the college, we awarded her an honorary fellowship. I sat beside her at the evening dinner that followed the ceremony and asked her where she was staying. 'Oh no,' she said, 'I am taking the night bus back to Oxford.' She certainly knew about resilience and she taught me a great deal.

I debated with others the possible steps that the college could take to improve the lot of women, and the outcome was the Women in Surgical Training organisation, which I chaired. In words that I wrote at the time, we declared that we were keen to ensure that women viewed surgery as a realistic career choice and that they received support and advice as appropriate. I wrote that the college needed to say to women:

- Yes, we do want you to consider a surgical career.
- Yes, it is entirely appropriate and acceptable. Gender should not have any relevance in deciding upon a surgical career.
- Yes, we know that you are going to have babies and that is entirely acceptable and appropriate.
- Yes, you can do some of your training on a flexible basis.

I might express the above sentiments rather differently today, but this was 1989.

We decided to invite interested women to come to the college for a day. I truly thought that there might be a small uptake of places at our first conference and was shocked when I heard we had almost two hundred delegates. These conferences continue even now and the delegates increase in number every year. The organisation later changed its name to Women in Surgery, but in essence it is still the same as it was originally, and it is thriving, with about six thousand members today. I recently attended its 30-year reunion and was delighted to see many women who clearly enjoy the career that I have also loved.

Students are always welcome to come to these events, to join the organisation and to meet and talk to those who have succeeded in their desired career. I recently read about the loneliness of top-ranking female tennis players, because tennis is a rather solitary business and does not have the locker-room camaraderie of football and other team sports. I, too, at times experienced a sense of locker-room loneliness, and to some extent Women in Surgery stands in the way of that risk of isolation. I remember one time towards the end of my career, while I was changing into theatre clothes, hearing two women trainee surgeons having a supportive chat. It was the first time ever that I had been present when two female colleagues were able to give each other support, and I was truly moved by that superficially quite trivial experience.

My initial expressed hope was that the organisation would soon be redundant, that it would become completely normal for women to be surgeons, not worthy of comment, and they would no longer require support. However, it seems that the organisation is still a much-loved and-wanted aspect of college activities. The recent college working party looking at discrimination supports the view that it does still have an important role to play.

I was privileged to spend several years on the governing body for surgery and to participate in instituting changes in training and examinations. But I am especially proud to have played a small role in advancing the position of women who wish to pursue a surgical career.

10
What Is a Professor?

Over the course of my career, I had met many Professors of Surgery, but I had never wanted to become one. Indeed, I was adamant that it was not for me. I wanted to be a clinician whose patients came first and who was skilful in the operating theatre. On the other hand, I also wanted to be on the advancing edge of my specialty, and for this reason I had always engaged in research from the very beginning of my surgical career. I had contributed to the medical literature on a regular basis since my first publication in 1964 in *The Anatomical Record*. That first paper described an aorta that divided into four instead of into two, and it set me on the road towards further investigative work. I did eventually ask myself, *Why not become an academic and a professor?* After all, I had worked in an academic department when I was a lecturer and had enjoyed it. Even if I was a professor, I would still be a clinician at heart and that would always come first.

I had previously come to the conclusion that Professors of Surgery could not possibly be good at all the diverse components of their work. Sadly, the one component that was paramount for me, operative surgery, did not always seem to be the driving force for them. In Liverpool, during my undergraduate and junior doctor period, Charles Wells had been the professor, and he was first and foremost a surgeon. But the idea that a Professor of Surgery could also be the surgeon that others turned to with a difficult case, who was in truth a surgeon's surgeon, was not a popular one.

Above all else, it seems to me, universities expect their professors to have a large research output and the income to support it, and to have a top-ranking citation record for that research. The idea of teaching comes in somewhere, but it is not a priority, and carrying out operations, especially complex, difficult and lengthy ones, may simply be seen as a drain on the time available for other important matters.

Some professors I had met seemed to think that ritual embarrassment was the best way to train future surgeons. Their hunting ground was the Surgical Research Society, where they were often apparently in competition with each other to make the most humiliating comment after the delivery of a paper. *Is the quality of research influenced in the slightest way*, I would ask myself, *by the ability of a young surgeon to deliver their paper from memory? Is it good 'continuing medical education' to attend meetings at which you only listen to papers on subjects about which you are an expert?*

When I first moved to St Mary's, I worked with Hugh Dudley, who was then followed by a charming surgeon from Leeds, Pierre Guillou. Pierre was a skilled surgeon and academic, but I always feared he would return to the north if the opportunity arose, which is exactly what happened in the end. I was very sorry to see him go, because to me he encompassed all the necessary skills for his work. Clearly, St Mary's needed to find a replacement professor, and an appointment committee had to be convened.

By that time, I had been involved in the 'hiring' process for several professors, and in 1993 I found myself sitting on the committee set up to appoint the successor to Pierre Guillou. The timing was particularly tricky because the independent St Mary's Medical School was about to be transformed into the medical arm of the Imperial College of Science, Technology and Medicine, better known as Imperial College London. We were the first medical school to merge with Imperial in this way; it was a major and transformative move. We went from being isolated and self-determining to part of an internationally recognised institution with its own governing body.

There were many components to the merger, and the heads of all the departments could expect a busy and potentially tricky period of adjustment. Not everyone supported the move. I did, because I had little doubt that without it, we would eventually simply disappear as a medical school. The staff at St Mary's were dedicated teachers and I hoped to see that dedication become the foundation of the new medicine component of Imperial. I understood the need for a new professor who was a little older and already familiar with the negotiations that would ensue. Neither of the two shortlisted candidates had much experience of chairing committees, and certainly not of walking on eggshells without cracking any of them.

After hours of discussion, the committee broke up without making an appointment. We were all sworn to secrecy. I returned to my office in the early evening feeling depressed and needing to catch up on the work of the day. I was still there some two hours later when I received a phone call asking if *I* would accept an appointment as the new Professor of Surgery. I was stunned and horrified. I explained that I had no wish to become a professor. I had never been a candidate or so much as filled in an application. I had settled into my new life in London, and just when I thought I had reached a level where I could finally relax and enjoy simply being a surgeon, this most unexpected invitation appeared out of nowhere. Never in a million years did I anticipate it and I did not want it.

Despite my feelings, I could see the reason for the suggestion and understood why I might be seen as a good fit. I tried to view it from the position of the Medical School and to appreciate what I might have to offer. After a very long period of prevaricating, I eventually — and quite reluctantly — did allow my name to go forward. The next few months, however, were to be far from straightforward.

I recently came across a diary that I had kept of the events as they unfolded in 1993. It begins:

> *September 1st dawned bright and clear and I was in the Lake District. This is — in theory — the first day of my new career as a Professor of Surgery, so why the Lake District? Perhaps I should write a prologue. If you can imagine the word prologue spoken in a Frankie Howard voice then you will be able to hear words behind words which is, believe me, an essential component of an adventure into academia.*

That prologue went back to 14 April 1993 and a dinner that I had organised for the St Mary's surgeons who were attending my presidential meeting of the Association of Surgeons. I had invited the dean to join us as a guest, and during the dinner I learned from him that there was to be no St Mary's surgeon on the selection panel for the new Professor of Surgery. This seemed to me a very serious omission, as the new professor would be working with those surgeons daily. I expressed my concern and, in due course, was invited to join the panel.

The preliminary discussions had centred on the possible specialty of the appointee and whether that specialty would fit in with the established specialties and workload of the department. For example, it would not be wise to appoint a transplant surgeon if the hospital was not carrying out transplants. The forward planning for specialties in London was tending towards grouping major specialties in one place and such decisions were being taken by a review group, rather than the local surgeons.

The committee met on 26 May 1993:

The great day began with a discussion of the candidates in the Dean's office, lunch and then four hours of the selection committee looking at the two surviving candidates, one a lightweight still looking for training and the other with a reputation for being difficult. So no appointment was made and at 6pm, sworn to secrecy, we dispersed and Neil Goodwin [Trust CEO] *and I drank a cup of tea in my office in a disconsolate mood.*

Two hours later the Dean sought me out to ask me to take on the job. My reaction was one of complete disbelief and although I was persuaded to think about it overnight, I had made up my mind [to decline].

I did seek advice from my old boss, Professor Robert Shields from Liverpool, and he appeared to support the idea, while at the same time warning me to be prepared for some criticism, which he said was already circulating. One professor was apparently already proving vocal in his opposition. So much for the secrecy we had all agreed to.

It is important to explain why some people felt opposed to the possibility of my appointment. It was not because I was female. At that time, most doctors who wished to become professors in their specialty would work their way up the academic ladder and would have first spent some time as a senior lecturer. It was not a well-defined career path and there was nothing to prevent an outsider such as myself coming in, but it was felt that such a move might send an adverse message to those already on the academic route. In addition, an NHS consultant might not fully understand the requirements of an academic role and would certainly not be familiar with all of them.

From my viewpoint, all of these concerns could, with support, be easily overcome, and my strengths lay in slightly different areas. I had always had a research profile, I loved teaching and I was a decent surgeon. In addition, I knew a great deal about the training and examining of surgeons and about the ways the surgical colleges worked. All useful stuff for a medical school that was about to take a massive leap into the unknown by becoming part of Imperial College.

27 May 1993
Next morning I was persuaded to go on thinking about it and was at the same time bound by the rules of the selection committee to remain silent to the outside world, an increasingly difficult task as the days went by. Pierre Guillou was probably one of the most positive influences in his strong support.

I was, however, far from persuaded at this point, and even somewhat irritated by the fact that I was spending every spare moment trying to work out the pros and cons of the situation. I well remembered that Pierre had once given a talk at the Royal Society of Medicine in which he had basically said the job was impossible as there were so many components to it, which left me feeling distinctly uneasy.

After many hours of contemplation and discussion, I eventually wrote to the Rector of Imperial and the Dean of St Mary's, to formally decline the invitation. I then went to a meeting in Glasgow and returned to a flurry of my usual activities. The rector and dean were however clearly of the opinion that I was the ideal candidate, and I found myself being unwillingly drawn back into the arena. I loved my job as a consultant surgeon and was resistant to the idea of change. It did not enter my mind that it might be good for others to see a woman in a leadership position in surgery. Nor indeed that if I were to be appointed, I would be the first woman to become a Professor of Surgery and to head up a department of surgery in the UK. Looking back on this, I can see the significance of it, particularly in the eyes of the up-and-coming women in the profession. It is, I acknowledge, essential to see women in such leadership roles.

The debate smouldered on and I took refuge in the things that gave me pleasure. One such fun day was the 28 June:

> *This was the first day of 'Sing for Stroke' week and Josie* [my lab technician] *and I had organised students, a piano, music etc. I spent two very happy hours in the main entrance hall of the hospital playing requests* [in return for donations] *while people sang.*

But behind the scenes there were still objections, and although the dean and rector seemed committed to persuading me to take on the role, many of the big guns in the world of surgical academia remained opposed. I had unwittingly landed in a hornet's nest and my greatest disappointment was that not one of the three professors on the original selection panel had yet seen fit to discuss it with me.

I spoke with one of them, who I had thought my friend, and told him of my disappointment in people's behaviour around the issue. I did not mince my words and he clearly listened. Over time he somehow managed to resolve some of the trickier issues in question, to the extent that opposition to me taking up the post slowly began to wane. He was senior and well respected, and no doubt the other professors listened to his words. Throughout it all, the rector and the dean continued to endorse my candidacy, and by 5 August I was verbally appointed. But by this time I had learned to be cautious, and so refused to move into my new office until I was officially appointed sometime later.

> *It is now 18 September and I still do not have a [formal] appointment. Pierre has gone and I am trying to fill the gap without actually sitting in the office on the tenth floor. There is no way that I will move into the Professor's office until I am appointed.*

In the meantime, Pierre had gone to Leeds and I needed to make new appointments in the school, which I did.

> *I have appointed Graham Sutton and Simon Paterson-Brown as temporary senior lecturers, and they have been superb. Warm-hearted, hard-working and determined to sort out the job descriptions, the teaching, et cetera.*
>
> *I have fixed the secretarial problem and Val will become my academic secretary. Varina [previously the Professor's secretary] will look after the senior lecturers.*
>
> *I have seen many of the staff on the tenth floor and tried to help them and tried to understand their problems and their research!*
>
> *Ara Darzi has been enormously helpful and industrious.*

There were some lighter moments too:

> *I met one of our staff nurses in Norfolk Place, who said congratulations but asked, 'How will you have time to fit it in?'*
> *'I will have to give something up.'*
> *'Yes, that's good, so long as it isn't Jack!'*
> *That made my day.*

And on 19 September 1993:

> *Visiting new patients, one of whom was in the Lindo wing. Found a lovely Malaysian staff nurse up a ladder changing my title to professor. I said I am trying to ignore that, to which she replied, 'Oh, you mustn't, you deserve it!' Cheered me up after a sad day sitting beside*

> *Danny* [my mother-in-law, who was dying at this point] *and fearing that I may never see her again.*

It took until 13 October for me to receive written confirmation of my appointment.

> *It's official. I have a piece of paper and two press releases! Josie* [my research assistant] *summed it up.*
> *'I do hope you have been good.'*
> *'Why on earth do you say that, Josie?'*
> *'Because they sure as heck will find out if you haven't.'*

The next few days were particularly hectic, with press interest, photographers and friends all apparently wanting a piece of me. A *Guardian* reporter asked me to tell her about all the discrimination I had experienced during my training. I told her that I did not feel I had met with any discrimination so far. She responded, 'My editor's not going to like this at all!' I persuaded her to write the good news for once and, in all fairness, that's what she did.

One important change was that I had to leave my Harley Street practice, as it was clearly something I would no longer have time to maintain. One fun evening around that time was spent with the Parkside Women's Dining Club, which consisted of about 30 female consultants of all disciplines from the local hospitals. We laughed a lot, they toasted me and I in turn toasted the 3,400 male consultants who were apparently referenced in one of the newspaper articles about my appointment.

Jack and I were committed to a trip to Spain that autumn, and although I could have used my time better in London, it did allow me the opportunity to surprise my old mentor Edgar Parry, who happened to be in Alicante at the same time as us. I showed him the press release and was touched by his delight.

With a lot of help from colleagues and friends, I moved into my office on the tenth floor of the hospital and I officially began work on 25 October 1993:

> *Began my first day in the chair by opening the door and welcoming all comers. Flowers on the table and people dropping in for a couple of hours. Then down to the business of ward rounds and clinics and emergencies – the real world. Peter Taylor came up to my office with two difficult cases and it was a reminder of how much we just don't know. But it is fun to learn and it was great to see him.*

Peter had once been a trainee with me and was now a consultant, but he was still happy to ask for help and advice when appropriate. He was a simply superb surgeon and a delightful human being, and he fulfilled my wish to see our trainees become better than their trainers.

> *27 October 1993*
> *Although time did not really permit I decided to go up to Leicester for a carotid investigation meeting. I returned in time for the Vickery lecture given by Geoff Slaney, and Jack came along to the lecture. In the car to the Barber Surgeons, Professor Miles Irving talked to me about the 'confidentiality' surrounding my appointment. He is remarkably supportive and indicated that I will be invited to the Association of Professors of Surgery (there had been rumours that I would not be).*

Next day I was at the council meeting of the College of Surgeons, and without exception I was warmly greeted and congratulated by the surgical leaders. It was tremendously reassuring to hear the elected representatives of the surgical world expressing their delight at my appointment. Of all of them, the one who gave me the greatest pleasure was Harold Ellis, a senior surgeon, who said he very much supported the idea of a senior, research-orientated clinician with a strong clinical reputation taking on an academic department.

16 November 1993
A cup of tea beside me and a moment that I don't really have snatched to write a little something. I wonder whether I can cope with all this. There is so much to do and so much more that needs to be done. Such a pity that I was denied the long quiet summer to get to grips with the job. No point in such thoughts – simply get on with it girl!

Amidst all of this activity, Jack remained his patient, tolerant, supportive self. We managed to fit in a delightful weekend in the Lakes not too long after my appointment, which we both sorely needed.

Hugh Dudley came to visit me in my new office and was remarkably supportive. He told me of his delight in the appointment and said, 'The whole hospital is behind you. They want you to succeed,' which was kind of him.

Work continued apace for the rest of the year, and in early January I turned up for my first meeting of the Association of Professors of Surgery, at which I was hospitably welcomed.

The next day, however, was perhaps the one I felt the most anxiety about, as it was the first time that I was to attend the Surgical Research Society as a professor. This was *the* academic surgical powerhouse and I was delighted when my department presented no fewer than seven papers, and better still the whole team subsequently sat together at dinner too. It was a huge boost to my morale.

All new professors have one particular inescapable ordeal to face, which is their inaugural lecture. We were holding a symposium at St Mary's on vascular surgery, and, to me, it seemed ideal to slot my lecture in then. I gave it a deliberately enigmatic title and just beforehand it felt as if the whole world was descending on the appointed lecture theatre, possibly out of curiosity inspired by my unusual title.

11 February 1994
The day of the John Mannick symposium, the debate and my inaugural. A big attendance all day and standing room only for my lecture. I called it 'restoring old wrecks' and in it I linked my job with the restoration of Highgate. It was well received and preceded by a very generous introduction from the Dean.

Bob Williamson [of gene therapy fame] *said it was the best inaugural he had heard, and although I am sure that cannot be true, it cheered me up immensely as he* [unlike me] *is truly an academic.*

The lecture was about the steps required to build a complete surgeon, and I used the construction and restoration of Highgate, my Lake District house, to illustrate the various different elements involved. I explained that as I was giving the lecture early in my career as a professor, I could not be expected to talk of my achievements, but only of my hopes and aspirations.

I was particularly concerned to stress the role of academic departments in building the skillset needed to become a well-rounded surgeon. To my mind, the essential research component of such departments and of surgical training should not be the only requirements; I spoke of how communication should be prioritised too, particularly across traditional boundaries. I wanted to see collaboration with other disciplines and I wanted to ensure we allowed for ambitious ideas or even wild dreams, while exerting sensible control, of course. I have always felt that academic departments should to be able to roam beyond the constraints imposed (largely) by available funding. We also need to train the young to be resilient in the face of the unexpected and the frankly depressing.

This was my last slide, a cartoon by Mel Calman:

In all of this Jack was wonderfully supportive and I could always trust him to point out the funny side of things too. It was my great good fortune to have such a happy and peaceful home life. He was retired and winding down by that stage, while I was at the beginning of the busiest decade of my professional life.

15 February 1994 (Shrove Tuesday)
Jack and I dined and 'pancaked' and I had my last wine for 40 days. He sent a fax to The Times: *'I am in urgent need of 40 half bottles of wine. Can any of your readers oblige?' They didn't publish it!*

My professional life continued at a fast pace. Patients were still central to my work, but I now had many additional responsibilities to find time for too.

17 March 1994
Sleep had been disturbed by phone call about a patient with a major problem at the Royal Marsden and the X-rays came by hand to me at 7am. Thus began a working day that ended at 10pm. And my first food since 6.30am. Crazy!

This entry is where my diary of that momentous period comes to an end, but of course, the job was only just beginning. It proved to be a lot of hard work throughout and there was always the fine line to tread between giving my all to patient care while at the same time running a busy academic department.

One particularly happy and unexpected event of 1994 was my invitation to accept an honorary degree from the University of Liverpool. When I first received it, I could not help recalling just how close I'd come to disaster in my second year there several decades previously, when I had felt so adrift in a strange new world. If someone could have told me then that I would end up with such an honour!

I had received my original MBChB (Bachelor of Medicine and Surgery) in Liverpool's Philharmonic Hall back in 1960, but the hall was undergoing renovations in 1994 when my honorary doctorate was awarded, so the ceremony was instead held in the Roman Catholic cathedral, one of the city's two cathedrals. The song 'In My Liverpool Home' famously includes the words 'If you want a cathedral we've got one to spare'. The Catholic one was originally meant to be a vast Lutyens-designed building, but progress stopped after the crypt had been constructed. Years later, 'Paddy's Wigwam', a modern circular construction, was superimposed on the site. It was a splendid occasion, and to my delight, we processed from the lower level into the cathedral proper while the organ played.

When I arrived for the ceremony, I was directed by an attendant into a room full of important-looking people donning gowns. Search as I might though, I could find no sign of a gown with my name on it. Suddenly the attendant reappeared and apologised, saying in a wonderful Scouse accent, 'So sorry, love, I took you to the wrong room. I brought you to the second division but you're in the Premier League.'

Such is the essence of Liverpool – it was perfect.

My new role included all of my previous responsibilities, with the addition of many new ones. I was in charge of the research carried out in the department, and perhaps more worryingly, for its funding. I also had overall responsibility for student surgical teaching and for examinations.

In order to qualify as a doctor, students need to pass a large number of examinations, one of which is a clinical exam. The process at that time involved patients kindly agreeing to be interviewed and examined by prospective doctors, while being observed by a consultant or professor. Mostly this was normally a quite enjoyable day for the patients, who would receive a small remuneration for their involvement. It was similar in many ways to the FRCS examination, but of course this was taking place in every medical school in the country. Gathering 20 or 30 suitable patients was a big task and we were always extremely grateful to those who volunteered to take part. It was sometimes interesting to ask the patients about their experience, and they were generally remarkably accurate in their assessments of the new fledgling doctors.

The patients were always asked not to tell the student their diagnoses, and one man took this guidance so seriously that he failed to tell the student about his chest pain, thinking that would give the game away. The pain was in fact his only reason for being a patient, so consternation ensued all around.

Clinical examination of the knee is a standard component of the exam. A lump can occur around the knee joint for a number of different reasons. It could, for example, be arthritis, a Baker cyst or an aneurysm, and the student ought to be able to correctly diagnose which it is. On one occasion, we had three knees in the line-up. After some time it became clear that the students were informing their waiting friends of these diagnoses, so we moved the patients around to different places in the ward. My next candidate examined the knee of the patient in bed 8 and looked at me very seriously as he announced, 'Ah, I feel a large pulsating swelling behind the knee and I believe this is an aneurysm.' Of course, unknown to him, we had moved the aneurysm from bed 8 to bed 12, so I suggested he forget all the 'helpful' advice he had received and start again with an open mind. He did go on to pass!

I was responsible for the examinations and was required to examine at my own and also other medical schools, with the aim of ensuring a level standard throughout the country. It was just one of the many new tasks I had acquired with the job. Although I have never been good at delegation, it was imperative now and I was greatly aided by the superb staff around me in every role. My wonderful PA Val kept me and my various commitments in order, and I was fortunate to have a number of other such loyal colleagues. I appointed Gerry Stansby to a vacant senior lecturer's post and he proved to be completely reliable and industrious, and very much my right-hand man.

He was central to the shift of the department's research emphasis away from general surgery, which was my predecessor's specialty, to vascular surgery, which was easily accomplished by basing it on the clinical workload.

I was very keen to retain my clinical practice and skills, so I continued to host outpatient clinics and to operate. When I did outpatient clinics, it was my habit to collect the patient from the waiting room and take them to the consulting room, introducing myself as we walked along. On one occasion, a tall gentleman from overseas appeared to understand who I was and he answered all of my questions without difficulty. He had been referred because of an aneurysm, so I asked him to take off his clothes and lie on the couch. He stripped naked and I got on with the examination. Once it was over, I said he could get dressed and return to the desk.

At this point, he asked, 'And when I am I going to see Professor Mansfield?'

It is hard to imagine what he thought was my role, but he quite clearly could not imagine that the professor was going to be female.

In a similar vein, I was once the speaker at a dinner and found myself seated at the top table, next to a man whose place card said 'Mrs —'. So I said, 'Clearly you are not Mrs —.

Who are you?' He told me and then responded, 'And clearly you are not Professor Mansfield. Who are you?'

I received invitations to speak from around the world and I enjoyed the international nature of my job. Jack would almost always accompany me and was invaluable in so many ways. We frequently met former trainees of his. He was good company and our hosts always appreciated his presence. We rarely had time to travel beyond the requirements of the visit, but on some memorable occasions we were able to do so. The trip I best remember was travelling to Syria where we enjoyed a very special holiday, after I had spoken in Beirut.

On another such visit to India, there was a period after the talks for questions. A man in the audience stood up and said that he wished 'to address my question to the woman in a *man's field*'. Never before had I thought about the possible significance of my name, and I thought he was very clever and funny. Some of my colleagues were not at all amused, however.

I was also honoured by several important organisations and colleges in the USA and Australia, and in response I would visit them and usually give an address. One or two such organisations were embarrassed by the fact that they had no gifts appropriate for a woman; I have a small collection of ties which were apologetically offered to me in this way.

My three step children were by this stage living independent lives, and in 1997 the first of our now six grandchildren arrived. Jack and I were spending the weekend with Peter Knight, our anaesthetist friend, and his wife Jo, who had formerly been a theatre nurse, at their home. When we heard that Lesley had given birth to a baby girl, Poppy, we sped to Portsmouth at once for the very happy event. There is something immensely exciting about a first grandchild, though of course all of them are equally precious.

Every six months I would receive a group of 20 young vascular surgeons from either France or Germany. They would arrive on a Sunday evening and leave on Wednesday evening, spending those three days in theatre watching me operate. Over the years, I had many such groups visit and I observed an interesting and very consistent difference in the behaviours of the groups from those two countries. A group from Germany was always deferential to the professor and would never question the wisdom of any decision that I would take, whereas the groups from France were only too willing to interrogate my decisions and actions. I found this quite amusing.

The nights also had a regular pattern to them, with one of the evenings always spent eating at a local restaurant. One time, a German group expressed a desire to try Indian food, so a very good Indian restaurant was booked and a private banquet organised. It was called the Bombay Brasserie and was just a five-minute walk from their hotel and also the hospital. I arrived with the local team in good time, but the Germans were nowhere to be seen, which was puzzling. After a while, the proprietor said, 'I wonder if they have gone to a different restaurant, also with Bombay in the name', as there were three in the area at the time. We hit the jackpot on the first attempt – they were indeed at the Bombay Tandoori on Edgware Road, where they had just placed an extensive order. They had asked the owner if he was expecting a group of 30 from the hospital and, not one to miss a great opportunity, he'd quickly said 'Oh yes!' It cost us money to extract them.

On their final evening, the groups would come to my home and a caterer would provide the meal. Despite having generally spent the full day operating, the evening would without fail end around my piano. A great sing-song is such a wonderful way of bringing people together.

Eventually, around four years later, I decided that it was time to start looking for my successor. I had always said I would only do the job for five years. I wandered into the Dean's secretary's office and asked for guidance, and she simply handed me the file on my and my predecessors' appointments. It was very revealing.

The search for my successor concluded with the appointment of Ara Darzi, and his subsequent meteoric rise to fame (he is now Lord Darzi) has demonstrated the wisdom of his selection. I had known Ara when he was progressing through his higher surgical training and had long recognised that he was a very special talent. He seemed to have skills in every dimension that could possibly be required of the head of a surgical department. In addition, he is a truly delightful person.

In the autumn of 1998, I received a totally unexpected letter indicating that I was to become a CBE. Jack and I diligently obeyed the rules and kept it a secret, but knowing that it would be public knowledge by then, we arranged a lunch party for friends in Cumbria to celebrate on New Year's Day. It was huge fun.

The special day was 2 March 1999, and apart from a garden party that I had attended in my capacity as President of the Association of Surgeons, this was my first real visit to the inside of the palace. I had lots of instructions from friends who had already been honoured, and the most unexpected was to make sure I visited the loos; they are indeed something to behold. We were also advised to arrive early, so that my guests could get good seats.

A major part of my memory of the event is the level of organisation that went on behind the scenes. I should not have been surprised, but it was superb and our various instructions were given in an enjoyable rather than a frightening or intimidating way. For example, we were taught how to curtsey with great good humour. My guests were Jack, Lesley and Jason, and having arrived early as advised, they were sat in the very front row. I can still picture Lesley with tears in her eyes today.

I was entertained very well in the line-up, as I was sharing the day with Lenny Henry when he too received his CBE. It was my good fortune to be presented with my CBE by Her Majesty the Queen, and she took care to exchange a few well-chosen words with each recipient.

The reason for my unexpected honour was 'for services to surgery and to women in medicine', and it pleased me that I was recognised as serving women across all of medicine, and not just in surgery. We invited family and a few close friends to have lunch with us afterwards, and it was a very special day.

My five years as the UK's first female professor and head of a department of surgery were ending, and it had been both an interesting and a challenging period. The members of the department made many contributions to the advancement of surgical knowledge during my tenure. There were 265 papers contributed to the literature, and 105 contributions to surgical books. There were almost two hundred presentations to academic surgical meetings, such as the Surgical Research Society, the Vascular Society and the Association of Surgeons of Great Britain and Ireland. The majority of these required some involvement from me and all of the presentations were rehearsed at our regular meetings. For some surgeons, it would be the first opportunity to speak publicly about their research and it was important to give them a helping hand and to build their confidence. I retained my interest and involvement with research after that, but it came as something of a relief to hand on the responsibility, which was arduous at times, to the very capable Ara Darzi.

11
Winding Down

And so, on 3 April 1999, the time came to empty out my office on the tenth floor of St Mary's and prepare it for the arrival of my successor, who was moving in two days later on what just so happened to be Easter Monday. Jack and I bought him a film director-style chair with his name on it as a welcome gift.

I was certainly not about to become a lady of leisure and, in fact, some of my work-related activities would even see an upsurge after my tenure ended. Although I was no longer the head of the department, I was to remain a professor of vascular surgery and I would still be a practising surgeon. I was a member of the Council of the College and a vice-president too. I was still examining undergraduates in their final exams and lecturing around the country and indeed the world. But best of all, there was now more time for patients and for operating.

One of my main leisure activities ever since my teenage years had of course been walking, mainly in the Lake District and occasionally elsewhere too. Having restored my house in Cumbria, I had the perfect base for enjoying the fells. I loved to set out early in my walking boots, ready to ascend a climb. Jack and the children also adored exploring the hills and Jason became a regular walker and even a competitive fell runner. We all shared a love of the open air. There was nothing better than a tough day of walking, followed by a good meal back at the house with a log fire blazing.

In the year I stepped down from chairing the department of surgery, I decided to repeat the Coast to Coast walk that

I had undertaken previously, this time to raise money for a research fellowship at the Royal College of Surgeons. By this stage, Jack was quite disabled with arthritis and unable to walk long distances, but he was nonetheless generously supportive of my endeavour.

In preparation, I decided to do one of the toughest days as a practice run, in order to check that I was still fit enough to undertake the whole trip, and it taught me an important lesson. As Jack delivered me to the start in Patterdale, he asked if I had checked the weather forecast. 'Yes, it's fine,' I replied. 'Well, it looks a bit like snow to me,' he replied, looking doubtful. I was equipped for anything, or so I thought, and set off regardless. He arranged to meet me later on at an agreed time and place.

Only when I had climbed to more than 2,000 feet did I realise that Jack was correct. At the top, I was in a full-on blizzard and snow was quickly gathering underfoot. I was worried and probably should have simply turned round and retraced my steps. Instead, after checking that I still knew how to navigate with a compass, I decided to continue with my original route. Using a map in a gale is difficult and wearing spectacles in a blizzard makes it even more so. At one moment I saw a golden eagle flying quite close to me; it was a once-in-a-lifetime experience, although it did cause me for a second to question my own sanity. The snow was getting thicker, and as I contemplated my planned route, I realised that it would be foolhardy to continue on such a steep course. I opted for a longer and much slower route, which was safer in the conditions. Eventually I arrived at the agreed meeting place and was unsurprised to find that Jack was not there, as I was almost three hours late. My mobile phone had died hours previously from water in its innards. On arriving I was relieved to spot a phone box, which looked like a beacon of hope, though it was designated 'AA or emergency calls only'. I chose to try the AA. The conversation went as follows.

'Where is your car?'

'I don't actually have a car, but . . .'

'No car? But this is the AA!'

'I'm calling as I need your help!'

'OK, then give me your membership number.'

And on it went. They did eventually phone Jack, as I had asked, but they didn't give me any confirmation that they would do so. I was left in a state of considerable uncertainty. I eventually rang the emergency number and made sure that they knew I was safe, just in case Jack had called in helicopter rescue.

Luckily I eventually made it home and the day ended well, but it taught me quite a lesson. Conditions change quickly on mountains and can be hazardous, even for experienced walkers. Of course, I had known all that in theory beforehand, but this was real and had been quite frightening.

Happily, my fitness did not prove to be an issue and so on a pleasant summer's day in 1999, I set out from St Bees on the west coast in Cumbria. I was wearing the College logo (an eagle looking, rather inappropriately, backwards) on my T-shirt as I embarked on the almost two-hundred-mile-long journey to the east coast at Robin Hood's Bay. It is the best long-distance trail of my experience with all the superb scenery that England and its National Parks have to offer. I was walking alone, but my 12-day programme had been published to those who wanted to give support, and there was an open invitation to join me for a spell along the way. So, each morning I would get to the agreed start point wondering who might turn up. I thought that my former patient Linda, whose aorta I had replaced years previously, was the most impressive of all those who took up the challenge.

One day, another patient of mine, who was not able to walk any distance somehow managed to appeared on a Yorkshire moor, announcing out of the blue that he was taking me to lunch at a nearby pub. It was so kind of him, but clashed somewhat with my habit of eating not much more than fruit and vegetables while on the move. As soon as I politely could, I made my excuses in order to get on with the walking. No sooner was I back on track than I heard a shout for help from the bracken, which was shrouded in mist. I could see an arm waving at me. I was running behind. I needed to make progress. But no, I simply could not ignore a cry for help, so with some reluctance I went to investigate . . . only to find it was my friend Professor Robin Touquet from St Mary's. Moreover, he was not injured but had been gesturing with a flask of medicinal brandy, in case of need. He was one of my most treasured colleagues and an enormous asset to the hospital and to his trainees too, so it was very nice to see him.

I had accommodation booked at Catterick, but at the end of that day, a dear friend from the Royal College of Surgeons, turned up and announced, 'You are not staying *there.*' Instead, a local surgeon was able to offer me a quite luxurious bed at his home. It turned out that his wife had a dinner party planned that evening; I had to warn her that the only clean clothes I had with me were my walking outfit and shoes for the following day. She didn't mind at all, and that was the best, and by far the most comfortable, night's sleep of the whole trip.

I was delighted to complete the walk on schedule, and found the then President of the College Barry Jackson waiting at St Bees with Jack, to greet me on my arrival and to watch me put my toe in the water, which is the required symbolic end to the walk. The local surgical fraternity had gathered in the pub and I enjoyed a great celebration with them. I had enjoyed a wonderful walk across England; in my opinion it is the best long-distance trail that I have followed.

Some years later, I was waiting with a few friends early in the morning for the start of an event called Wake up and Walk, which was organised by the American College of Surgeons in San Francisco. A young American surgeon came to talk to me and asked if I knew anyone who had any information about the Coast to Coast walk in the UK. Not only had he picked the perfect person to ask, but of greater coincidence still, he turned out to be none other than the surgeon son of Dr Stanley Crawford, whom I had visited in Houston to learn about fixing thoraco-abdominal aneurysms all those years before. John and his wife went on to enjoy the walk and we were glad to be able to give them some hospitality.

I also went on to walk the length of Hadrian's Wall to raise money for the Stroke Association. It is less than half the distance and has none of the grandeur of the Lakes' mountains or the moors of Yorkshire. What it does have is a truly fascinating history, but with a schedule to meet, I was frustrated to pass much of it by without the time to delve deeper.

My favourite Cumbrian hill is Blencathra, or Saddleback, which is visible from my Lake District kitchen. It is my most frequently climbed hill, and a place where I find great peace and with which I have a deep connection. I have a wonderful song called 'Blencathra the Mountain' saved on my mobile phone, which is brilliantly evocative of that magical place. Throughout my life the Cumbrian fells have consistently provided me with joy and with solace too, when times have been hard.

Jack was an enormously supportive husband and accompanied me on my travels whenever he could. I tried to reciprocate when possible, and one such occasion was a trip to visit his old school. He had been at Westminster School and in his senior years he ran the medical dinner there for the old boys. The attendees were former students who had become medical doctors, and sixth-form boys (they were all boys then) who were hoping to get into medical school. Of course they wanted to make a good impression on these senior doctors, who might be able to help them in their ambitions. I was simply 'the wife', and would watch with great amusement the shock these boys displayed when they discovered I was a professor at Imperial, where many of them hoped to go, and not only that but a Professor of Surgery too!

Jack had held a pilot's license in his youth when he flew in the RAF, and even in his later years he remained interested in flying. One plane that particularly delighted him was the Concorde. Its daily departure was visible from Hillingdon Hospital, where Jack worked. He so wanted to fly in it, but the costs were prohibitive.

In 2002 he travelled with me to San Diego, where I gave my final eponymous lecture, and we returned via New York. Unbeknown to him I had booked dinner at an excellent New York restaurant, the Gramercy Tavern, and then a stay in a hotel near the airport. The next morning, we turned up for our flight home and he slowly realised that I had organised something special: we were to travel home on a Concorde. At the end of our flight to London, we were both completely entranced by the experience and I declared that in the future that was how I would always travel. I never did repeat the trip of course, but it was a truly wonderful aeroplane and we were both saddened when it eventually ceased to fly.

I continued to be in demand to give lectures around the world, and although I enjoyed visiting and meeting new people, I was not really an enthusiastic traveller. No sooner had I arrived in some far-flung destination than I would be thinking about getting back home. At heart I am a home bird and nowhere suits me better.

I did, however, actively decide to undertake two visits to Lebanon. During the war, I had followed the fate of the area with concern when Pauline Cutting, who had previously been my Senior House Officer, came to be based there. In addition, my wonderful colleague Dr Aghiad Al-Kutoubi had left St Mary's to become Professor of Radiology at the American University in Beirut, and it was a special opportunity to have a reunion with him. During our trip he arranged for us to visit Syria, which was truly wonderful. Aghie had been a special friend at St Mary's, because of his professional skills and knowledge but also because of his engaging personality. He was a very important support for me.

Jack had of course retired some ten years before me, being my senior by a decade. The old phrase 'for better, for worse, but not for lunch' came to mind at that time, but as I was not even going to be at home for lunch during those ten years, there was at least no opportunity for marital strife there. I did, however, fear that the removal of Jack's work, which he loved, would prove to be difficult for us both.

I was completely wrong. He sensibly decided to take on two new projects upon his retirement. The first was to cook, and the second was to build us a house. A story, entirely fictitious, had been told at his retirement celebration by Bill

Hegarty, an anaesthetic colleague. He said, 'Jack and Averil had an agreement that whoever got home from work first would cook dinner. And so, Jack was often to be seen driving round and round and round, until Averil's car finally pulled into the driveway.'

But in the first week of his retirement, Jack declared that he would commit to always cooking on Friday, 'because Fridays are hard'. This perhaps requires some explanation. Each week, as the weekend began to approach, there was always a feeling in the surgical world that we needed to finish any outstanding work before the lull of the weekend. Although surgical work would continue every day of the year, we were well aware that staffing levels and availability are reduced at weekends, so there was a wish, indeed a determination, to always get things done before the end of Friday wherever possible. So, Jack began with Fridays and gradually took over the rest of the weekday cooking, and what's more, he became very good at it. By that point in life, both of us enjoyed cooking and good food, and with it a refreshing glass of wine. Our first house in Fulmer had been previously owned by the wine expert Tony Laithwaite, and on our arrival we'd found the wine rack filled with the best that the *Sunday Times* Wine Club had to offer. 'Hope you enjoy both the house and the wine,' said the accompanying note. It was a lovely gesture and a sound commercial one too, as Jack always bought our wine from Tony thereafter.

I had mistakenly thought that the second (and rather more major) project of building a house was to be a mere hobby. I rather assumed that Jack would build it and then sell it, hopefully making a little profit. Not so. He wanted to build it and *live* in it, which I first realised when he asked me to choose colours for the bathroom and kitchen. It turned out to be a special house indeed and Jack was woven into the very fabric of it. It was in the garden of our old home in the outskirts of London, and he was present every day alongside the builders, whom he knew well. He had researched and incorporated many ecological features into it.

One of our daughters-in-law recently remarked to me that Jack always lit up a room when he entered it. So he did, and on this occasion, he lit up a whole house. Our second grandchild, Helen, was born while her parents were living with us and we had many happy family times there, the culmination of which was a party for our twenty-fifth wedding anniversary. We held the party just before we finally sold the house and moved into a place closer to my work; Jack was becoming more disabled and the garden was by then no longer a pleasure for him but a chore.

I have never been troubled about moving house, which is perhaps a familial trait, as my parents also moved many times. It seemed to me to be a normal part of life. Moving to a house within walking distance of my work was a real luxury, although it did result in an occasional phone call along the lines of, 'I know you aren't on duty, but as you are just down the road, could you possibly pop in and . . .'

Living, as I still do now, in that London mews house was a great revelation for us. It is a true community with frequent parties and a book club, where neighbours are friends who care for each other's wellbeing. I had purchased the house back in 1982 for a very small sum, simply to have a base close to the hospital for when I was on call. Emergencies are common in vascular surgery and can take a few hours, so being local is very valuable. My mother later moved into the house and was there until she died in 1991, and although a Northerner through and through, she did very much enjoy her time living in central London.

During my final couple of working years, I assumed the role of Associate Medical Director of the St Mary's NHS Trust, in order to ensure that the process of setting up revalidation of the staff went smoothly. In the mid-1990s there had been an investigation into excess deaths among patients in Bristol following paediatric cardiac surgery. The GMC responded to this by insisting that doctors were to be regularly checked, in a process that they called revalidation. The system has many shortcomings, and although I tried to influence the powers that be to set up something more reliable and workable, what we got was 'revalidation'. It was my job to see it introduced at St Mary's.

Fortunately, I selected an assistant who was capable and, given guidance, able to do most of the work very well. I knew I was on to a good thing when I asked her at the interview what she liked doing best at work and she replied, with enthusiasm, 'Writing reports.'

The role brought me into close contact with the medical staff of the whole hospital, and I would soon become aware of those involved in any kind of problem. That problem could be personal, or range from a threat of litigation through to being investigated by the GMC. All of the various scenarios were highly stressful for the individual concerned and the doctor often felt, and frequently was, unfortunately, somewhat abandoned by friends and colleagues. I was able to provide support and assist with their progress through the courts or the GMC investigation. I discovered how valuable it was to be able to help and advise in such difficult circumstances, and also saw just how much that help was needed. My advantage was that I was senior (read: old, grey and not a threat) and also knowledgeable about the workings of colleges and the like. All I sought was fairness for those concerned and to relieve some of the stress where I could.

I came close to being sued myself on just one occasion during my career and it made me realise how very difficult that threat can be. In my case, it arose because of a complication following surgery. I had carried out an aortic operation that involved the internal iliac artery, which supplies blood to the pelvis. The patient developed a weakness in his leg afterwards and this was something that none of us had seen before. The neurologists thought that the new arrangement of the blood vessels could have partially deprived the nerves to the leg of their blood supply. I explained all this to the patient and also said that I had never seen such a complication before and neither had my colleagues. I apologised that it had happened, even though I could not have prevented it. It delayed his recovery, though slowly the power returned and he was restored to health. Meanwhile, however, I received the dreaded letter saying he was suing me. The experts quickly decided that I had no case to answer, but even so, those few weeks were for me completely dominated by the intense anxiety I felt at the prospect of possible litigation.

After stepping down as head of department, I continued to be a working surgeon for two more years, though I was was no longer on the emergency call rota. Emergencies constitute a large portion of the life of the vascular surgeon and until stepping down, my nights were often spent in the operating theatre dealing with such emergencies. So, at last, after almost 40 years of being on call, it was a surprise to be able to count on a full night's sleep. It was a welcome change but at the same time not one that came without regret, as much of the interest from being a surgeon stems from such urgent cases, and in a way I missed that side of my work a great deal.

I made the decision to step away from surgery completely when I reached the then mandatory retirement age of 65 in

2002. I well remember my last operating list. I had hoped for some easy, gentle cases ahead of bowing out for the final time. But the team had other ideas and wanted me to look after some quite complex operations, and so it was. By this time Peter Knight had retired and been replaced by a wonderful colleague, Martin Price, who was both a good anaesthetist and an excellent teacher. He was at the 'top end' (i.e., giving the anaesthetics) for the day and we had a very happy time. It ended with a spontaneous party in the surgeons' room at the end of the day. A crowd of friends turned up to see me off and none of us could really believe that it was truly my final list.

My last ever outpatient clinic was populated by patients I knew well, who had discovered that it would be my final one and had somehow contrived to squeeze in a last appointment. One couple who had known me for some years as the result of my operating on one of them seemed to have been sitting in the waiting room all day, but no matter how hard I tried to get them to come in for their appointment, they managed to evade me until the very end of my shift. They wanted to be my last ever clinic attendees and they had very kindly brought along an ice cold bottle of champagne and glasses. They opened the champagne with the words, 'Well, if they strike you off the medical register now, it won't matter.'

My colleagues, in particular John Wolfe, were generous in arranging a wonderful send-off, with talks during the day and a splendid dinner in the evening at the Royal College of Surgeons in Lincoln's Inn Fields. I was overwhelmed by the generosity of my friends and colleagues, who had travelled from various far corners of the world to attend the celebration; they were joined by Jack and all three children and a couple of patients too. There was even a band there to entertain everyone, provided by some obliging medical students.

Clearly a speech was called for, and in response to a toast given by Baroness Barbara Young, I recited a version of 'The Lion and Albert', with each verse relating to a particular person who had been important to me. I had carried a notebook with me for almost a year and made notes and tentative verses about all my colleagues. I had performed Stanley Holloway's monologues as a child, and as I came from Blackpool, this one seemed to fit the bill. I began:

There's a famous seaside place called Blackpool
That's noted for fresh air and fun
And Mr and Mrs Ralph Charles Dring
Lived there with young Averil their kid

A grand little lass was young Averil
Of sisters and brothers she'd none
But uncles and aunties and cousins
In plenty, so she'd lots of fun

I received some amazing presents, including an electronic piano, but by far the most significant was the gift of a Shaker music stand. I had declared, rather unwisely, that I was going to learn to play the cello in my retirement. I actually remember saying, 'I can play ten notes at once on the piano, surely one at a time can't be that difficult.' I have had to eat my words! Michael Grigg, a superb vascular surgeon in Melbourne who had worked with me at St Mary's in the late 1980s at the end of his training, and his wife Sherryl Wagstaff, an ENT surgeon and my closest friend, arrived for my retirement party with the beautiful Shaker music stand 'for your new career as a cellist'. The die was cast!

Jack and I entertained all the overseas visitors and my closest colleagues at our house on the following Saturday, as we were keen to make the most of their visits. But then, at the end of the day, they left and that was it. I was no longer a consultant surgeon, I no longer needed to be available at all hours of day and night and I could have a glass of wine whenever I wanted, without fear of needing to drive – I was released! But as I had never felt oppressed by my work and really had loved almost every minute of it, I wondered whether withdrawal symptoms might start to set in quite quickly. Luckily as it happened there was none of that; I simply and contentedly moved on to a new phase of my life.

I had achieved more than I could have possibly anticipated as a young student. I hoped most of all to have trained and perhaps even inspired some good young surgeons, and to have encouraged women to believe that they could achieve their goals. I had saved lives and improved practices. I anticipated that I would miss the people most of all, both patients and colleagues, but in the event, many of them maintained contact. I had no wish to linger beyond my sell-by date. In any case, I had plans for the future. I did not intend to be idle.

12
Retirement

I had worked for just about 40 years and there were very few gaps in my medical experience over that time. Work had largely but not entirely been my life, and it was the 'not entirely' bits that were now to become rather more important. With the benefit of hindsight, I can say that retaining other interests was the most valuable decision, and it has allowed me to have a splendid retirement.

On my sixty-fifth birthday I found time to put pen to paper, or to be more exact, fingers to keyboard. This is what I wrote on that special day in June of 2002:

> *The day began with the ascent and inevitably the descent of my favourite local fell, Blencathra* [or Saddleback, as it may be known to some]. *The weather was as inclement as any midsummer day could be, but that did not dampen the enthusiasm to accomplish something that I had long since promised that I would do. It is after all a reason for rejoicing that I am physically still able to do so.*
>
> *I was accompanied by a long-standing and close friend and his arrival was a complete surprise, as the result of collusion between him and Jack. So a good start and afterwards the three of us toasted our survival for 65, 71 and 74 years with champagne and a sandwich lunch.*
>
> *So why the keyboard?*
>
> *Well, it is because the day concludes my clinical career with the NHS, which has been uninterrupted, apart from working overseas for two years, since I qualified as a doctor in 1960.*

I went to medical school in 1955 from a working-class, non-medical background with the intention of becoming a surgeon.

Twelve years after qualifying I became a consultant surgeon and during those 30 years of continuous practice, I have seen many changes. It is more important however to record that I have been happy with my lot. Not every moment of every day and night, but generally pleased with my choice of career, which has been immensely enjoyable.

The reason I feel it is important to record this fact is because it seems that younger doctors are increasingly not so happy with their choice of career. If you are unhappy you cannot work so well, you become demoralised and perhaps eventually you give it up and try something else. Studying medicine demands hard work and dedication and I cannot imagine that you give it up without enormous soul-searching and recognising a major personal loss. The NHS also suffers a major loss and the causes of the unhappiness need to be seriously sought and, if possible, rectified.

These comments are not based on any scientific study and are entirely personal but on this, my birthday, I feel I can try to look at where change has possibly lessened the attractions of the job.

I want to introduce with some care the word 'fun'. I do so recognising that it could offend sick patients, who I am sure would not want the treatment of their diseases to be regarded as fun for their doctor. That is most certainly not my message but in the carrying out of our work, which can be harrowing and exhausting at times, we need a lighter aspect.

The lighter aspect for me has come from the feeling that I was doing something for people. The desire to help people is the commonest driving force in the selection of a medical career. I see that desire as genuine, so when it appears that your efforts are either not recognised or, worse still, criticised, the effect can be profound.

It was accepted at the beginning of my career that the doctor would do their best. Doctors were not seen as the cause of disease but as honest brokers trying to resolve a problem. They were free to try something new, and thus broke new ground in treatment in a way that may never be possible again. In my own specialty of vascular surgery, someone had to be the first to clamp an aorta and replace it with Dacron, and in many such high-tech surgical specialities, the results which initially were poor are now expected to be perfect.

The newly and recently qualified doctor now has a strict limit placed on their hours of work in a way that would have shocked my boss at that stage . . . 'I suppose you could go out on Tuesday evening for an hour or two provided you are back to do a night round.' No, I am not about to advocate a return to that, but there is a price for the shortened hours, which in my view contributes to unhappiness. First there is no 'mess' in the way I knew it and, as a result, far less camaraderie. Stress can often be relieved by sharing it with a friend, and the late evening pot of tea and plate of sandwiches proved to be a gathering point where stress was overcome by talk.

When you were phoned at night it was usually about one of 'your' patients and you always knew whether you needed to get up and fix a drip or whether it could wait. You knew your bosses' likes and practices, and you had usually seen the operation. Not so today, when the doctor on call has huge numbers of unknown patients to care for. They may not know the consultant or registrar responsible for the patient and they are highly unlikely to have seen the operation. In consequence they cannot offer advice over the phone and must always make a visit. That visit takes longer because the notes have to be read through and often a complete stranger contacted for advice.

Caring for your own patients is less stressful, more professionally satisfying and pleases the patients more. When patients are pleased they complain less and another source of unhappiness is reduced.

Criticism, complaints and media accusations all conspire to make the public and us believe that we are incompetent and lacking in that fundamental thing, the desire to help, to do good. I have never had personal contact with a doctor who sets out to do harm. Of course, I know that *they exist, but the majority of even the worst cases seen by the GMC and others did intend to do good. Errors are not deliberate but all of us will make them. The concept of a 'no blame' culture is only just becoming acceptable but, meanwhile, heads have to roll.*

If the error that you will inevitably make turns out to have dire consequences for the patient, then we must all feel devastated for the patient and their family. But there is another victim, and it now seems that the doctor who perpetrates the 'crime' must also see their life and not just their career in ruins.

I think that, by and large, doctors are still respected and trusted by the public, and many patients want us to make difficult decisions on their behalf, and to guide them. Doctors make decisions for their patients all day, every day and do so with the best of motives. Young doctors make more of those decisions than anyone else and must be supported in so doing.

I could have continued with private work beyond the age of 65, but I decided not to do so. Most of the surgery I did was major and required a team, and I did not want to set up and manage a whole group of doctors and nurses in my late sixties. Another route that many surgeons take is to become involved in medical litigation. Healthcare professionals can be taken to court if it is thought they might have been negligent, and reputable clinicians may contribute to the process by providing an opinion as to the rights and wrongs of a particular case. I tried it but concluded that I would simply be doing it for financial reward and not because I enjoyed it, so it wasn't an option for me.

I had learned how important it is to not be idle in retirement some years previously, when I was secretary of the Liverpool Medical Institution. One of my jobs was to prepare citations for the life members. I visited them all at their homes. There were seven in total; four had put on their metaphorical slippers and were to be found sitting alone by the fire. The other three had developed almost new careers, advancing their interests or hobbies in new domains. Those three were lively and interesting and far more the sort of person I wanted to become.

My second 'career' had always been music, and although I continued to play the piano, I was not able to participate in an orchestra as a pianist. My best hope was to find an orchestral instrument and learn it in the hope of becoming a member of an amateur orchestra. I decided on the cello because of the wonderful sound it can make, but perhaps I could have chosen a lighter, less cumbersome instrument! I chose the lightest case but even that was at least 10 kilos, which I didn't even consider when I began. Since then, the cello has become hugely important in my life, even if it has been frustrating at times too. I did not learn as quickly as I might have done in my youth, and as many parents will testify, the initial sounds are at best disappointing and at worst frankly discordant.

Jack's sister Jill was teaching at Sherborne School at this time, and the music teacher there was charged with finding me my first London teacher, who turned out to be one Pippa Mason. She was advancing her expertise at music college and she handed on her new knowledge to me. We became friends, and years later, I asked her to play at Jack's funeral.

When I first began to learn the cello, I would rush off to the shop to purchase recordings or sheet music, but one of today's little miracles is of course the availability of music on the internet. The internet even allowed me to continue to have lessons during the Covid pandemic, thanks to Zoom.

From the start, I went to the Oxford Cello School in the summers. I made slow progress but loved being there. The OCS is a long-established summer school for cellists of all ages and abilities. I joined the large group called Adult Improvers. They run a highly complex timetable and all the various courses intermingle. Some of the participants are still at school, others are semi-professional and yet others are preparing for exams. We stayed in a boys' boarding school and played at all available moments of the day and evening. Then we would head to the pub for some well-earned refreshments, along with the tutors. The cello has been the source of a number of wonderful new friendships for me; I have especially enjoyed meeting fellow members of the adult improvers group at the Oxford School, with whom I have often shared a restorative glass of wine at the close of day.

I will always be on the back row, but I am very grateful to John Lumley for letting me have a place in the Bart's Orchestra, which I love. Its official name is the St Bartholomew's Academic Festival Chorus and Orchestra, and Jack and I had previously sung in its choir. When I told Pippa that I was to join an orchestra, I expected a shriek of horror, but she was delighted. 'That is just what you need. I will teach you how to cheat! If you cannot play all the notes, then make sure you play the first note of the bar correctly and on time. And look as though you are playing the rest.' At least I did not have to learn to read music and I was familiar and competent at timekeeping. As the years pass I have improved and I love the feeling of being in the midst of and contributing to that wonderful orchestral sound.

The orchestra is just one of an astonishing number of opportunities to play with other amateur musicians that are available thanks to hardworking and generous organisers. One such is Sue Hadley, who puts on music events in Primrose Hill in London. She plays cello and is of a similar vintage to myself, and I so admire her cheerful organisation and the galvanising effect she has on us amateur musicians. My first experience of one of her events was something called Cello Love, which is a very fun weekend designed for cellists only. Sue's regular orchestras and awaydays provide me with much happiness and the chance to engage with likeminded friends.

Jack was never so keen on my playing the cello and he rightly felt that it resulted in my neglecting the piano to some extent. When our grandchildren came along, I tried my best to encourage them to enjoy music. They would often sit on my lap in their nappies and bash sounds out on the piano. I wanted them to feel that music was an integral part of existence for them, as it is for me. At my eightieth birthday party at the home of one of the children, the one gift I wanted most was a concert put on by the grandchildren, and this they organised superbly. I have to say that my wonderful grandchildren are the most treasured and unexpected gift of my old age.

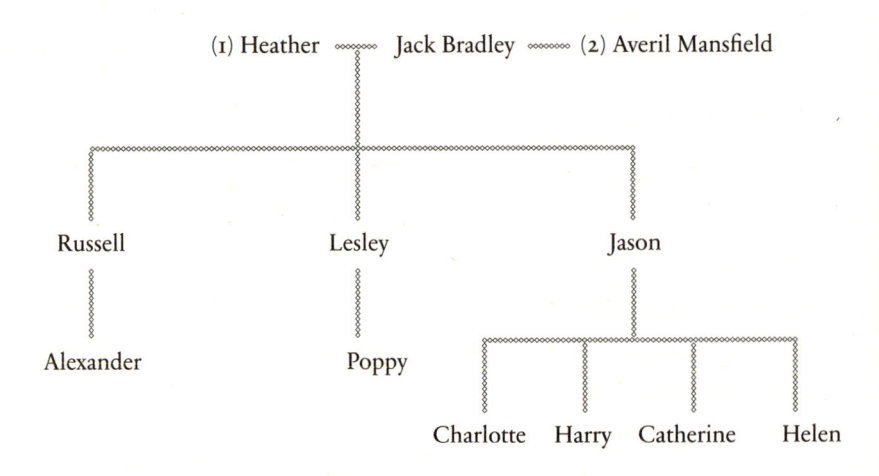

```
              (1) Heather  ∞  Jack Bradley  ∞  (2) Averil Mansfield
                                  │
        ┌─────────────────────────┼─────────────────────────┐
      Russell                   Lesley                    Jason
        │                         │                         │
    Alexander                   Poppy        ┌──────────┬──────────┬──────────┐
                                          Charlotte   Harry    Catherine    Helen
```

234

'Amateur musician' was not to be my only occupation in retirement, because I was also appointed to chair the Council of the Stroke Association, a national medical charity. My interview took place in a rather dark room in the House of Lords, and I was asked how long I would do it for, if appointed. I replied a maximum of five years. 'Oh,' said a male voice from the darkness. 'Are you trying to tell me I stayed too long?' It was my predecessor, who, it transpired, had held the post for the last decade.

It proved to be a steep learning curve and involved many hours of work and a great deal of travelling. I had never been in the driving seat of a major charity before and there was much to learn. One of my first tasks was to appoint a chief executive to replace the retiring Margaret Goose. She had generously planned her retirement so that she could work with me initially and oversee the transfer of responsibilities from herself to her replacement Jon Barrick.

Both of them were dedicated, hardworking leaders of the charity and both taught me about the value of a close understanding between chair and CEO. Knowing the boundaries and understanding the sensitivities of the relationship between trustees and staff was crucial. The trustees were meant to indicate the direction of travel for the charity, but the staff had to put those ideas into practice.

The Stroke Association was a good fit for me because I had always regarded stroke prevention surgery as the most valuable work I did. I had already been a trustee and so knew quite a lot about the organisation. In 2002, in common with many similar charities, there was only a fairly basic governance structure. With the new CEO, we took a long, hard look our practices and over time developed a system that we hoped was more robust.

The origins of the association were a number of very well-meaning, altruistic founders. Initially the organisation was small and then it began to grow. One particular problem was its link with chest and heart as the Chest, Heart and Stroke charity; in order to expand, it needed to concentrate on stroke and it also needed to be UK wide. Some trustees of long standing were very resistant to change and Jon Barrick and I had an uphill battle to persuade them of the good reasons for reform. When three trustees resigned as a result of these changes, I too offered my resignation, but it was rejected by the remaining trustees.

I spent many days visiting Scottish and Irish stroke physicians and their units in order to determine a way forward. One such visit included the then Scottish Minister of Health Nicola Sturgeon, who I concluded was a tough lady who was 'going places'. It was challenging work indeed; I remember going home to Jack and asking him if I was mad to be doing so much when I was meant to be retired. It all proved worthwhile, though; establishing a charity to focus uniquely on strokes was clearly the way forward.

A major difficulty for the charity was the lack of public understanding of the meaning of the word 'stroke'. I developed the habit of asking the person sitting next to me on a bus or a train what they thought a stroke was and almost always they would slap a hand across their chest, indicating a heart attack, rather than a brain attack. We received great help from a publicity campaign around the FAST (Face *drooping*, Arm *weakness*, Speech *slurring*, Time *to dial 999*) acronym.

I visited every corner of the UK and included places outside the NHS system in my visits, such as Jersey and the Isle of Man, in the hope of establishing a unified and universal approach to stroke care and research. I met many dedicated people on these trips – physicians, therapists, nurses, carers, patients and many of the staff who worked for the association. The volunteers were especially admirable, as considerable dedication is needed to reliably turn up every week to provide, for example, a club for people recovering from a stroke. I also greatly admired our patron, the Duke of Kent. It is not easy even for medical professionals to converse with those who have lost their capacity for speech following a stroke. But time after time the Duke would visit stroke units and he would stop and chat to every single patient. I found that inspiring.

As often happens in a new and growing charity, our finances did not always line up with our ambition and this was to be a major challenge for us to confront. A charity needs a firm financial foundation and staff must of course be properly and reliably paid. There are some wonderfully generous philanthropists in the UK, but they need to be approached with a robust plan of action. Fluctuations in fortunes can result in considerable difficulties in running a charity, and although legacies are great, they do not aid planning, so we needed to grow our financial foundations and ensure we used those donations responsibly.

Jon Barrick was a totally dedicated leader who worked hard and supported all his staff well. He also brought talented people into the organisation and one of those, John Harvey, made major progress with large donations, which gave us the stability we needed. He proved to be a great asset and a friend.

My five years with the association were busy and enjoyable, but when the time came for a new broom to move in, I was happy to go to the 'headhunters' to talk about the criteria for my successor. They asked if they could put my name into their database for other chairs, but I declined. The very next day, a letter arrived asking me if I would allow myself to be considered for the Presidency of the British Medical Association, the trade union for doctors in the UK. Initially I incorrectly blamed the headhunters for this very unexpected approach.

Why me for the BMA? I asked myself. I had been a member throughout my working life, but really my only connection to them had been a direct debit. I had no idea whether this was just one of several exploratory letters sent to possible candidates, or whether in essence it was a job offer.

How did I feel about the BMA? I wasn't supportive of all of their policies, so did I want my name linked to the organisation? They appeared to be in favour of the huge reduction in working hours that came as a result of the European Working Time Directive. I saw the benefit of more reasonable working hours, but not if it removed our professionalism. For me, the patient's needs would sometimes dictate that I simply had to continue to care for them, and I wanted to be able to make my own decisions about such a response. For me, that was at the heart of being a professional. It also seemed to me that the BMA were willing to consider strike action, which I did not agree with.

I thought long and hard before having lunch with the chief executive in order to consider my options. Eventually, I decided to let my name go forward and hoped to be able to be influential from within, should I be appointed.

I was indeed appointed by the council, and by happy coincidence, I was to be installed as president in Liverpool in 2008. By this time, I had formed the opinion that the president had no real executive function, but that there might be some behind-the-scenes opportunity to influence the organisation, which I thought could be interesting. Perhaps rather cheekily,

I thought it was somewhat akin to the relationship between Her Majesty the Queen and the prime minister.

I had to give a presidential address, and this offered me an opportunity to state my views to the association as a whole. I was able to invite guests of my choosing and to pay homage to them for their influence and thank others for their support. Among the guests were my first husband Jonathan and his second wife. He had been a huge support during my training years and I was very pleased to be able to acknowledge this in public.

Edgar Parry was there with his wife, and I could similarly give recognition of the vital role he had played in my career. He was willing to give guidance to a young woman with the (what then seemed) crazy ambition of becoming a surgeon. For a gifted surgeon or any other craftsman, passing on skills is central to maintaining and advancing trades and professions. But it is far easier to do the job yourself, and great patience is required to guide somebody else's faltering early attempts instead. He and others in Liverpool taught me more than the skills that are needed. They taught me about attitude. I sincerely believe that attitude comes from the top. Go into a ward where there is a caring sister or manager, and the ward exudes warmth and kindness. It is sadly not always the case, however; in fact, the reverse is sometimes true.

Sir James Paterson Ross, surgeon to the Queen, once said that 'surgery, like religion, is caught rather than taught' and that 'the personal relationship between a student and his chief is of greater importance than the details of an education or training programme'. In Liverpool I was absolutely taught about being a professional, and I hope that I caught the attitudes that enable one to become the kind of doctor that all of us would want to be treated by.

The installation took place in the concert room of

St George's Hall and I was able to speak of the importance of the city's musical heritage and its influence on me. I also sought to explain why I had accepted the honour of becoming President of the BMA despite my concerns:

> *Let me set a scene. Suppose I were to operate on Hamish Meldrum's [he was Chairman of the BMA Council then] aneurysm (so far as I know he does not have one!) this evening, and during the night he started to bleed such that he needed to return to theatre. How would he feel if a total stranger, superbly qualified but unknown, turned up to look inside? He would be understandably unhappy. There is something about a professional contract that is different from a commercial one. Unlike politicians the public generally trust us, and that trusting professional relationship is something I want to say a few words about.*

I then asked two questions: Are we still a profession? And does it matter? The answer to both was of course yes. I also reflected on specialisation and the need to maintain contact between different specialties, and not become isolated in our own cocoons:

> *We are greatly privileged as a profession. We regularly enter into the deepest places in our patients' minds and indeed their abdomens. They have to trust us. They have no real choice. Dame Janet Smith said, 'I think the public ought not to even have to think about whether they trust their doctors — it should be something that they are able to take completely for granted.' But that trust must be based on integrity, compassion, up-to-date knowledge and a commitment to ethical research.*
>
> *For me, the foundation of our position in society is based on altruism, the solid underlying concept of our jobs. It is a hard taskmaster and not without controversy. But it is where most of us began and is essentially how we wish to be viewed — as people who put patients first. As a trainee said in evidence to the RCP [Royal College of Physicians]*

working party, 'Medical practice requires neither humility nor altruism. Good medical practice, however, requires both.'

We like to be viewed as going beyond the call of duty. Whatever else we do, we all want to be seen as treating patients in true Osler ideals with compassion and competence. There are those who see such ideals as overly arduous and unrealistic. Doctors have lives too.

To artificially divide work from life or life from work is, for me, to create expectations that lead to tensions that are perhaps unnecessary.

We are today protected from exploitation by the concept of working in teams. But handing a patient over to another member of the same team does not remove responsibility from us for their proper care.

One of the most important tenets of professionalism is the way in which we behave and thus the handing on of behaviours and values to the next generation of doctors. I benefited greatly from the positive role models I met in my training. They treated both their patients and their students in a humane fashion and not the harsh belittling fashion regarded in some quarters as surgical behaviour. Entertaining, certainly, in Doctor in the House, *but such destructive behaviour needs to be consigned to history if we are to retain and hand on our professional values.*

I also told this true story:

On one occasion, I stood in the corridor outside theatre awaiting the start of an operation on a leaking thoracic aneurysm. Three off-duty trainees asked if they could come to watch. I was delighted until they said, 'But what shall we do, as we are already out of hours?' I was stumped. So I said, 'If I were doing this operation on BBC TV, would you watch?' They agreed that they certainly would and that it would be much better to see the unedited version. They were not being exploited; they were seeking professional learning. As I have often remarked to uncertain trainees, if I were playing a concerto at the Royal Liverpool

Philharmonic Hall tomorrow, I would decide how much I needed to practise, not some government minister.

I concluded with my thanks and these words:

Some, and perhaps many, of you will disapprove of some, and perhaps all, that I say, but I trust that, like Voltaire, even if you disapprove of what I say, you will defend to the death my right to say it.

It was only a one-year appointment, and there is little one can do in such a short amount of time, but it did lead to my taking on the position of Chair of the Board of Science. This was a BMA role, though largely separate from its trade union activities. It was not, however, separated from politics, because one of its functions was to try to influence those in government to address the nation's most pressing health issues as we saw them. I held the role for five years and I thoroughly enjoyed the challenges that it presented.

The BMA aims to be both a professional organisation, trying to promote the highest standards of patient care, and a trade union, trying to get the best deal out of government for its members. Their annual representative meeting is in essence a trade union congress. Members put forward proposals that are debated and then voted on. A successful vote determines the policy of the BMA and means the committees of the BMA have to put such motions into effect.

The Board of Science is similarly constrained by the annual meeting, but the policies are generally for the benefit of society and patients. Fundamentally, it deals with public health, and to chair this meant another pretty steep learning curve for me. The staff in support, however, were second to none. This made the task easy and pleasant, and our progress was rapid. One colleague there in particular, Nicky Jayesinghe, was and still is superb. She has a law degree, is married to a GP and is fantastically organised and good with people. How clever of the BMA to appoint her.

Nicky was the highly skilled power behind the throne and she organised the board and its workload with consummate ease, recruiting experts in a fashion that made them feel she was doing them a favour. No one said 'no' to Nicky and she charmed everyone into producing a top-class result. She led a very happy, well-chosen, well-motivated and clever team, which included the wonderful Darshna Gohil.

Together with the board members and the department staff, we teamed up on a wide variety of health issues, including drugs of dependence, statistics, e-cigarettes, and growing up in Britain, and most of these topics resulted in a publication of some kind. I also worked to draw attention to the research funds available from the BMA and, in order to give them due prominence, we decided to have a research awards event to celebrate them, and also to thank our donors and encourage new ones. One of the biggest difficulties as a researcher is often finding funding to get started. It is relatively easy once you have a track record, but at the start of a career it can be a real challenge. The BMA essentially provides start-up grants and they fulfil a real need.

Soon after I retired, I began to plan for the centenary celebration of the first female fellow of the Royal College of Surgeons of England. In 1911, Eleanor Davies-Colley was that first woman. Since then, a slowly growing number of women have been following in her footsteps, though they did not get so much as a mention in the history of the college at that time, and if you walked around the building, you would be forgiven for thinking that every surgeon who had ever lived was male. I gained support for a lecture theatre in Davies-Colley's name, and set about raising the money that was required to establish it. I was enormously aided by Jacqueline Fowler on the college staff, and also by the enthusiasm of many other supportive surgeons, especially female ones. We even had a reception in 10 Downing Street hosted very generously by Cherie Booth, wife of the then Prime Minister Tony Blair. It was a splendid occasion and a rare opportunity to cross that well-known threshold.

One of the features in the lecture theatre was a rather wonderful mural by Paul Cox, which was funded by a charitable foundation that supports works of art and which I have included below.

We also rescued the original brass plate from Davies-Colley's hospital, which had found its way into a skip when the hospital was demolished to make way for a supermarket. We celebrated both the centenary and the new theatre in 2011 with an international meeting. Sadly, the theatre eventually fell victim to the college's subsequent redevelopment, but the mural survives and is now on display prominently in the college, as are portraits of various female council members.

Jack was as ever very supportive of my post-retirement endeavours, but it was increasingly evident that he was having difficulties. He had struggled physically for some time, but now he was concerned that his mind was less sharp too. A close medical friend came by when I was out and in a house full of tea, my favourite beverage, Jack was unable to find any. The friend expressed his concern and Jack too became aware of and unhappy about these developments. I decided there and then not to take on another major role, and to focus instead on enjoying our time together – even for lunch!

When he came to need major heart surgery, Jack was ready to accept the risk of dying as a result of the operation, rather than be further limited in his activities. I was not so sure, but I did not try to oppose his decision. On the weekend prior to his admission, we visited all the children and grandchildren, and he was so happy to see them all. Family was hugely important to him and seeing the next generation coming along gave him great joy. I have since wondered whether my planning of the family visits suggested my uncertainty about the outcome, but he had no hesitation and went in for the procedure. After a rocky spell in intensive care, he improved and went first to the ward, and then was able to come home. It seemed that he had 'got away with it', and every day was an improvement on the previous one.

On the fourteenth post-operative day, he was sitting on the couch while I prepared lunch for us when he suddenly called out to me, 'Something has gone terribly wrong.'

Indeed it had, and he collapsed unconscious. I had no choice but to attempt resuscitation. I dragged him onto the floor and dialled 999. It was 40 minutes before the paramedic arrived and they were 40 minutes of hell, throughout which the telephonist gave me strong verbal support and reassurance as well as instructions.

Both their and my attempts were to prove futile, however, and Jack died later that afternoon. Fortunately, the children were all able to get to the house in time and we shared those terrible final minutes together. I witnessed many deaths during my career, but none of them came close to the trauma of losing Jack.

There has not been one day in the following years when he has not been in my thoughts. Grief is a normal but powerful emotion. It is often associated with feelings of depression, but it is not a disease. It is acute in the early months, and then you learn to live with it and to park it. Just now as I write this, Lesley phoned; when I told her what I was writing about, we both ended up in tears. You can pause grief, but it can't be written off. I am fortunate to have a loving family and such good friends.

Within a few weeks of Jack's death, our mews book club was born. It might have been coincidental, but I doubt it. We are 12 women who meet once a month, with each person hosting once a year. We are a disparate group with a wide age range and broad interests. There is nothing remotely intimidating about it and we gather together for the friendship as much as for the stimulus of reading. We have read close to a hundred books since then and I do not think I am alone in seeing it as a priority above most things.

One winter's day in 2016, I took the bus to Hampstead to try out the string quartet section of the University of the Third Age (a charity that creates opportunities for people to keep learning in retirement). I walked up a short steep hill with my 10 kilos of cello on my back and I became very short of breath. I felt that I was being rather foolish and determined not to take the same route again.

When, just a few days later, I walked (with no cello) up a gentle hill from the Athenaeum towards Piccadilly to get the Tube, and found myself having to stop because of chest discomfort, I did not at first connect the two happenings. This time I attributed it to having had a good three-course meal and a glass of wine. But in the following days, I was able to work out that it was always after around two hundred metres on the flat that the discomfort began. I remembered my father's words of a 'heaviness' or even of 'an elephant sitting on my chest'.

As is so typical of my profession, I took no action, even though I was concerned that the symptoms were reliably repetitive. I had given notice of my wish to demit chairing the Development Trust, a charity at St Mary's, and towards the end of November I handed it over to Dafydd Thomas. Two days later, Russell, my eldest stepson, had his gallbladder out and I went to their home to release his wife Elena from childcare. Between Wimbledon Park and the house, I had to stop a couple of times.

I spent the weekend at Highgate and then went to 'the parade of past presidents of the Vascular Society' in Manchester. There I had breakfast with a good friend and fellow surgeon who had worked with me in her training years, and when I told her of my symptoms, she gave me the good advice that I should see a cardiologist. 'Now!' I finally did so in early December, and I was shipped into the Hammersmith Hospital immediately. I was not even allowed home except to pack up an overnight bag!

Even on the angio table, I expressed concern that I might be wasting everyone's time. 'Would you like to see your angiogram, Professor?' They asked. I could immediately discern the tight stenosis, or narrowing, in the Left Anterior Descending (LAD) artery, a vital coronary artery.

The procedure was straightforward and the cardiology team efficient and caring. I now have a stent in my LAD and a bucket of pills to take. My initial response was, 'Me? Heart problems?!' I used to say to my students, 'Choose your parents wisely', and I fully appreciate that, as both of my parents died of heart attacks, the important genes are loaded against me. Modern medicine is amazing and my physical recovery was very good. However, the effect on my psyche was considerable. For the first time in my life, I had to confront the fact that I'd had a lucky break and that the condition was serious. Superficially, I dismissed it and returned to normal activities. But it took much longer for my confidence to return. I had no real risk factors to modify and so had to rely on those pesky pills to keep me safe. I have never been a great believer in the 'statins for all' philosophy that some doctors promote, but I am a good patient and I do keep on taking my tablets. I have never feared dying, but I do have concerns about the manner of going. And while I may not fear death, I don't want it just yet!

The National Health Service has quite simply been at the heart of my working life since 1960, and even as a child, I realised the huge benefits that it would bring to the people of the UK. I was interested in its instigator, Aneurin Bevan, and when, in 2012, my colleague Dafydd Thomas found a bronze of Bevan for sale, Jack and I decided to purchase it and to donate it to the BMA. It now resides in the members' lounge in their headquarters in Tavistock Square.

To be given a lifetime achievement award by the NHS Heroes organisation with his name attached was a particular pleasure, and the connection with Bevan went some way to suppressing my very uncertain response when I was told I was to receive it. I have never been a fan of awards ceremonies, tending to regard them as opportunities to create celebrities based on fairly tenuous evidence, and also as attaching a big performance to the act of simply doing one's job.

I also admit that I was flattered though, and of course, by the time I knew about the award, so did my family and friends. ITV were running the event and had secretly asked Russell if I was available on the date in question, and he had said that they should ask me as I was usually pretty busy. Some colleagues had already recorded little snippets about me, so I went along with it, swallowing my misgivings.

In the event it was all great fun and a fascinating experience. There was one rather packed day in the summer of 2018 during which I was taken by an ITV crew from my beloved Lake District to my childhood home in Wembley Avenue, Blackpool, on to my primary school and then to Liverpool Medical School and the Royal Liverpool Hospital, all for filming. Twelve hours later, I sipped a very welcome G&T in a Liverpool bar before being driven home. It was an exhausting but interesting day, packed with memories and experiences.

I have often meditated on the power of a TV camera to make us do things. I do feel sorry for the lady who then owned my childhood home and had welcomed us into a sparkling house, only to never appear on the screen, and for the school that laid on staff on a bank holiday, but which also didn't make the final cut.

The event itself was superbly organised and my only concern was that I might not recognise whichever celebrity would be given the task of presenting my award. I did not have my PA Renee there to drop a useful hint in my ear if needed. I need not have been concerned, however, as it was presented by Camilla, the then Duchess of Cornwall, and even I managed to recognise her. She was charming, funny and altogether delightful. At the dinner, I had the joy of being accompanied by three members of my family as well as a former trainee. The celebrity chosen to sit at our table was Gloria Hunniford, who was a warm and lovely presence. My granddaughter Catherine was a delightful companion for the evening.

Pat Young, my friend whom I first met at the Hammersmith, moved to live after retiring in her native Yorkshire. She was a great character who taught many of us how to nurture friends. When her husband became ill and bed-bound, she was determined to care for him at home. She began to look ill and blamed it on the lack of sleep and exhaustion. She had to be in a wheelchair at his funeral in 2017, as she was too breathless to walk up the aisle of the church.

I accompanied her to see a consultant and offered to leave the room when he asked her to strip, but she asked me to stay. The skin puckering over the breast cancer that neither she nor her medical advisors had found was obvious to me. My heart sank, as it was abundantly clear that this was an advanced and inoperable cancer. She was given a few weeks to live but managed a further four years, thanks to modern treatment coupled with sheer determination. Her oncologist Dr Andy Proctor was brilliant, as indeed was the whole team in York.

Throughout this period, she continued to give friendship and support to those she loved and who loved her. She cared deeply about the wellbeing of her friends and, needless to say, we her friends cared deeply about her. If Pat had ruled the world, there would be no strife or deprivation. I think we all learned a great deal from her as a remarkable human being. In her last two weeks, with her family beside her, she was gently nursed by May, who had been a staff nurse at the Hammersmith Hospital where Pat had been the ward clerk, and also a sister on the vascular unit at St Mary's. In her hands and surrounded by family, she was able to leave us peacefully and with dignity.

Another special friend is Sherryl, a surgeon who lives in Melbourne, Australia. I knew her husband Michael Grigg before she even met him, when he was working with me at the end of his training in London. Both of them are now important parts of my life and we have many shared values.

On one occasion, Michael and I were invited as speakers to a conference at the Royal Society of Medicine. He was to speak first and wrote a script in which, from the front row, I was to rather shockingly interrupt him with the words, 'Hang about, I don't understand a word of what you are saying!' He then invited me to join him on the platform and we continued as a double act.

He was a skilful surgeon with many other attributes and I hoped we might persuade him to stay in London. But had he done so he would never have met Sherryl, and I would have been deprived of a very close friend. She and I have a special bond, which is in no way affected by the fact that she is many years younger than I am. When Jack died, she asked, 'Do you want me to come to the funeral, or shall I come when everyone else leaves?' After a death there is a flurry of activity, which then suddenly stops, and it is then that a good friend is invaluable.

My longstanding Lake District connection means that I have several special friends there too. Among them are some wonderful characters. I was drawn to one who expressed his willingness to agree to any request with the words 'Nay bother'. It was clear that, like me, he (perhaps unwittingly) had decided not to join the 'society for saying no'.

My wonderful next-door neighbours Rose and David

Harper provide me with inspiration for how to be warm and understanding friends. Rose was, in addition to being a mother and a farmer's wife, a professional gardener. Some years before Jack died, he and I had the honest discussion about what should happen on the occasion of our deaths. We both wanted to be buried in the fields around Highgate and we even did a trial dig to see whether it would be possible, given how rocky the land is. I truly recommend such a conversation to all, as it took some of the uncertainties out of the event. After Jack died and was duly buried at Highgate, Rose designed a garden as a memorial. Friends gave trees in his memory, and on a wild and wintry day, a small group of us planted the 84 donated saplings. It is now known to us all as the 'Gravy Garden' because my youngest granddaughter Charlotte, then aged about three, pronounced the word 'grave' as 'gravy'. It has developed into a magical place thanks to Rose and her generosity and skill. David recently retired after a lifetime of farming, and if you ask him how he is, he invariably responds 'grand' or 'never better', despite his aching joints.

My really longstanding friendships tend to be with women. I have kept in touch through the years with a number of women from the various activities of my youth. Liverpool was such an important part of my life and I cherish the continuing friendship of Pat Morris, widow of Derek, my solicitor and friend, and also my former anaesthetic colleagues John Crooke and Raymond Ahearn.

The women fall into groups of activities in my working years and the biggest groups are the secretaries and the nurses. I know the name and story of almost every secretary with whom I ever worked. They were and are such a vital component of my life and they form the backdrop to everything I have achieved. Offices for consultants were a rarity back then, so my office in the early years was often the top of a filing cabinet in the secretary's office, or something similar. Life revolved around the secretaries, and they were always open for a chat and sometimes a moan whenever the need arose.

When I wrote my thesis, it was in the days prior to word processing, and 'cut' and 'paste' meant exactly that, with scissors and Sellotape. After creating a huge roll of paper, I vividly recall delivering it to Sue, a long-suffering secretary in Liverpool, for typing into its final form.

My St Mary's secretary Val knew me well and would always protect my daily five-minute catnap by saying, 'She's in a meeting.' One memorable day, she strode into my office and announced she was no longer going to do my emails. I was to do them myself. I was shocked. 'I will show you how,' she said. That was such an important step, which I particularly valued after retiring. She was so important in my life and I moved mountains to get her into the post of my academic PA when I finally became a professor.

Another wonderful secretary was Renee. I needed a secretary for my private practice, and her boss at the time was retiring. He mentioned feeling almost tearful about having to say goodbye to Renee; I realised I was on to a winner! And so it proved to be. She worked from my London home and was invaluable. In her desire to educate me about 'celebrities', she would say, 'You are not doing anything on Wednesday night, so I have bought tickets for you and Jack to see . . .' My life became very well organised and so did my paperwork, and Renee became like a member of the family.

One weekend, she and her husband went off to stay with friends in the north and she left a note attached to the computer screen that said, 'Gone for some wind chill.' On their return she tragically suffered a massive stroke and fell to the floor. Her husband called an ambulance and also me, and I met them both at the hospital. Looking back at that day in the late 1990s, I realise just how much better stroke care is today than it was then. The hospital to which she was taken (a large district general hospital) did not have an out-of-hours CT scan service, so she was transferred by ambulance to another hospital and it was close to midnight when her husband and I followed desperately behind in my car. We were completely ignored by the hospital and there was no attempt at all to let us have any information about Renee. I eventually went off in search of her, only to find that she had died. It was left to me to convey this terrible news to her husband. This totally unacceptable treatment of both patient and family was a driving force for me when I chaired the Council of the Stroke Association some years later. Urgent and humane care was essential and is thankfully now much better established.

    I still keep in touch with and cherish my relationship with a number of former colleagues and friends, such as Dafydd Thomas, the neurologist, and Alasdair Fraser, a gynaecologist, both of whom have St Mary's in their hearts. It is that kind of place. Another cherished link I still have with the hospital is the Music Society, and such student societies have been a vital and consistent part of my adult life. I had been afraid when I retired that I would be deprived of connections to students and colleagues, but it proved to be possible to retain many of these relationships, which I value greatly.

On 15 March 2020, I started to keep a diary of the Covid pandemic. It was the morning after I'd had a sleepless night worrying about a planned gathering of 'the girls' at my place in Cumbria. We are all medical and I was confident of their support when I said we should cancel our plans. But it was a tough decision because we had no experience to guide us. I wrote:

> *I woke up this morning to the realisation that although it is Monday, it and all the following days to come will feel like Sunday. It feels as though the world has stopped spinning on its axis. How can an invisible virus alone and unaided bring civilisation to a halt. This is truly global.*

There was a slow realisation of the seriousness of our situation, followed by a trickle and then a torrent of postponements, which eventually became cancellations. Could my cleaner come? Initially yes, then no. Could I get my hair cut? Initially yes, and how I wished I had done so before the inevitable no came along.

One interesting response to the pandemic was the desire to get in touch with friends and loved ones, partly to ensure they were surviving and partly to make sure they knew how much we cared. One female surgeon friend wrote to me, 'Just wanted to remind you that you are a really important part of my life. I couldn't have imagined that from having your photo on my wall in 1993 I would have the privilege to get to know you and (hopefully) carry on your inspirational work.'

I similarly felt the need to make sure special people knew how much I cared about them. Slowly but surely, the situation and its gravity became clearer. My friendly dustman called and asked if I might end up going back to work.

On the 25 March 2020, all I wrote in my diary was the following:

India is in lockdown.
The Olympics are postponed.

We began to stand on our doorsteps at 8pm to applaud the NHS. I began to make cakes, leaving them at my neighbours' front doors. Then came the shock that first Prince Charles (as he was then) and then Boris Johnson too had caught the virus. A former colleague phoned to tell me that I had predicted the pandemic all along, which seemed unlikely to me.

The delivery of a £25 veg box became the biggest event of my week. It was splendid and my neighbours would come to view it on my outside table, and to share its contents. I was equipped for a siege, it seemed. I looked up the definition of the word siege: 'surrounding and blockading of a place' – not so accurate, perhaps as there were no enemy hordes out there, only nasty invisible viruses. Then I looked up 'virus'; the term is attributed to a Dutch scientist Beijerinck, and his first shot at a name was 'contagium vivum fluidum' (contagious living fluid) of course the change was later made to 'virus' (venom).

I asked myself what I would like to leave behind if these were to be my last days, and I contemplated writing my life story for the first time. I also determined to devote some part of every day to the following: cello, piano, writing, exercise, cooking and reading.

My neighbours and I could have taught Downing Street a thing or two, as during the pandemic no rules were broken on our mews, but if the weather allowed, we would sit at our outside tables and communicate at a distance. In inclement weather we met on Zoom. Nothing was allowed to interfere and no penalty notices were issued.

I coped with the isolation surprisingly well and attributed this to having plenty to do, as well as picking up the new means of communication. I considered how different it would have been in the previous flu pandemic, when there were no easy means of keeping in touch. The sense of isolation for many people must have been profound.

The lowest point for me was Christmas Day in 2020, and even that was eased by the lovely and unexpected arrival outside my house of my youngest grandson Alexander, with his parents. He played Christmas carols for the residents of the mews on his violin, standing in the cold in the middle of the street. Sadly, they could not come inside and share my solitary meal. We stuck to the rules!

Emerging from the restrictions was also not easy, and my first foray to the shops and the bank felt like sailing into the unknown. As I write this, we are rapidly heading back to normal life, even though there are many cases still around. I have asked myself what I missed most during the lockdowns and it was, perhaps not surprisingly, being able to mingle with others, especially as part of an orchestra.

On 13 August 2020, in the midst of the pandemic, I received an email from a lady called Cathy from the BBC, inviting me to be a castaway on *Desert Island Discs*. My email response began simply: 'Wow!'

I was amazed, thrilled, overwhelmed and rather scared, but there was no doubt on this occasion that I would accept. It is such an iconic programme and which of us has not at some point idly contemplated what our choices would be, if the opportunity were to arise?

The first and most important task was to make those choices, which was much more difficult in reality than it had seemed in theory. It is not simply a matter of listing your favourite music; as a listener, I knew that the associated story was what the programme was about. I had a list of about one hundred essential recordings that had to be whittled down to just eight. In the early days of *Desert Island Discs*, it would have been so much more difficult to make that selection, but today, with the likes of YouTube, it is possible to listen to so many recordings with ease, without so much as leaving home.

The final few choices were aided by my grandchildren Helen, Catherine, Harry and Charlotte all sitting around a table with their 'devices', and we had a few laughs together at Grandma's shortlist. They could all be described as classical music, including Peter Maxwell Davies, Brahms and Shostakovich, apart from two. I had to include Abba's 'Dancing Queen', to remind me of my grandchildren, and a Flanders and Swann song about the famous London omnibus. I made that particular choice as I knew all their songs by heart and because I had made my first Lego creation during lockdown – a red London bus, the set for which was sent to me by my good friend Sherryl. I became quite addicted to Lego during the pandemic!

Once the decisions were made and sent off to the BBC, I then simply waited for a date. The pandemic had a hand in that, as one of the other chosen castaways unfortunately developed the virus and had to postpone his slot, so I was moved forward. I opted to go into the BBC for the recording, but had to be alone in a studio with only sound and no sight of Lauren Laverne.

I found that it was quite an emotional moment when the theme tune played; there was no going back. Lauren proved to be a very skilled interviewer and made the whole experience enjoyable for me. My luxury choice was a grand piano and I recalled how my father had given me my very first piano with the words: 'A grand piano is useful. You can play it, you can eat off it and if times get really hard you can sleep under it.'

Then came the wait for the broadcast. I was certain that I had said some foolish things, so I decided to listen to the live event alone in my office. But it was not as bad as I had expected, so I was able to relax afterwards over a (socially distanced) glass of bubbly with some neighbours. I had made a cake to resemble a desert island, complete with palm trees, which was placed on the table outside for friends to help themselves. The experience proved to be a nice boost to morale in the difficult time of the pandemic.

One surprising consequence of being on the programme was the post that followed. It exceeded the mailbag of any other event in my life by quite a considerable margin. It had the extra advantage of regenerating various long-lost friendships. Many old patients got in touch through a range of means, and colleagues from every stage of my career wrote letters or emailed me. This went on for months following the actual broadcast. There was even a farmer, local to me in Cumbria, who listened to the podcast some weeks later while riding on his tractor and who wrote to say thank you. The programme clearly has an amazing reach. I was sad to be unable to share the experience with my lovely Jack, but that aside, it was a joy and a fantastic privilege.

My working life has been dedicated to patients, balancing their needs against the needs of myself and my family in what today's young refer to as the work/life balance. I tried hard not to let either patients or family down, but I freely admit that when patients had urgent and compelling problems, I felt that I had no choice but to respond. Quite frequently, I would be the only expert available, so it was a matter of doing the operation or walking away. Vascular surgery is often a life-or-death situation, stroke or no stroke – or, at the least, a loss-of-limb scenario. I found I could not turn away and, if humanly possible, I would always do what I could.

I was not unique in that attitude. For me, and I think for most doctors, altruism is at the heart of everything we do. I know that some resent this responsibility, but for me it was a privilege, even though it could sometimes prove onerous.

Looking back, I realise that I had the best possible career for me, one that I loved with no edge of resentment about the demands it made on me and my family. I also had great good fortune to be supported by others throughout my life. My wonderful parents were quietly determined that I should achieve whatever I was capable of, even though they initially thought I was aiming too high. Once they realised that I had the ability, they were wholly supportive.

My primary school back in Layton was, in my opinion, the best possible foundation for me to develop from. It provided everything that a good education does and drew out of me the determination to succeed. Choosing Liverpool as my university was also good in so many different ways. Liverpudlians are by nature warm and welcoming, and will always support the underdog. I can almost hear them saying, 'If you must be a surgeon despite the fact that you are female, then good on you. We will support you. Go for it, girl!' I certainly never met any discrimination in that city, and whenever I was the best person for a job, I got it. Humour is the constant background to life in Merseyside, and the pleasure is always mine when I return to Lime Street Station, climb in a taxi there and engage the driver in conversation. Liverpudlians could always see the funny side of my unusual career, but they were never cruel. My take on life is that we all need to inject some fun and humour into our work, and indeed into our lives, whenever possible.

Clearly, being a surgeon is not without its tragedy and sadness, and I certainly spent many a sleepless night fretting that I was unable to cure a particular patient. There would be times when, despite my best endeavours, the outcome was not as wanted, or even fatal. If you are human, you must inevitably ask whether it was because of your own inadequacies that the failure occurred. Support from colleagues and family is vital in such circumstances, and all of us have a role to play in supporting others through difficult times.

Both of my husbands were tolerant and supportive, and accepted the fact that patients were always going to be at the centre of my life. My acquired family have been wonderful in their understanding of my work. I simply hope that they were not too deprived by my dedication to medicine. Jack was the most perfect soulmate and undoubtedly the love of my life. He gave me unstinting support. Through him I acquired a family of children and grandchildren that are my ongoing delight today.

My hopes for the future of my profession are that we can retain our professionalism and that we can always value altruism. I have been immensely proud of the NHS and admit to concerns for its welfare. I am now more likely to be a recipient of healthcare than a deliverer of it, and I would want our service to be a comprehensive, considerate and kind health institution that we can be proud of.

I also hope that today's young doctors can enjoy their work as much as I did . As a child, I thought I knew what I wanted to do for the rest of my life, and it turned out to be the perfect career for me. I enjoyed it in every aspect and I felt that it was a privilege to have a part to play. I never resented the large demands on my time and energy and at all times, I was treated with respect.

My hope is to have passed on to the next generation of surgeons certain skills and, perhaps more importantly, certain attitudes. Concern for the welfare of patients comes at the top, but not far behind comes concern for the welfare of the others with whom we work; treating them with kindness and sensitivity and never with disdain. There is no place for discrimination of any kind, nor for bullying.

Writing this book has provided me with an opportunity for reflection. It has also given me the unexpected chance to say a huge thank you to the many people – staff, patients, family and friends – who have touched my life and allowed me to touch theirs.

Finally, my message to the young is that you can achieve your dreams no matter what your background. Take every opportunity to discover what it is that will give you fulfilment, then work towards that goal. Hard work, humility and humour seem to me to be a recipe for success, and I wish you every happiness.

Acknowledgements

I am indebted to the family, friends, colleagues and patients who make up my life story as it is told in this book. There are many important people who do not get named but who are still of great significance to me. I could not name every secretary, trainee, nurse, colleague, patient, friend, teacher and neighbour – but each one of you is a valued piece of the jigsaw that constitutes my life. I am grateful to you and could not have done it without you.

I had considered writing down the events of my life in order to give my grandchildren a reasonably accurate account of it. I was aware that no memory is 100 per cent accurate and that they can become even further distorted as time passes. Those vague thoughts were propelled into action by a number of people. Out of the blue in February 2021, I received an email from Lauren Gardner suggesting that as the result of listening to my *Desert Island Discs* programme, she thought I should write my memoirs. She then progressed this idea into reality. Then I was guided along by Katie Fulford, who has continued to the present.

The next person I must mention is Sam Ramsay Smith, a retired surgeon who had spent some years writing his own story and who had been a young student and then doctor in Liverpool, where our paths crossed. He gave me good advice and strong support throughout the whole process.

Behind the scenes I sought advice from my friend Carol O'Brien, and she has been a wise and experienced counsellor.

ACKNOWLEDGEMENTS

Then into my life came Claire Collins of Ebury Publishing at Penguin Random House, who has been consistently supportive and encouraging. She in turn introduced me to Paul Murphy, who proved to be pivotal. I was not new to writing, but to date everything I had written was of the scientific genre, where extraneous words and phrases are an anathema. Paul taught me how to introduce colour and emotion into my story and proved to be a very patient and skillful teacher. I am immensely grateful to him.

Among the others who have been of great help are David and Liz Reilly, both doctors who have known me for years. David is a surgeon and a far better writer than I will ever be. They gave thoughtful advice about both content and title. Peter Taylor is mentioned in the book and had ideas for stories to tell. Likewise, Linda de Cossart and Colin Bicknell, Kathy Dixon, my Australian friends Sherryl and Michael, my daughter-in-law Julie and my neighbours Gill, Bernie, Diana and Meira all made contributions. My sincere thanks to all. I hope you will not be too disappointed by the end result.